With a loving heart, generous openness, and the absolute conviction born of experience and observation, Rue is offering both practical suggestions and a paradigm stretching point of view to anyone seeking a greater understanding of a daily life of Unschooling with joy. I personally can't think of a single question that is not covered somewhere. The format is easy to read, full of warm anecdotes, challenging ideas, and the core idea that the heart of Unschooling is parenting with absolute Trust. ~Robyn L. Coburn, unschooling mom of Jayn

The most useful book published for new unschoolers since The Unschooling Handbook. Rue addresses clearly and persuasively the most common questions and objections in an easily accessible format. The personal experience and conviction brought to each answer shines through along with her deep love and respect for her children. I'd recommend this book to anyone embarking on an unschooling lifestyle or wondering how to counter objections from family or friends. ~Danielle Conger, unschooling mom of Emily, Julia, and Sam

I can imagine that some might think that such a life with children is just too good to be true. But I know from my own experience that it is possible! Take her advice to heart! ~Kelly Lovejoy, unschooling mom of Cameron and Duncan

"It's simple, but not easy." Without even leaving home, your life can change all kinds of ways. Relationships between parents and children can go from rough and antagonistic to peaceful, productive and sweet. It's not easy, changing one's life for the better, but this book shows that it's simple. ~Sandra Dodd, unschooling mom of Kirby, Marty and Holly

Parenting A Free Child: An Unschooled Life

Rue Kream

To Jon – For emptying clogged dream catchers.
TINACOL

To Dagny – For never changing the radio station when Zeppelin's on,
and even though you think The Doors sound like old people
playing bad music.

To Rowan – For hoozgenflutzky. I don't know what that means,
and you still smell like pea soup.

Contents

Preface   **1**

Why choose unschooling rather than homeschooling?   **3**

Do your kids want to go to school?   **5**

How are unschooled children different?   **7**

Are we qualified to unschool?   **9**

Should I send my daughter to school, just for Kindergarten?   **12**

Should we try unschooling?   **15**

Will unschooling fill the need for my kids to interact with a
   group of children regularly?   **17**

Why do the opposite of what the majority of our society does?   **19**

Can I unschool with a chronic illness?   **21**

How can I support my daughter as she transitions to
   unschooling?   **23**

What do I do while my kids are having fun?   **25**

Will my kids stop learning if I stop lessons?   **26**

Am I spoiling my daughter?   **28**

What do you and your kids say when someone asks what grade
   they're in?   **30**

What about socialization?   **32**

Is it bad for kids to have very busy schedules?   **34**

How can I stop my child from making so many mistakes?   **35**

How can I get my daughter to do something more constructive?   **37**

All my kids want to do is play. What do your kids do?   **39**

What is a typical day?   **41**

How do you ensure that your kids eat properly?   **50**

What do you do when your child is hungry before dinner or
   doesn't want to eat what you make?   **53**

Do your kids watch TV whenever they want?   **55**

Do your kids watch whatever they want on TV?   **57**

Should I tell my kids I'm lifting restrictions on TV?   **60**

My son wants to play video and computer games all the time.
   What should I do?   **62**

Do you make your children brush their teeth?   **65**

If I want my son to take a bath before bedtime and he ignores
    me, there comes a point when I have to pick him up and take
    him, don't you agree? *67*
What about housework? *69*
If I don't make my child clean up her messes, how will she learn
    take responsibility for them? *72*
Do your kids take care of their pets? *74*
How did you handle the 'Why?' stage? *75*
Are you 100% honest with your kids? *77*
What do you think of boys playing with dolls? *79*
Do you have your kids work it out themselves when they argue? *80*
How are your children learning manners? *82*
Why should I do things for my child that he can do for himself? *84*
How do you feel about punishment? *86*
Do you just let your kids do whatever they want? *88*
What about the idea that we should remember who the parent is
    in our relationships with our kids? Can't we unschool but still
    enforce bedtimes, impose consequences, and have our children
    do chores? *91*
Isn't it a parent's duty to make choices for her child? *95*
How do you handle whining? *97*
How do you handle temper tantrums? *99*
How do you handle episodes of rage? *102*
What's wrong with using natural consequences? *104*
Wouldn't you rather see a child spanked than run over by a
    car? *106*
I've spanked my daughter. How do I change our relationship? *108*
How do we begin to parent more peacefully? *109*
Don't you ever have a bad day? *112*
Do unschoolers have any expectations for their kids, academically
    or otherwise? *114*
Do your children take standardized tests? *117*
What do you do about relatives quizzing your kids? *119*
Aren't you afraid there will be gaps in your kids' knowledge? *121*
How are unschooled children exposed to all the topics they
    would be exposed to in school? *123*

Don't you worry that your kids will be unprepared when the time comes for them to leave the nest? What about college? *125*

How do unschooled children learn to read? *129*

Do you make your kids sound things out? *132*

What do you think of incentive programs? *135*

Do you censor what your kids read or what movies they see? *138*

Should I tell my daughter to look it up when she asks me how to spell something? *140*

Shouldn't I give my kids the advantage of reading and writing well? *142*

What should I do about my daughter's terrible handwriting? *144*

What about math? *146*

Do unschooled kids learn the multiplication table? *148*

Do your kids get an allowance? *150*

How would an unschooler handle this situation? *152*

How do you handle it when your child wants to quit an activity that cost money to join? *153*

Dagny and Rowan answer some questions *156*

Things I wish adults would not say or imply to children, and one thing I wish they say more often *158*

Favorite games, resources, and craft supplies *160*

Parenting A Free Child

"I think creativity is a way of thinking, of being. It doesn't mean you have to be an artist or writer, it means you approach life with the ability to be open, to solve challenges new ways and try new things."
~Ren Allen, unschooling mom of Trevor, Jared, Sierra, and Jalen

Preface

For our family, unschooling has little to do with education and much more to do with our relationships, the way adults view children, and the philosophies we choose to live by. The principles that guide us do not apply only to a list of academic subjects. They permeate every part of our lives and our interactions with each other.

Jon and I treat Dagny and Rowan with respect. We trust that they know in their hearts what is of value to them. We choose to live in ways that keep us connected and involved in each other's day to day lives. We question the ideas that are accepted and passed down as fact from generation to generation. We believe that learning will happen in its own time and is not more important than loving or hoping or laughing. We live without subjects, in a world where life is not separated into neat little pieces but instead swirls and flows together in ways we could never design.

Trusting and respecting our children as whole people leads us to approach every aspect of our family life with fresh eyes. What are we trying to accomplish? What are our priorities? Are there new solutions to dealing with the issues that come up when living together as a family?

Our unschooling is our parenting is our life together.

I'm certainly not an expert in parenting or in unschooling (is anyone?), but rather a parent who has put a lot of thought into how children in general are treated and particularly into how my own children will be treated. In other words, I'm much like any other unschooling parent. We do not have a perfect life, and I am not a perfect mother. Overall, though, we have a good life with close relationships and a happy, peaceful home. We haven't found that these things come without any effort or thought or mistakes on our

1

parts, but working together we've been able to find ways of living with each other that contribute to the harmony of our family.

In *Escape From Childhood*, John Holt wrote, "Now I have a vision – of the world as it is and as it may be – to share with any who may want to look at it. I can't plant this vision in their minds; everyone makes his own model of reality. But the light I throw on experience may help some of them to see things somewhat differently and to make a new vision of their own." My goal in writing this book is to throw light on my experience. I hope it contributes positively to your vision, your model of reality, and the peacefulness of your family.

"A person's freedom of learning is part of his freedom of thought, even more basic than his freedom of speech." ~John Holt

Why did you choose unschooling rather than some other form of homeschooling?

I always knew that the way 'everybody' lived didn't feel right to me. I used to imagine that, when I grew up, I would live on an island with my family. From a very young age I struggled to understand what life really meant. As I grew, I came up with some answers. Life for me is truly feeling the earth underneath me and seeing the things around me. It is enjoying every moment with the people I love. It is making another person smile. It is thinking and dreaming, feeling pain and feeling joy.

When Dagny was a baby, I started to ask myself new questions. Does it matter if we know our multiplication tables? Is accumulation of knowledge the goal of life? Should there *be* a goal of life? Why should we spend her childhood apart from each other when we both want so much to be together? Can we step off the well-worn path and find our own way?

When I learned that unschooling was a possibility, I was thrilled that we could continue to live as we had been since Dagny was born. I found the answers to my questions, which in reality I had known all along. Children belong with their families. Nothing is more important than living in connection with the ones you love and sharing life's experiences. We can't help but learn as we live full and interesting lives together.

When we rejected the kind of life that comes with a roadmap, we were able to question what it was we wanted from our lives and to determine what we do not want. We want joy. We want to know that we lived consciously and in the moment. We do not want to mold our children. We want them to have the freedom to choose their lives. We do not want to ever feel that we wasted time we could have spent together.

Our major reasons for unschooling have nothing to do with academics, but of course there are reasons we choose not to teach our children. We believe that children (humans) seek out knowledge in the same way they seek out fun or food, and we believe that adults can do a lot to interfere with that desire to learn. We don't believe that repetition is necessary or that there is a list of things that every person needs to know. We believe that turning the relationship of parent and child into a relationship between teacher and student is detrimental. We want our children to own their learning and to learn for their own reasons, not to please a teacher.

Jon and I have determined what it is we live by, what matters, and what does not. It has evolved and will continue to evolve as we face new challenges and joys in our lives. We want to choose the lives we lead, and we want our children to have the opportunity to do the same.

Ultimately I'd say that the reason we choose to unschool is because we want our children to be truly free.

"A free bird leaps on the back of the wind and floats downstream till the current ends and dips his wing in the orange sun rays and dares to claim the sky." ~Maya Angelou

Have your kids ever said they'd like to go to school?

Dagny did go to school for kindergarten. She still feels unhappy that we didn't know unschooling was an option. She remembers eating in the loud lunchroom, being made to count to 100 every day when she already knew how, hearing about how someone threw rocks at a girl in her class on the bus, being scared by the fire drill, being forced to take 'naps,' and having to sit next to someone who irritated her. Rowan was only two at the time, but she remembers enough to make school seem unattractive.

My sister has two birds. On warm days she puts their cage outside, where they can feel the air and hear the call of the birds in the trees. No free bird has ever tried to climb into the cage with them. That's the image that comes to mind for me when people ask me about my free children going to school.

It does sometimes happen that an unschooled child will ask to go to school. In many cases, parents find, after discussing it, that what the child really wants is a lunchbox or to be able to ride on a bus, in which case it is easy enough to give her what she wants. In other cases the child is feeling lonely, and more of an effort needs to be made to connect with some new friends. Curiosity can also play a part. What goes on behind those doors? Maybe it's more fun than parents would have them believe. Often a visit to a school for a day is enough to give a child a taste of what it is actually like.

Some children feel pressured by relatives or neighborhood children. In that case, I would suggest that a conversation with the other person involved is a much better course of action than sending the child to school.

If it happened that Dagny or Rowan found that she could get something out of school that she couldn't get at home, I would support her just as I would if she were interested in any other activity. In the meantime, it's not something I worry or even think about. They are happy with their lives and revel in their freedom. I don't foresee their choosing the cage when they so enjoy soaring through the sky.

"Thank goodness I was never sent to school; it would have rubbed off some of the originality." ~Beatrix Potter

In what ways do you think unschooled children are different from traditionally schooled children?

My brother-in-law, who is a middle-school teacher (and also an unschooling parent), once told me that my children have a spark that he does not see in the children in his class. Rowan and Dagny have an enthusiasm that schooled children seem to lose in second or third grade. They take ownership of their knowledge and believe that they can learn anything they want to learn. When Jon asked Dagny whether she could play a song on her guitar that was on the radio, she answered, "I could if I knew how." That seems to be how she feels about everything – if she decides to learn it, she'll find out 'how' and there's no doubt that she could do it.

Children in school cannot talk when they want to. They cannot leave when they want to. They cannot eat when they want to. They cannot run, drink, draw, read, sleep, sing, dream, or play when they want to. In school kids are limited in what they are supposed to learn. They are taught things that don't interest them. They are judged on their knowledge, and their minds and bodies are not their own. They often retain knowledge only long enough to pass a test or write a paper. They are given a narrow view of what is valuable and are taught that just being interested in something is not enough to make it important.

Unschooled kids are used to determining what to do with their own time, bodies, and minds. The unschooled children I know are so interested in the world around them that they inspire me to be more interested too. Because of this interest they are also some of the most *interesting* people I know. They don't worry about whether it is 'cool' to be interested in something. They look for new experiences rather than shy away from them.

The unschooled kids I know don't compare themselves to others. They don't need to have the latest clothes or listen only to the most popular music. They are very self-assured and confident. They are comfortable with people of all ages and in many situations.

They also have a very different viewpoint when it comes to classes. One day Dagny's guitar class was cancelled; her Grampa said something about how she must be excited not to have to go, as just about any school kid would be, for example, on a snow day. Dagny wasn't at all excited. She was upset to miss it. The difference, of course, is that going to class is part of following her passion for music, not something she is required to do whether she likes it or not. She found a teacher whom she likes as a person and who is interested in her as a person too. They share an interest, and she enjoys her time with him.

In *A Sense of Self: Listening to Homeschooled Adolescent Girls*, author Susannah Sheffer interviewed homeschooled girls in order to compare their experiences with the experiences of schooled girls who reportedly lose much of their self-esteem in the middle school years. In her conclusion she writes, "Homeschooling can give young people the chance to ask the question, 'Who am I? What do I really want?' It is through the process of asking and then gradually answering that question that the girls I've interviewed have developed the strengths and the resistance abilities that give them such an unusually strong sense of self. They can say, 'I like who I am,' not just because they have learned to repeat such a statement but because they have had a chance to think about who they would like to be and to work at becoming that person. This is the chance I would like to see all young people have."

This is the chance unschooling gives our children.

"While we are postponing, life speeds by." ~Seneca

We just can't decide whether we should unschool. We've read so much our heads are spinning. We're not sure we're qualified to keep our kids home – what if we don't know enough? Sometimes my kids ask me a question regarding something I don't know a lot about. Often I can give them some information, but not a complete answer. I don't know whether to bring it up later. I'm not sure how to find my kids' interests, and I'm afraid we're going to fail at unschooling. We're thinking about doing lessons in the morning and unschooling in the afternoon.

I recommend making a decision one way or the other. If all the information you're reading is overwhelming you, take a break from that and just think about it simply: Do you want to be home with your kids? Do they want to be home with you? If so, the rest will fall into place.

You are their parents. Unschooling at its best is an extension of good parenting. In *Teach Your Own,* John Holt wrote, "Human beings have been sharing information and skills, and passing on to their children whatever they knew, for about a million years now. Along the way they have built some very complicated and highly skilled societies." You don't need to know anything more than you know right this minute. You know your kids. You love them. Who could be better qualified to help them as they grow than you?

There's no way to 'fail' at not going to school. A huge amount of stress and worry comes through in your questions. It sounds as if you're putting a lot of pressure on yourself, and by extension on your children, to do this 'right,' when in fact all you have to do is take them out of school and *live* with them.

Pretend that your children are on summer vacation. Find work that you love to do, and let your kids help you if they want to. Look for the learning that they do, even in the places you wouldn't imagine it, and trust that their interests are inherent to them. Enjoy each

9

other. Get yourselves out to new places, try new foods, spend a day in your pajamas, watch movies, or pretend you're tourists and visit local attractions. Offer lots of new sights, sounds, smells, and tastes to your kids.

I don't think it's possible to unschool part-time. Unschooling requires a trust that children want to learn and that they will learn what they need when they need it. Undermining that trust by saying, "This is something I don't believe you will learn unless I teach you," will not allow your children to feel the ownership of their learning that unschooled children feel. It will give them the message that ultimately you are responsible for their learning. It may also give them the message that the required 'subject' is something so uninteresting that no one would want to learn it if not made to.

Dagny and Rowan ask me lots of questions I don't know the answers to. I do the same with their questions that I do with anything that might come up when I'm having a conversation with another person. I tell them what I do know and sometimes think of a person we could ask if they want to know more. If they bring it up again when we're near a computer and are still interested, we look it up together. If they've gotten me interested, I look it up myself. Then I'll usually say, "Hey, do you still want to know whether mosquitoes hibernate?" (Some do.)

If your child is not interested in it later, that's ok. You don't have to encourage her to follow up on it. Maybe the amount of information you came up with was enough. Maybe she just wanted to know how much you knew about it. Maybe she was just making conversation. Almost certainly she'll add your little bit of knowledge to some other bits she picks up from someone else or hears in a song or reads or sees on TV.

I've noticed that most of the things my kids (and I) learn are learned in a 'bits and pieces' manner. When they are interested in something, they start noticing it everywhere. They make connections and see patterns. They pull information from a vast number of sources and put it all together in a way that makes sense to them. You are not their only source of information. It is not necessary for you to have all of the answers, and knowing that you don't will only help your children to accept that it is all right for them to say, "I don't know."

"For every person wishing to teach there are thirty not wanting to be taught." ~Sellar & Yeatman

We were planning to unschool, but now that kindergarten age is approaching I'm thinking maybe we should send our daughter. We have a nice school down the street. They sing every day, have lots of toys, and we know the teacher. She's dying to get my daughter in her class. I do think socialization is important, and I'm thinking of just sending her for one year.

Here are some questions that come to mind:

What if your daughter doesn't feel like singing every day? To me, this question is very important. It's a small example of the kind of thing that schools do to 'benefit' children. It should be fun, right? Well, truly, what if she just doesn't want to sing? What if she doesn't even want to hear anyone sing? I certainly feel that way sometimes, when I just want some peace and quiet. Luckily for me, I can move to another room or ask the person who's singing whether she would please stop. Not so a child in a classroom.

Even the parts of school that are created with the idea of giving children some enjoyment are not going to be enjoyed by every child at every time. Just as importantly, what about those moments when your daughter wants to sing and it is not the designated time? Is it ok with you for her to be made to sit quietly when she wants to sing?

Is there a reason you can't have lots of toys at your house? Couldn't she have toys that she can use when she wants to and in her own ways, at home? If money is an issue, what about home-made toys? How many toys are really necessary in order to have a good time, anyway?

Are you willing to put your family's life on the school's schedule? To wake your daughter when, if left to herself, her body would take another hour or two of sleep?

Are you willing to have to ask permission or give an excuse to spend a day with your child?

Why does this teacher want your child in her class? Is she opposed to homeschooling? If so, do you feel confident that she will not sabotage your intention to keep your daughter home next year? A child's teacher can be a huge influence in her life.

Is your daughter willing to live with no privacy for most of her day? To always have someone know where she is and what she is doing, what she has brought with her and where she keeps it?

Is your daughter willing to choose her clothing based on the decisions of some authority of the school? In many schools hats are not allowed. No tanktops, no short skirts, no clothes with brand names. Is this something that your daughter is comfortable with?

Do you believe that the majority of socialization that takes place at school is positive? Just about everyone remembers being told, "We're not here to socialize," at some point in her school years. In addition, with 25 to 30 children under the supervision of one teacher, an awful lot of meanness passes unseen in a classroom and on the playground. Not just the major bullying that seems to be on the news every few weeks, but the smaller unkind acts that eat away at a child's sense of self and safety.

Do you feel confident that in being taught some academics your daughter won't lose some of her innate curiosity and belief that she can learn things on her own? Right now she probably thinks there's nothing she can't do. Will she retain that spirit after a year of schooling? Right now she probably thinks that figuring out new things is exciting. Will she still think so when she has been trained to come up with the 'right' answer in order to prove her worth?

Is your daughter comfortable with having to ask someone's permission to use the bathroom? Aside from being embarrassing for some children, there are also occasional times when the answer will be no due to time constraints. Are you comfortable with the possible ramifications to her health?

Are you and she comfortable with her being required to eat on the school's schedule instead of following her body's natural rhythms? Learning to wait for lunchtime instead of eating when the body signals that it is hungry does not lead to healthy eating habits.

Are you and she comfortable with the fact that the amount of time she is given to eat lunch is hardly enough to eat a candy bar, never mind a nutritious meal? In some schools lunch period is about 15 minutes. Add to that the crowded, noisy lunchroom, and I can't imagine you've got a recipe for healthy digestion.

Are you and she comfortable with her having to sit down when she wants to run, draw when she wants to jump, be inside when she wants to be outside, write when she wants to sleep?

Are you concerned that what you'll have to un-do will outweigh whatever benefits you think your daughter would get out of going to school?

Finally, is there anything your daughter could want or need that cannot be provided for outside of a school environment? I can tell you that we have never come across a thing.

"Grade school is the snooze button on the clock-radio of life." ~John Rogers

My daughter went to kindergarten this year, and she really loved it. I missed her and want to keep her home this year. She's willing to unschool, but I'm not sure she really wants to. What if I keep her home and she's unhappy? Maybe I just don't want her to grow up. What if you're wrong and school would have been a great experience for your kids?

Maybe she'll love being home too. It can't hurt to give it a try if she is willing. If she is unhappy you'll know, and you can reconsider if that happens. I wouldn't worry too much about 'what ifs.' School brings plenty of those, too, and worrying about them is a waste of energy and doesn't bring anything positive into your life.

I think following your heart is the way to go. You want to be with your child – that's wonderful! Only good things can come from that. She will continue to grow and change whether she goes to school or not. The difference is that you will be a much bigger part of each other's lives while she grows if she stays home. Your lives will be intertwined just as they were before your daughter went to school. Not wanting to miss out on her growing is not the same thing as wanting her to stay little forever.

Our society encourages us to distance ourselves from our children when they are very young. Unschooling allows your relationship to develop naturally. Outside of the school environment, your daughter can grow into independence in her own time.

I think just about everyone feels some nervousness when making a big decision. For me, I know that once I really commit to a decision I feel more peaceful about it almost immediately. Someone once said about unschooling that it's like deciding to jump off a cliff and then realizing you can fly. I say: grab your daughter's hand and jump.

What if I'm wrong? I can compare that 'what if' to a reality. Rowan and Dagny have amazing lives. They are happy and fun loving and incredible people who are completely open to life; they are living lives of their own choosing. Whoever they might have been had they gone to school, who they are is just right.

"I don't think schools teach young people anything about friendship, intimacy, and trust." ~John Holt

My son is in a private preschool. I'm not happy about the teasing that is part of life at school. I keep thinking there's more we could be doing with that $500 a month. On the other hand he seems to like it well enough, and I do think it's important for my kids to interact with a group of children consistently as they grow up. How can unschooling fill this need?

Unschooling might not fill *your* need to have your child interact with a group, but, if it is his need, unschooling will fill it just fine.

What kind of socialization are you paying for? Is spending his day with a bunch of unhappy kids who take out their frustrations on the kids around them (in teasing and probably in other ways) a positive experience for your son? Top that off with some adults who think kids should have to go through it and you couldn't *pay* me $500 a month to go — or any amount of money to send my kids.

The pattern I see over and over is that children enjoy going to school until they are eight or nine, but for the remaining years the majority of them just mark the time until it will be over. If your child enjoys being with groups of kids, there are many opportunities for group activities. Sports, music, park and recreation programs, library programs, and homeschooling groups can all provide group experiences. One great resource for finding other homeschoolers in your area is The Homeschool Social Register (http://www.homeschoolmedia.net/register/index.phtml), created by unschooling dad Dave Hirschman.

I'd spend some time thinking about *why* it's important to you that your kids spend time consistently with other children of the same age. Is there something you think they can learn only in that environment? Is it because you still have a bit of school left in you? What if one of your children were more introverted and wouldn't want to spend consistent time with a group?

17

You really can't do much in life without socializing to some extent. An unschooled child is able to socialize with a wider variety of people than the average school kid, and his sense of self and freedom is encouraged instead of trampled. He's also able to choose just how much socialization he is comfortable with.

Here's an embarrassing little tidbit: Before Dagny was born I had decided that it was very important to me that we involve her in a lot of sports activities. It somehow didn't occur to me that she might have absolutely no interest in sports. As it is, she's mildly interested in some sports but has never wanted to join a team, and luckily for her I came to my senses long before she was able to bounce a ball.

When I look back on why I thought it was important, I have to admit to myself that it was because when I was in school the popular kids were all jocks, and I didn't want Dagny to be one of the 'unpopular' kids. Thinking about it now, it's hard to believe I had those thoughts. Our children are who they are and will be who they will be. We now live in a world where people are not categorized, and it is a much nicer world to live in.

There *is* much more you could do with that money! Movies, travel, ice cream, helping others in your community, craft supplies – $6,000 a year could mean a lot of fun together.

"No doubt another may also think for me; but it is not therefore desirable that he should do so to the exclusion of my thinking for myself." ~Henry David Thoreau

You want me to lie to the school board? Isn't that teaching my children that lying is acceptable? Even if I don't think the majority of society is doing the right thing, societal norms are present. You can't fight the government, so why teach our children at home when that's exactly what the government and society doesn't want? Our children are just people, and we don't want them to think they are so special that they don't have to get through school just like everyone else.

You are the governor of your own existence.

There is no reason you would have to lie to the school board. An unschooling life can easily be translated into the language of institutional schooling. If you have difficulty doing it, there are online resources available to you. In many places it is unnecessary to report to the school board at all.

However, if I were in the position of having to lie in order to give my children the right to grow up in freedom, I would do so. I don't say that lightly. Honesty is very important to me. However, if the government put me in the position of having to choose between honesty and my children's happiness, physical and mental well-being, and freedom, I would not hesitate to lie.

What would this model for my children? I believe it would model that we cannot and must not let our beliefs be determined for us by other people. I believe it would model that we cannot and must not give away our freedom. As my good friend Racheli Gai once said, "Repression requires compliance."

What the government or society wants does not factor into my decisions. What will bring us peace and happiness in our lives does. If we let others dictate how we spend our lives, have we really lived them? Who we are is in great part made up of the choices we make.

19

I do treat my children as if they are special. They are special. Yours are too!

"Adversity introduces a man to himself." ~Unknown

I have a chronic illness, and I worry that my limitations will interfere with my children's learning. Can I unschool with a chronic illness?

At 21 I was diagnosed with fibromyalgia and myofascial pain syndrome. I suffer from joint pain, muscle pain, insomnia, memory problems, and a tendency to drop things. I've learned to function on little sleep, to push through pain, to ask for help, and to laugh instead of cry when I feel out of control.

My health did not play a part in our decision to unschool, but as time passed it came to play a big part in our lives, and therefore in our unschooling. My condition is just one more reason that we feel that unschooling provides an ideal life for our family.

Some of the less significant benefits of unschooling with a chronic illness are the logistical ones. Mornings are generally most difficult for a person suffering from fibromyalgia, and unschooling allows us to schedule our mornings around these difficulties rather than around a timetable set up by the school system. My symptoms are also very unpredictable. It is impossible to know when I'm going to be most mobile, and spending our days together allows us to take advantage of every moment that I am feeling well.

Much more meaningful to me are the ways in which unschooling while dealing with a chronic illness has affected our relationships, my children's characters, and our family's outlook on life. The sense Jon and I always had of being a team, facing life's joys and obstacles together, grew to involve our children. There has never been any of the feeling of "us" and "them" that seems so prevalent in our society between parents and children. We work together to find ways around the problems caused by my illness and also to make our home the happy and peaceful place we all want it to be.

Dealing with my illness has contributed to my children's development of empathy, caring, and thoughtfulness. The consideration that they show me has extended to quiet acts of thoughtfulness for others – bringing someone a pillow when she looks uncomfortable, offering to help carry something when a person looks overloaded, or running to open a door for a mom carrying a baby. These are not things we taught or required them to do.

Dealing with fibromyalgia has reaffirmed for us that the unschooling philosophy is sound. We never worry that unschooling might cause our children to miss out on important areas of learning. Our lives provide opportunities to learn lessons much more valuable than how to diagram a sentence or solve a math problem. How could we *not* trust that we and our children will learn what we need to know?

"The greatest sweetener of human life is Friendship." ~Joseph Addison

My daughter will be leaving school this week, and we plan to unschool. She's concerned about keeping in touch with her friends, but I'm considering limiting the amount of time she spends on Instant Messenger, because it's important to me that we get lots of family time. I'll probably also limit TV and video games, because I've heard that, while they're deschooling, kids sometimes binge on those things. I'm also worried because she is feeling doubtful about the unschooling lifestyle. She's afraid that she'll be below her peers in subjects like math and science. How can I assure her that she will learn what she needs to know when she needs it?

If your daughter is concerned about losing touch with her friends, I recommend doing everything you can to help her to stay connected with them. Not only will she be happier because her social needs are filled, but your relationship with her will benefit as well. She will see that you take her wants seriously and that what's important to her is important to you.

Instant Messenger is a wonderful resource. It's not only a fun way for kids to keep in touch — although that would be a good enough reason not to limit it. It provides yet another opportunity for you to see that learning is *everywhere*. Instant Messenger is real-life writing, which is likely to improve spelling, typing, and communication skills. It can encompass computer skills, social skills, geography, current events, and pop-culture.

I would not be concerned about getting enough family time. Right now your free time is greatly limited by school, commuting, and homework. Next week you will find that you have huge amounts of time together. Restricting your daughter will be counter-productive if you want that time together to be spent happily.

Deschooling refers to the period of time when a family is leaving school behind and getting used to a new way of life. The commonly

23

touted formula is that a person needs one month for each year she was in school (or schooled-at-home) to shed the narrow thinking that school can encourage and to begin to be comfortable with her new freedom.

There's a reason kids are drawn to TV and video games while they are deschooling. They need time to adjust to freedom and just be. If you stop her from doing what she is interested in doing, you will be interfering with the process and building resentment between the two of you.

Spending a few days with a large group of unschoolers at the Live and Learn Unschooling Conference is a wonderful experience. Anyone with doubts would benefit from attending. Information about the conference is available at www.liveandlearnconference.org.

The unschoolers we've met are happy and interesting and friendly. They are the best possible proof that living without comparisons and subjects and all that school brings is not only possible, but a fabulous way of life.

There are also Internet resources available. She could visit www.unschooling.info, where she could talk to unschoolers of all ages. There are a number of websites created by grown unschoolers. A few are:

> http://www.chancey.info/
> http://smokylake.com/Christy/homeschool.htm
> http://www.homestead.com/peaceandcarrots/
> http://www.quovadis-gathering.org/main.html
> http://community.nbtsc.org/

Finally, there's time. In time she will see that she is learning, see that life is not divided into subjects, and see that, if she follows her passions, the rest will come naturally. But first and foremost, *you* have to trust in unschooling enough to know that, if what she feels she needs to know is how to develop and maintain her relationships with her friends, it is just as valid as doing math and science.

"Our children are watching us live, and what we ARE shouts louder than anything we can say." ~Wilfred A. Peterson

We're new to unschooling. My kids love it. They're spending time playing together, reading, building things, watching TV, just having fun. The problem is me. I like to plan things, and I worry that I'm being lazy with them. There are things I would love to do with my time, but I feel too guilty to do them. Do you have any advice?

Do you want your children to feel guilty for doing the things they love? Peace Pilgrim once said, "Live this day! Yesterday is but a dream and tomorrow is only a vision, but today well-lived makes every yesterday a dream of happiness and every tomorrow a vision of hope." Yes, we are parents, but we are also people living our one and only lives. Let your children see you live each day with happiness and hope.

You can still plan things. Plan things no one has ever planned before, see whether your kids want to plan anything, and be willing to ditch the plan if something better comes along or if the kids don't share your enthusiasm for the idea.

If you're feeling as if you're being lazy, maybe you should look at what *you're* doing while your kids are having all this fun. Unschooling is for everyone. You get to play too! Play with your children, and play yourself. Try to do something you've always wanted to do but thought you wouldn't be good at. Go to a new grocery store and buy things you've never seen before. Rent movies you've never heard of without reading the packages. There's nothing stopping you from doing anything you want to do, so sit down and think: what do you want to do? Then you can make a plan to do it while your kids happily play.

"Joy springs from within. No one makes you joyous; you choose joyfulness." ~Unknown

I'm finding that I'm not enjoying homeschooling any more. I don't want to do lessons, and neither do my kids. I think we may be moving towards unschooling, but I'm worried that they'll stop learning if I stop lessons. What about spelling and history and geography? If I can't motivate them now (at 7 and 5), how will I do it when they're older and really need to get to work?

I think a lot of people evolve into unschooling just as you are describing. And I think, for most of them, there is a lot of confusion and doubt and general angst while their minds take in a lot of new ideas and question things they've taken for granted.

Are you enjoying life with your kids? We focus on joy in our family. Everything else falls into place if we focus on enjoying each other, doing things we love (this includes the parents, too), and making our lives what we want them to be (which in our case is happy, peaceful, connected, and interesting, among other things).

I would find it hard to motivate myself to do lessons too. Lessons are boring, no matter how much you try to make them interesting. They're an artificial moment in your day. We have never done a lesson, but history, geography and spelling are part of our everyday lives. Unschooled kids don't necessarily learn things at the same time as a schooled (or schooled-at-home) child, but when they do learn something, it is because it has meaning in their lives.

I don't believe anyone can go an hour without learning something. Whether they choose to be open to that learning is another story. The unschooled kids I know are totally open and look for new things to learn. They think the world is interesting, and they want to soak it all up. Learning is not a chore or something they do only between 8:00 and 2:00 on weekdays. Forcing them to do lessons would destroy that part of them.

When do your kids 'really need to get to work?' What's going to be different when they're eleven or fifteen? Dagny's eleven and is every bit as enthusiastic and interested as she was as a toddler. The things she's learning are often more complex, but some things are the same – she's learning them because she wants to, because they have meaning to her. She'll own that knowledge.

History, spelling, math – they all come up in little bits and pieces that the kids put together into a whole that makes sense to them. Drop the lessons, and look at what your children do. As unschooling mom Anne Ohman once said, "It requires an active effort on your part to shift your own perspective and your old definition of *learning* – you need to work on seeing learning happening in what your children love to do." Make that effort, and you will be amazed at how motivated to learn your children really are.

"Never fear spoiling children by making them too happy. Happiness is the atmosphere in which all good affections grow." ~Thomas Bray

I know I'm supposed to help my daughter follow her interests, but when I help her get whatever she needs for all of her many projects, I feel a bit like she's being spoiled, especially if she ends up not completing the project.

While shopping for some other things at the craft store a couple of weeks ago, Rowan came up with an idea for a project. She picked out some silk flowers and a little fake frog, and made plans for an indoor flower garden. She spent a long time choosing colors that she felt worked well together. The stems were quite long, so she thought she could plant them and water the garden and then pull the flowers up slowly so it would look as if they were growing. We talked about how water drains in a container garden and whether that would be necessary with fake flowers. I asked her what else she needed, and she said just some dirt and a big container.

That night Rowan said she'd like to get the container, so Jon took her shopping. She wasn't happy with the selection at the store they went to. She had a specific size and shape in mind, and nothing the store carried was quite right. Since it was getting late, they decided to try the next day and came home.

She wasn't sleepy, so she got to work on the water feature for her garden. She used a recycled frozen food container to make a pond. The frog she bought was made of Styrofoam, and she was concerned that it might get ruined, so she came up with a way to make him float on top of the water without actually getting wet. It took a couple of tries, but in the end her solution was very ingenious.

We went to two stores the next day and finally found the perfect bin for her garden. She filled it with some peat moss left over from another project and went to work arranging her garden. It looks great, and she's very happy with it.

About a week later Jon mentioned that he had been telling someone about Rowan's project, and the response to our taking her to shopping for a bin was that we were 'spoiling her.'

Do we spoil her by making sure she has what she needs to express her creativity? It surely doesn't seem that way. While watching ABC's *Extreme Makeover: Home Edition* one night, Rowan told me that hearing the stories of the suffering that the families on the show go through makes her think a lot about her life. One of the things she said, with an amazed and grateful tone, was, "I never even run out of paper!" She's thankful for little things that many people take for granted.

Were we spoiling her by getting her a big bulletin board for what she calls her penny project? She is collecting pennies from the birth years of people she knows, so she can arrange them into a kind of monetary family tree. She hasn't glued them on yet, but the board is ready and waiting for her. If she never ends up using the board for that project, it'll still have been worth the $5 I spent. She knows that I believe her ideas have value and that I want to help her when she wants me to.

Helping a child to fill her wants and needs does not 'spoil' her. Denying children what they want and need arbitrarily – doling it out based on their behavior or the parent's whim – creates a neediness and a feeling of lack that can cause children to behave in some pretty unpleasant ways. In those cases the problem is not that the children are spoiled but that the parents have put them in a position to have to beg, sneak, lie, or nag in order to get what they want. The child loses touch with what is actually important to her as she gets caught up in the battle of wills and the need to fill a hole that didn't have to exist in the first place.

It's okay to be kind to our children. It's okay to give them a feeling of abundance. Knowing that their own needs and wants are valued will only make them want to help others to meet their needs and wants too. Kindness begets kindness.

"Man's mind stretched to a new idea never goes back to its original dimensions." ~Oliver Wendell Holmes

People always ask my daughter or me what grade she's in. We don't know what to say. What do you and your kids say?

We usually say that they don't go to school and therefore are not in a grade. This, of course, leads to other questions: What do you mean they don't go to school? Do you have to report to someone? Do they take tests? How do you know they're learning? How do you know you're qualified to teach them?

Some people ask these questions because they are sincerely interested. Other times it's obvious that the person is only asking because she's instantly decided that what we're doing is wrong and she wants to argue with me about it. My answer may differ based on my perception of why the person is asking, but in either case I project a happy and confident attitude, because I am happy and confident in our decision to unschool. Both Dagny and Rowan stand a little taller and have smiles in their eyes when they say, "We're unschoolers." To those who are open to the idea, knowing that we are happy with it makes the idea even more attractive. For the others, well, it's hard to argue with someone who is so obviously thrilled with her life.

Some unschoolers choose to answer based on what grade the child would be in if she went to school. By doing this you can generally avoid the follow up questions. We do not do this for a few reasons. One, it doesn't feel honest. Two, I don't keep track of what grade my kids would be in if they went to school. We do what we can to keep school as fully out of our lives as possible. Three, I'm opposed to the whole idea of grading. Four, why not spread the word about unschooling?

I try to tell as many people as possible about how we live. Sure, many of them look at me as if I'm crazy and my children are doomed to a life of ignorance. Every once in a while, though, we come across someone who lights up. You can almost hear the new thoughts exploding in their minds as they consider the idea. I am eternally grateful to author Sandra Boynton for discussing her family's unschooling on a television interview. Without her it might have been years before I learned that it was possible for my children to live their lives in freedom.

Any time my family's unschooling is received in an open-minded way, I feel that I am giving back what I received and hope that other children's lives will be changed for the better as our children's were. The more of us who share the joy that unschooling can bring, the happier the world our grandchildren live in will be.

"Simply being different isn't wrong. Don't try to be a duckling if you're born to be a swan." ~Unknown

If your kids don't go to school how do they learn to get along with people their own age? We don't want our children to be different. It's easier on them if we help them fit in. This can only happen if they go to school and get socialized and learn how to be around other children. Why would I want my daughter to be a misfit?

"Don't you worry about socialization?" It's the number one question people ask me when they hear we are unschoolers, and it's not a difficult question to answer.

Nowhere but in school do we expect people to socialize with only those who were born in the same year. Separating children by age may make administrative issues easier for the schools, but assuming that all children of the same age are ready to learn the same things and should spend their time together does not benefit the children in any way.

Rowan and Dagny are open to friendships with babies, toddlers, young children, teenagers, adults, parents and grandparents. Their friendships are based on interests and values and common ground rather than on age or circumstances.

What if we turn the question back at the parents of schooled children: "Aren't *you* worried about socialization?"

Dictionary.com defines socialization as *the adoption of the behavior patterns of the surrounding culture.* The culture of schools is a closed culture; it is a culture of conformity. In adopting the behavior patterns of this culture, schooled kids are socialized to cover up their differences, but they are there just the same. The necessity to conform is one of the most detrimental aspects of institutional schooling. Is it truly easier to fit in? Easier to repress whatever aspects of yourself don't fit the mold? Not in my experience.

Outside of school's closed culture, unschooled kids don't need to change who they are in the hopes of getting other people to like them. They are free to be themselves.

The age segregation in schools socializes children to look with disdain at those who are younger (much to the detriment of their relationships with their siblings) and to conform themselves to whatever expectations people have for their age group.

Outside of school's closed culture, unschooled kids accept people for who they are, regardless of age. One afternoon not long ago Dagny and Rowan snuggled up together so that Dagny could read her a story. That in itself made me smile. They are friends as well as sisters. At one point in the story, Dagny came across the word *solemn*. She hesitated, unsure of the word. Rowan turned to her and said, "Oh, that's solemn. It means sad." and Dagny thanked her and continued with the story. Rowan is four years younger than Dagny, but Dagny has not been socialized to think of her as inferior, or to be embarrassed if she knows something that Dagny does not.

With the possible exception of a select few, every child in school feels she is a misfit at one time or another. In school it matters how you dress, whether you're athletic, whether you're too smart, what kind of shoes you can afford, and what kind of music you listen to (among other things). Kids are categorized by teachers and each other from the first day of school through graduation. While some of the categories are more positive than others, most have a negative connotation of some sort ('Brains' aren't cool, 'Jocks' aren't smart), and all are limiting.

Outside of school's closed culture, unschooled kids never have to feel the confinement of a label or the desire to be something they are not.

If you were hoping for a shorter answer, here it is: Am I worried about socialization? Yes, but not for my own children.

"Don't underestimate the value of Doing Nothing, of just going along, listening to all the things you can't hear, and not bothering."
~Pooh's Little Instruction Book

One of the reasons we didn't send our kids to school is because we saw so many overscheduled school children with no time to play. Now our unschooled kids are involved in so many activities (ballet, soccer, music lessons, homeschool group outings, etc.) that we're barely ever home. Is it necessarily a bad thing for kids to have busy schedules?

That depends on the kids. Some people love to be busy. The fact that you're worried about it, though, is enough of a reason to put some time into thinking about whether you and your kids have enough free time. Our society doesn't think kindly of free time, although I have noticed some commercials lately on the kids' networks promoting it. Recess has become existent in name only in many places (I don't consider 15 minutes of being outside recess) and tossed aside altogether in others. Adults are working longer and longer hours, and it has become accepted as the norm. There does exist some pressure to be *doing* all the time.

I don't believe this is a healthy way to live for most people or a way of life that is conducive to a connected family. If you have concerns about over scheduling, talk with your kids. Do they feel too busy? How do they want to spend their days? Make sure that their need for downtime and time with your family is being met. Make sure that they know you want them to do what *they* want to do and that they don't have to do anything just to please you.

Also consider whether your own need for downtime and family time is being fulfilled. It's quite possible that your needs will differ from theirs, and your needs are important too. If even one person in the family is feeling over scheduled, you can all work together to come up with a solution that gives everyone what s/he needs and wants.

"Anyone who has never made a mistake has never tried anything new." ~Albert Einstein

My child keeps making one mistake after another. I'm giving him freedom like you suggest, but he just can't seem to do anything right. How do I make sure he follows the right path?

I believe that each of us has to determine what our own 'right path' is. If you are still trying to determine that for your son, he does not have the freedom that I feel a person should have. There are many things I've done that others might see as mistakes but that I know in my heart are not (unschooling, for example). Trust that your son knows and wants to do what is right for him.

Mistakes are important. Every time I make a mistake, I learn something I didn't know before. In school a mistake can cost a grade or cause embarrassment. In life a mistake is a chance to try again armed with more information.

Kelly Lovejoy, Live and Learn Unschooling Conference coordinator and unschooling mom, calls mistakes 'learning takes.' Simply changing your perspective can help you to see the value in making a mistake and gives you the confidence to try things you're not sure you'll be able to do well. When our children see that we're willing to try new things and accept that we may make mistakes, it can inspire them to try things they may fear they'll have trouble with too.

I've also found that, if I can let go of the idea of making a mistake, I can sometimes see things turning out differently than I planned in a positive way. For example, I did a decoupage project using some favorite photos. At first I was disappointed because I couldn't get the pictures to lie smoothly. As I continued, though, I noticed that the overall effect made the finished pieces look aged and more interesting. Many times I've mistakenly added an ingredient to a recipe and found that it tasted better than the original (of course, I've had the opposite result as well!). So instead of automatically assuming I've made a mistake, I've learned to think of it more as experimenting without having a particular outcome in mind.

I would be careful of thinking things like "he just can't seem to do anything right." Even if you never say those words aloud, your child could internalize that it's how you feel about him. By focusing on the positives in your son, you can help him to do the same for himself.

"A man is not idle because he is absorbed in thought. There is a visible labor and there is an invisible labor." ~Victor Hugo

How can I get my child to do something more constructive? All she wants to do is daydream. How can I motivate her to be more active?

Some people are by nature more sedentary than others. Is it possible that you are comparing her activity level to someone else's? I would try to stop thinking of your daughter as inactive. It doesn't bring anything positive to your relationship and could very well contribute to a negative self-image for her.

Does she have the opportunity to be more active if she wants to be? Room to run around, swings, a jungle gym, a bike, a trampoline? I consider it my responsibility to provide the environment and let the kids decide to what extent they want to use what I provide.

I'm always suspicious of comments which suggest that a person is only interested in doing *one* thing. So the first thing I'd recommend is to think about whether it's really true that all she wants to do is daydream. I also question why you consider daydreaming a poor choice of activity. Here's what dictionary.com says about daydreaming: *A dreamlike musing or fantasy while awake, especially of the fulfillment of wishes or hopes.* That sounds pretty great to me.

In addition to what the dictionary has to say about it, I believe that daydreaming serves some other purposes as well. It's a time to listen to yourself and to imagine anything at all, as well as a time to process new ideas and think new thoughts. Unschooled children are lucky in that they have the time available to daydream as much as they'd like. So many school kids (and their parents) are overscheduled and exhausted, with no time for contemplation. It's not something that can be squeezed into the car ride between school and soccer practice. How wonderful to learn to be with yourself at a young age, to be at peace with silence, and to find value in your own thoughts.

I would encourage your daughter's penchant for daydreaming. You could make her a "dreambook" in which she can write or draw about her dreams and inspirations. Ask her to share with you what she is thinking about – but be prepared to graciously take no for an answer. Share with her some of your thoughts and dreams. Talking about your inner thoughts and finding value in what she values will have wonderful effects on your relationship and will give you both a glimpse of the inner life the other leads.

"Play is the only way the highest intelligence of humankind can unfold." ~Joseph Chilton Pearce

I insist that my kids are awake by 7am. I don't want them to think they can be lazy just because they aren't going to school. This means I have to set a bedtime, or they'll be cranky the next day. During the day they won't do anything unless I put it in front of them. They just want to play. They're not interested in disciplined learning. What kinds of things do your kids do?

There is nothing lazy about sleeping past 7am. Many people, myself included, feel most wide awake in the evening and most sluggish in the morning. Our body clocks are all different. To expect a child to live a happy, interested life (a.k.a. unschool) on your schedule instead of her own simply will not work.

The idea that a child should go to bed at a preset time every night really doesn't make much sense. The idea that the parent should choose what that time is makes even less. No one can possibly know when another person is tired. No one can know when another person has had enough sleep. The best way to ensure that a child gets the sleep she needs is to allow her to listen to her body: to go to sleep when she feels tired and to get up when she naturally wakes up. A child who sleeps on her body's schedule will not be overtired and cranky.

Playing is good! It's not *just* play. It's PLAY!!! Children do it because they know what they need. It's important, and it's fun, which is also important. We're taught not to value play and to think it's something people should outgrow. But it is valuable, and I hope to be playing all my life. What's more important than joy and imagining and thinking and dreaming and learning and hoping and being creative? Play is all of those things and more.

When you say they 'won't do anything,' I assume you mean that they won't do anything that looks like school. If you want them to do school work, why not put them in school? In choosing to unschool you have given them the opportunity to learn in ways that are much more natural, but also much more difficult for many people to see as legitimate learning.

I'd imagine that what my kids do on a daily basis isn't so different from what your kids want to do. What's different is how what they're doing is viewed. In our house fun is important, play is valuable, and learning is everywhere. We're not much interested in "disciplined learning," since the undisciplined kind is much more fun and leads us in directions we could never plan.

"There are only two ways to live your life. One is as though nothing is a miracle. The other is as though everything is a miracle." ~Albert Einstein

I don't understand what unschoolers do. Isn't it just a way for lazy parents to homeschool? What does a typical day look like for your family?

We try to live with our eyes wide open, taking in new things and appreciating the world and the people around us. We have fun. We talk with each other. We listen to each other. We clean the house. We cook together. We play outside. We go apple picking. We go to the Renaissance fair. We go to the Children's Museum. We watch movies. We read. We lock ourselves in our own rooms and ignore each other for a while. We paint. We swim. We play board games. We visit with friends. We write letters. We plan parties. We travel. We do laundry. We watch the clouds. We make up plays. We make things out of big cardboard boxes. We watch TV. We do crafts. We play dress up. We wonder. We take apart old phones. We invent things. We argue. We play 'who am I.' We take naps. We snuggle. We pay the bills. We think. We love each other. We live as though everything is a miracle.

I don't think you *can* be lazy and unschool. To unschool is to be available to find a map, read a book, time a swimming race, bake a cake, or play a game at a moment's notice. This was illustrated very nicely at our house one evening at the end of a long, hot summer day. The adults were pretty exhausted and lounging around the pool while the kids, with their seemingly boundless energy, continued to swim. The moon was out, and Rowan and Dagny started to talk about craters on the moon and how you can see them with a telescope, and gee, maybe we should look at them with our telescope? Jon jumped up and started walking towards the house, all the while muttering just loud enough for us to hear, "Damn this unschooling. Kids wanna see the moon, I gotta schlep out the telescope. Put 'em in school,

41

and if they wanna see the moon you just tell 'em to wait 'til they cover it in science class. Stupid idea, keeping these kids home…"

He cracks himself up, and luckily we think he's pretty funny too. But he's absolutely right (not about it being a stupid idea, of course!). Living in connection with active, inquisitive children keeps you busy. The parents of children who go to school do not take on the same responsibilities towards their children that we do. In choosing to unschool, we have chosen to respond to their interests and dreams in a way that will never make us lazy, as much as we might like to be at the end of a long, hot summer day.

The question "What is a typical day?" is asked so often I'm going to write down what we do for the next week. Keep in mind that your days will look different than ours do, and in fact our days look different from week to week, depending on the time of year, whether someone's feeling cranky or unwell, what we are interested in, and lots of other variable factors. There's not much typical about life, and life is what we do. No two lives are identical, and since unschooling is based firmly in the life you lead, we can't expect any two unschooling families to look the same.

Monday. We were all a little tired because we had a birthday party and sleepover this weekend. I got up around nine, and the kids did too. We all had breakfast and got dressed. I did some cleaning. While I was working, Dagny read and Rowan watched TV. Rowan asked me whether I'd play a game, so we played Battleship (she won), and then I finished up what I had been doing.

When I finished, I had some painting I wanted to get done. Rowan came into the room where I was painting and set up some watercolors so that she could paint too. Dagny had been reading again (she got new books for her birthday) but eventually joined Rowan in painting. Rowan did a couple of portraits of Dagny, and Dagny made a painting for my dad, and we all talked as we worked. When I finished, Rowan wanted to play another game, so we played Chutes and Ladders. We all ate and talked for a while, and Dagny read some more. Rowan and I played a bit on the computer.

I wanted to make ratatouille for dinner, and Dagny wanted to try a recipe for sweet potato biscuits. Rowan thought that sounded fun, so the three of us cooked together. We made some extra mashed sweet potatoes, and Dagny experimented with adding different ingredients until the flavor was just right. Jon came home, and we all ate dinner, which was delicious.

After dinner Jon and the kids went grocery shopping to get what we need for Thanksgiving and to buy some supplies for the jelly bean party we have planned for Tuesday.

When they got back Rowan decided to work on the piñata she was making for the jelly bean party. I was organizing some drawers when she told me that she didn't mind doing it herself but it sure would be fun if I helped, so she and I worked together for an hour or so decorating and filling a piñata we had made the night before out of paper, tape, and streamers. Jon and Dagny watched TV and used the computer, and Jon did some housework.

At about nine o'clock Jon and Dagny decided to go to bed (Jon to sleep, Dagny to read), and Rowan and I stayed up for another half hour. After reading *CinderEdna*, we decided to go up too. Rowan came in my room for an hour or so, read over my shoulder in bed and talked quietly with me, and then went to her room to go to sleep.

Tuesday. At the birthday party this weekend my niece Drue was upset because she didn't win the 'guess how many jelly beans there are' game, so we decided to have a jelly bean party with her and her brother Declan. In the morning Rowan and I set it up. She covered the dining room table with bits of ribbon and put out juice and cups. I filled four jars with jelly beans, and spread lollipops on the table per Rowan's request. While we worked, Dagny was reading.

After we had the party set up, the three of us played Chinese Checkers. In the middle of the game, the party guests arrived. We decided to stop playing since the marbles looked like a lot of fun to Declan, and we wanted to let him play with them.

The kids opened their jelly bean jars and did the piñata. My sister left for an ultrasound appointment, and we all decided to go play in our office, which has lots of fun toys in it. After a while the kids decided they wanted to watch a movie and after some discussion agreed on *Toy Story 2*. We got out some crayons and markers so they could draw while they watched. Drue made Dagny a picture of her family, and Declan made a picture of me. Rowan made a lot of pictures. A couple of the kids got hungry and got themselves some food.

After the movie, we went back to playing. Dagny and I played Mancala, while the other kids played a bunch of other games (Legos, Pizza Pileup, cars, house), and then Dagny and Rowan played Mancala. I made a snack plate and then used the computer while they played and munched on broccoli, apples, cheese, and bananas.

My sister came back with her husband and told us that her baby is a girl. Everyone's excited to meet Maeve. They stayed for a while, and all the kids decorated their jars. After they left we took down streamers and balloons from this weekend, and then Rowan and Dagny played with the deflated balloons and water. Dagny and I went to her guitar class, and then stopped to pick up some pottery we made last week. She reminded me that she'd like me to iron the pilgrim costume she made to wear on Thanksgiving.

Jon and Rowan played while we were gone. When we came home Jon and Dagny figured out how to play a new game, Abalone, while Rowan and I talked, watched TV, and used the computer. At about nine-thirty we all went upstairs – Jon to sleep, Dagny to read, and Rowan and I to lie in bed talking. When Rowan went to her bed, I read the book *Ruby Holler*, because Dagny had finished it and thought I would enjoy it too.

Wednesday. I got up at 9:30. Rowan was still in bed, and Dagny was downstairs playing her guitar. I listened to a song she's writing, and we talked about *Ruby Holler*. Rowan came down, and we talked about our plans. I got dressed while the kids played Abalone, then I played Uncle Wiggly with Rowan (she won again!). Dagny got out her costume and the ironing board while we played, so when we were done I started ironing her costume. After a few minutes she decided she'd like to try the iron, which she hasn't done before, and she finished up. While we ironed, we talked with Rowan about how people ironed a long time ago and when ironing boards were invented.

Rowan made a puppy out of paper, and thought about how she could make one that would move. She wants to use a battery. Dagny started on the fourth book she's read since Saturday. We talked to my sister on the phone about which books Dagny's read so far and how much she liked them (my sister gave them to Dagny). Rowan watched *Scooby Doo*, and I made some preparations for Thanksgiving tomorrow.

Rowan and I looked at a calendar and saw that December is the next month, and that after that it will be January and her birthday. We talked about whether you can use the same calendar two years in a row if you don't cross the days off, and why not. Then Rowan and I played Battleship (guess who won). Dagny stopped reading to watch us play and then decided to make jewelry. She showed me how to make a new kind of bracelet, and I made some with her. While we worked Rowan made Dagny a heart out of paper and markers. After I stopped, Rowan joined Dagny, and they made jewelry for an hour or so. Then Dagny went upstairs to read, and Rowan watched *Ed, Edd, and Eddie* while I went on the computer.

Jon came home early, and we all went to his parents' house for dinner. We had a nice time with the kids' grandparents, aunt, uncle, and two cousins, Cooper and Megan. We came home and stayed up until about eleven and then went to sleep.

Thursday: It was Thanksgiving. Dagny wore the costume she made. She really looked like a pilgrim and used a lot of 'dost' and 'thou' when talking with us. We spent the morning cooking and getting ready for our big dinner, with occasional breaks to do more important things like read *Eloise Takes A Bawth*. Dagny made the stuffing and the biscuits, and Rowan was in charge of mashed potatoes. The kids came up with ideas to make the table pretty.

We watched the parade and the dog show on TV. Watching the dog show is always interesting. We talked about why someone would want to show his dog and how and why dogs are judged on their appearance. Dagny and I are uncomfortable with the way the dogs are treated, and Rowan was concerned that they might not like all the noise. We all enjoy seeing all of the different breeds, though, and learning about what they were bred for and are capable of doing. My parents came over for dinner, and my mom showed Dagny how she makes whipped cream.

After they went home we watched *Bedknobs and Broomsticks*. I hadn't seen it since I was a kid and didn't remember it at all. There are lots of references to World War II, so we talked about Nazis and bombs and the kids asked whether England was invaded. There were also some little tidbits (like vultures whose job it was to pick injured players off the soccer field, but who kept being frustrated by the person getting up again) which led to explanations of things of general knowledge (vultures very rarely hunt, but wait for motionless prey). The kids found the clothing very interesting, too. The young boy wore short pants and the older, long ones. The young girl always wore a dress, and the women's dresses were very different than anything you would see today. There were women in uniform in the movie, which prompted a discussion about whether women were allowed to fight in World War II and what kinds of jobs they did do.

We all went to bed full and tuckered out.

Friday. Jon and Dagny got up early and went to my sister's house to install a light fixture in my niece and nephew's room. Drue said that Jon's just like Bob the Builder. We agree.

They came home, and we cleaned the house. Rowan and I got dressed. I played Go Fish with Dagny while Rowan did a puzzle; when she was done, she joined us for the end of the game. They made some jewelry. We made a list of some supplies we needed, then headed to the hardware store. We are beginning the renovation of our downstairs bathroom/laundry room. We spent hours picking out all of the things we needed, and the kids had a lot of fun picking out paint chips. They have a new line with Nickelodeon characters on them. Rowan's going to tie some of hers together to make a notebook. Dagny likes to sort hers into color groups and combinations that look good together. They played store games with them for hours in the afternoon/evening while Jon did some work in the laundry room and I did some errands. While I was out I picked up some crafts for the kids to do with their Grampa tomorrow.

Later, I worked on a cookbook project for my niece Amy's wedding shower, and Dagny helped me come up with ideas for it. Rowan made placemats out of graphic paper covered with contact paper. She made one for each of us. Jon was working in the laundry room and asked the kids to come in and holler down to the basement when the lights went out to help him figure out what circuit he needed to turn off so that he could do some electrical work.

We watched TV together for an hour or so and then headed upstairs to bed. Jon and Dagny went right to sleep, but Rowan and I lay and listened to the wind, which was howling. Rowan thought it sounded like a giant crying. The rain was lashing at the windows and was quite loud, so Rowan stayed awake with me a bit longer than usual and eventually went to sleep around midnight.

Saturday. The kids went right back to their paint chips this morning. They arranged them and opened up a paint store. Rowan was the customer and changed personalities every few minutes. They pretended the store had a robbery. Their friend's farm was recently robbed, so it may be that's what spurred this particular make-believe.

Jon worked in the laundry room most of the day. Rowan and I played Chinese Checkers. I had a date with my mom, so my dad came over to play with the kids for the day. They played store with the paint chips, pretended they were clothing, played cards, made foam gingerbread men, and painted treasure boxes. Rowan watched part of the *Rugrats* marathon on Nickelodeon.

When I got home, we found that our *Tuck Everlasting* DVD had arrived in the mail. We decided to watch it tomorrow because the kids wanted to watch the new *Rugrats All Grown Up* episodes tonight. I brought home a new toy. It's a whiteboard with three letter games on it. One of them is similar to hangman, but instead of a person the players draw a monkey. Rowan was excited to see that she could draw a monkey and made two for me. Dagny helped me work on my niece's cookbook, and Rowan decided to use some of the special paper to make a cookbook of her own. Jon helped her spell the ingredients she wanted to write. We all watched the first episode of *Rugrats* together. Dagny and I enjoyed a scene where the mom gets upset with the principal at her son's school, asking him if he just wants all the children to be the same and to stamp out their individuality. She was very vehement, and it was funny to see this small person cause the enormous, intimidating principal to back down. We talked about how much humor there is that shows how damaging the push for conformity in schools is, and we talked about how little it seems most people think to refuse it.

Jon played video games upstairs for a while. I went up to read, and the kids stayed in the living room to watch the other episodes.

Around ten they came upstairs, and Dagny and Rowan described some scenes they liked in the shows we missed. We read *Where Oh Where Is Kipper's Bear?* and *Where The Wild Things Are.* We talked about the fact that they're making a movie out of *Where The Wild Things Are* and wondered whether we would like it better than the movie version of *The Cat In The Hat,* which we did not enjoy.

Dagny and I had a conversation about colors, inspired by her cousin's name (Maeve). We were each lying in our own bed and yelling to each other unnecessarily loudly, which had us giggling a lot. She wanted to know what mauve looked like and how it was spelled; that led to a conversation about other colors with odd names like chartreuse and taupe. Then she wondered whether we could make someone immortal by covering him with layers of synthetic skin. We talked about the damage that occurs inside a body, to organs, etc., and she thought maybe there could be a chemical that would make someone immortal. Eventually everyone settled down to sleep, and I read *The Moffatts,* which Dagny had recommended to me.

Sunday: Dagny got up around 9:00. Rowan and I slept until 9:30. Jon got up before all of us and started working in the laundry room. Rowan seemed to be very sleepy and spent most of the morning watching TV. Dagny joined her for a while. We played games, ate, and lounged around most of the morning.

At three, we went to a pottery studio to meet our family and make dishes for my niece and her fiancé as a wedding present. When we got home, we all worked on the recipe book we are making for them. Rowan had fun with the special papers again, and Dagny and I finished up the project.

I'm sure I left some things out, but this was a pretty typical week (even with Thanksgiving). I don't put one ounce of thought into whether any of this 'teaches' my children anything. Of course they learn from it all, but that is not the goal of our journey. The journey is the goal.

One thing that doesn't come through in my descriptions of our days is how much we talk to each other. Whether watching TV, lying in bed, driving in the car, cooking, or whatever else our days bring, there is a habitual rhythm of conversation. We learn an incredible amount simply from talking with each other, as each of us carries within ourselves such a differing variety of facts, observations, and not so important tidbits. This steady flow of communication is not only one of our greatest tools for learning, it is also one of the things that most improves our connection and keeps us in tune with each other. How many things must go unsaid and unexplored when a child is not permitted to speak as the mood hits her? When at too many of the moments she is allowed to speak, it is only to answer someone else's question? How many opportunities for a parent and child to see into each others' minds and hearts are lost when they are separated from each other for most of their days?

A typical day is never typical, but it is always connected, always focused on joy, and always filled with love.

"Forbidden fruit causes many jams." ~Anonymous

My child would eat nothing but junk food if I let him. Sometimes he begs for cookies for breakfast! How do you make sure your kids eat properly? Is candy consumption a matter of unschooling or parenting? You seem to think by controlling things or making them unavailable, I am actually encouraging my kids to focus on them and desire them, but that hasn't happened in my family.

We made a parenting decision not to take away our children's freedom to make their own choices about what and how they would learn, what and when they would eat, and what they would do with their time. In order to separate our unschooling from our parenting, I would have to draw a line somewhere where learning ended and life began. I can't do that.

We make sure that Rowan and Dagny eat properly by keeping a variety of foods readily available and by trusting them to listen to their bodies. Knowing when she's hungry comes as naturally as breathing to a child, as does seeking out a balance of foods. It is not possible for a parent to know whether a child is hungry. Only the child knows. Allowing the child to hear and listen to her body will lead to healthy eating. When parents interfere with their child's eating, they often cause confusion over what hunger feels like and cause certain foods to have more of an allure than they would otherwise have. We can give food magic by negotiating for it and forbidding it, and it's a magic that guarantees there can never be 'enough' of the forbidden food.

My children have always made their own choices and have well-balanced diets. They do not think of food as good or bad, but as fuel for their bodies. They've never wanted any food badly enough to beg for it, because they have never had to beg for any food. They eat when they are hungry and stop when they are full. How many adults who were controlled as children wish they had that ability?

We always have candy, chips, and cookies in our house. As each holiday approaches we throw out candy from the previous holiday. Not once has all of the Halloween, Solstice, or Easter candy been eaten. Dagny and Rowan are more likely to choose a perfectly ripe pear, wheat crackers with cheese, or some other nutritious snack than they are a cookie. Overall, they make healthy choices, and equally importantly, have no issues regarding food or their bodies.

I kept track of some of the things Rowan said about food while I was writing this book. Here's a sample:

One afternoon she and I made brownies and lasagna. She likes to eat brownies while they're still hot, and they were ready before the lasagna. She cut herself a brownie and asked whether anyone else wanted one. She ate some then said, "I don't want to get full so I can have some lasagna, so will someone eat the rest of my brownie?"

At a birthday party she asked me, "Can you hold my Jell-O so I can get some broccoli?"

While playing video games, she said to Jon, "I want a cookie, but I only want half a cookie. Will you eat the other half?"

After dinner at Friendly's, when the waitress offered her the free sundae that came with her meal, Rowan said, "I don't want any ice cream. I'm full." (This happens regularly. We have quite a collection of free sundae coupons.)

At Papa Gino's when someone bought her a soda without asking what she wanted, Rowan said, "Would it be ok if I had a water instead?"

Do you truly believe that your child would eat nothing but 'junk' given the opportunity? Is he an unreasonable or self-destructive person? Assuming the worst of him doesn't seem a very kind way to think about your child.

I'd think it's quite likely that making things off-limits could increase a child's desire for them, and I'd argue that if your children are begging for cookies it *has* happened in your family.

There's also the possibility that children will feel the need to be dishonest with their parents in order to retain their approval. I know children who sneak sweets when their parents can't see them. I'd guess that most kids keep some things from their parents because they know their parents would be upset or disappointed to know how they really feel. Keeping my relationship with my children honest is hugely important to me. I want us to know each other for who we really are.

Then there's the fact that, if I controlled my children, I would not be allowing them the opportunity to choose the lives they will live and the people they want to be. I don't believe that's my right, nor would I want to deny them the joy of it.

Many of the ideas regarding food that get passed on to children don't make much sense. Why is it ok to eat cookies in the afternoon, but not in the morning? The truth is that not all cookies are 'bad' for you; but, even if they were, they have the same ingredients at 9:00 AM that they do at 3:00 PM.

I like to examine all of my knee-jerk responses. Very often they spring from the fact that I have not really considered an issue thoroughly and am simply saying what 'they' say or what conventional wisdom tells us.

I once heard a parent tell a young child that he couldn't eat just the frosting on his piece of cake; he had to eat some cake too. Today I heard an older child ask for gum at the store. Her mother responded that she couldn't have a piece of gum: she could only have a lollipop. Some parents take controlling their children to a level that lacks even a pretense of making sense. Whether it is because it's what their parents did, because they think that's what they are supposed to do in order to be good parents themselves, or because they speak without thinking, in the end each nonsensical rule a parent comes up with erodes the trust his child has in him. Beginning to question why and truly thinking about what you are saying are important parts of developing a relationship with your child (and a life) that has a solid foundation in truth.

"A smiling face is half the meal." ~Latvian Proverb

A family dinner is very important to us. What do you do when your child is hungry an hour before dinnertime? I don't want my kids to spoil their appetites. And what if they don't like what you make for dinner? Do you make them something different?

In this situation (as in most others) I would think about what my goals are. Is the goal to spend time with your children at the table, to share a conversation? Is the goal to nourish their bodies? Is it necessary that the two goals be met at the same moment? Once you have determined what your goals are, it is usually pretty simple to come up with a solution that suits those goals.

A hungry child should be fed. To withhold food from a hungry child is an abuse of the power you hold just by being a larger person. In any situation where a child has to ask me for help in order to do something, I feel it is my responsibility to happily give that help. Childhood is naturally frustrating enough without adding adult-imposed frustrations.

Eating when you are hungry does not 'spoil' your appetite, it satisfies it.

As for spending time together, some families do enjoy dinnertime around the table. However, many unschooling families find that so much of their day is spent in connection with each other that the dinnertime togetherness is not really necessary. If a family dinner is important to you, tell your children how you feel about it and ask them how they feel. They might be willing to eat when they're hungry, but still sit with you at the table to talk while you're eating dinner. Or they might be willing to have a small snack before dinner in order to be able to eat as a family. So many times a conversation is all it takes to solve family problems. The important thing is to be sure that your attitude encourages a conversation – an exchange of thoughts – rather than a lecture or an attempt to convert them to your way of thinking.

I would not insist that they sit and eat at the table with you. An unwilling participant doesn't add much to a dinner conversation; instead of a feeling of connection he is likely to feel resentment at being controlled.

When planning a meal we try to take into account each person's tastes. We serve the main ingredients separately – for example rice, vegetables, cheese, fajitas, toppings, and chicken for Jon, our token meat eater – so each person can choose what s/he'd like. If nothing that we've made appeals to one of the kids, we help her get something simple from the kitchen. Asking them ahead of time whether what we want to make is something they want to eat cuts down on last minute food preparation while the main meal is sitting on the table.

"You can live nicely without it. The same can be said about books, electricity, plumbing. But why? Life may well be simpler, but not richer." ~Dan Vilter, unschooling dad of Matthew

Do your kids watch TV whenever they want? So many studies show that kids are watching too much television these days. Really, I see little of value on TV, and I sincerely believe it is damaging to young children. I don't think having a TV has anything more to do with unschooling than having a giraffe does.

Rowan and Dagny have never had limitations on the amount of television they watch. For them, TV is just one option among many other options. It does not have any special allure. There's always something new and/or interesting available to do at our house, so when they choose TV, they choose it because it is what they really want to do at that time, not because they are allowed an hour of television a day and they're determined to use that hour. My sincere belief that they are intelligent and thoughtful and would be discerning in their television viewing has proved to be true.

I haven't heard of any TV studies that were conducted with unschooled children. The kids who are being studied spend somewhere around six hours of their day in school, an hour or more in traveling to and from school, and varying amounts of time on homework. Given that, two hours of television is indeed a big chunk of their 'free time.' From my perspective, seven or eight hours of 'un-free time' a day is much more damaging to a person than television could ever be.

Dagny and Rowan decide for themselves what has value for them. We trust that they know what they need and that they want what's best for themselves. I do my best to understand what it is they get out of something, but I don't have to understand it to accept that it is of value to them. I don't understand the value fixing a Jeep CJ for the hundredth time has for my husband, yet I still help him find the time and money because he enjoys it.

I can't trust my kids to learn in their own way and time and respect them as whole people and then cut off an avenue of interest or treat them in a way I would not want to be treated.

The difference between having a television and having a giraffe is that a TV is something I can provide for my children and a giraffe is not (although I would try to find some way for my child to interact with a giraffe if she were wishing for one). It's the difference between my deciding to limit something and the real life limitations that exist. What both TV and giraffes have to do with unschooling is that they exist in life, and as unschoolers we want to be open to life and what it offers.

In *Escape From Childhood,* John Holt wrote, "'Allowed to experience childhood.' At one level these words are true, but hardly worth saying. At any age, we experience being that age. Clearly the users of such words mean something else. Being allowed to experience childhood means being allowed to do some things and being spared having to do others – or *forbidden.* It means that adults will decide, without often or ever asking children what they think, that some experiences are good for children while others are not. It means for a child that adults are all the time deciding what is best for you and then letting or making you do it. But instead of trying to make sure that all children get only those experiences we think are good for them I would rather make available to children, as to everyone else, the widest possible range of experiences (except those that hurt others) and let them choose those they like best."

Your children's comfort levels will likely not be the same as yours in many areas of life. It's possible that they will watch more TV than you would choose to. It's also possible that they will watch less TV than you would choose to. Trust that they will find the balance that works for them. Children are going to form their own opinions and make their own value judgments whether we 'allow' them to or not. I would much rather support my children as they do so than block their ways.

"Mankind is at its best when it is most free. This will be clear if we grasp the principle of liberty. We must recall that the basic principle is freedom of choice…" ~Dante Alighieri

What about the content of TV shows and commercial TV? You don't let them watch whatever they want, do you? So much of it is not educational or is inappropriate.

Rowan and Dagny make their own choices regarding what they'd like to watch on television. We trust them to know what they need, what they are comfortable with, and what they should do with their time.

We learn many things from programs which might not be considered educational. My children use their imaginations while watching television and love to talk about character development and how different kinds of shows are made. TV has taken us to the Amazon, shown us animals we may never see in real life, given us a glimpse into other cultures, given us ideas for projects, shown us how things work, been a jumping off point for conversations about relationships, mainstream family dynamics, morals and a million other things, and made us laugh. I believe very strongly that enjoying your life is just as important as learning. In fact, the two are often intertwined, but a shared laugh from something that has no official 'educational value' is not less important to us than knowing the answer to 5x8.

I question the idea that everything our children do has to serve the purpose of increasing their intelligence. Why do we, as a society, place so much importance in making our children smarter? We don't try to make them taller so that they can reach more things. We don't spend twelve years trying to get them to use their toes as fingers so they can hold more things at once. Yet a huge business has been built around the idea that we need to do things to them in order to make them smarter.

Consumerism is often a concern for those who wish to limit their children's exposure to television. While it is true that some commercials and TV programs are sending messages that I don't agree with, it is not something that worries me. My children do not watch TV in a vacuum, and they do not watch mindlessly. Jon and I are there with them, answering their questions, talking about things we think are interesting or important or irritating, and listening to their opinions on what we are seeing.

Commercials provide a great opportunity for conversation about what our values are. They have prompted us to talk about the fact that we can accept what is being spoon fed to us, or we can think and make up our own minds about everything in our lives — not just what cereal to buy, but more important decisions as well.

Dagny and Rowan are extremely analytical in their TV viewing. They pick commercials apart: Why did they choose those kids? See how they used lighting to make that look better? Wow, that angle makes that look much bigger than it really is! Are there really people who believe that buying something will make them happy or more beautiful or popular or smarter?

Yes, television is a window into consumerism. But consumerism is all around us, and we've found dealing with it head on has given our kids a strong viewpoint on it. The fact that TV is a window into consumerism does not mean that it is not also a window into the world. As unschooling parents, we choose to open up the world for our children; limiting TV would be doing just the opposite.

It's common for parents to worry that their children will choose to watch something the parents find inappropriate due to its violent or sexual nature. We've found that Rowan and Dagny make very responsible decisions about what they choose to watch. They know what they are ready for. They don't choose to watch things that are disturbing or not interesting to them.

Do our children ever choose to watch something that I don't enjoy? Yes. I sometimes watch things they don't enjoy as well. We are different people and will surely have different opinions and interests from time to time. It is important not to let your own opinions negate another person's. The fact that I don't find enjoyment in a certain program does not give me the right to interfere with someone else's enjoyment.

"Forbid us something, and that thing we desire." ~Geoffrey Chaucer

If we decide to lift restrictions on TV, should we just announce that the kids can watch whenever they want now? I'm afraid all they're going to want to do is watch TV.

This is not something we've dealt with as we have never limited our children, but I have put some thought into how we might approach this situation.

There's something to be said for easing into it rather than making an announcement. If you make a big deal out of suddenly letting them watch as much as they want, you're setting up a situation in which they might watch more than they would really choose to if it hadn't been limited in the first place. There would quite likely be a heady feeling of freedom that would contribute to them watching a lot and maybe a feeling that they should squeeze in as much as possible in case you change your mind.

You could begin by saying, "Yes," whenever they ask whether they can watch TV, until eventually maybe they'd stop asking. This would also give you some time to get used to the idea and to see the benefits of not limiting TV in your own family.

I do have one problem with this idea, however. Personally, I would feel that I wasn't being completely upfront with my kids; I'd want to bring the subject out in the open. I'd be inclined to say something like, "I don't feel right about making decisions for you and I want to really think about why I am doing it. What do you think?"

If you find that your kids are watching a lot of television at first, I recommend continuing to do other interesting things yourself, inviting them to join in if they'd like. I would also snuggle up and watch television with them.

Nine times out of ten, I am in the room while my kids are watching TV, if not actively watching with them. Most commonly they are watching while doing something else such as drawing, playing with stuffed animals, making something out of a big box, or writing. Often what they are doing has something to do with the storyline of whatever they are watching. Throughout that time we talk about whatever comes up on the TV or the things we did that day or want to do tomorrow. Time spent watching television can be just as much a time of connection as time spent at any other activity.

"Allow children to be happy in their own way, for what better way will they ever find?" ~Samuel Johnson

I'm worried about my son. He has no interest in anything intellectual. All he wants to do is play video games and play on the computer, so I have to limit him to an hour a day. I also don't like how violent video games are.

Ah, those pesky 'have to-s.' I contend that you do not have to; you choose to.

I don't agree that video and computer games are necessarily *not* intellectual. In any case, while society places a lot of importance in all things intellectual, your son may have his own ideas about what is important. Is he kind? Mechanical? Artistic? Imaginative? Instead of worrying over what he is lacking, celebrate who he is.

I strongly encourage you to start playing video games with your son. Take his interest seriously. If you haven't played video games yourself, you will be surprised at the complexity of the games and the variety of things that can be learned from them. You may also surprise yourself by enjoying them. Most importantly, though, your son will know that what interests him is important to you, and you will be connecting with each other in a joyful way.

There is a huge selection of video games available, and I'm sure you could find many you would not consider violent. In reality, though, none of them are violent. As author and physicist David Deutsch says, "But whatever the type of game, it is not violence. Violence is where you hurt people. Games just appear on a screen; they don't actually hurt anybody." Children know that games are not reality, whether they're playing with 'guns' made from sticks or with video games.

We play on the computer just about every day. Some days we play for hours, some days much less. One of our favorite websites is www.homestarrunner.com. We all enjoy the humor. I can't help but notice how many things we've learned from playing there and how many connections we're making with other things we come across.

One of the main characters is named Marzipan, so we were very interested when we watched an episode of Martha Stewart where she decorated a cake with marzipan vegetables. I had heard of it before but never really knew what it was. Rowan made plans for her own 'garden' cake after seeing that episode.

The word play on the site is very dry and is probably my favorite part. In figuring out some of the jokes, Rowan has learned a lot about spelling and various meanings of words. A lot of the language the characters use has become part of our own family language. Timing in humor is something that has always come naturally to Rowan, so the way the characters use it is very interesting to her.

Dagny enjoys the 'history' section of the site, which shows how they developed their characters and what formats they started out using. Rowan has always been interested in voices and loves that two people do all of the characters' voices. She does a great imitation of Homestar. She likes to draw pictures of the characters and act out scenes. Both she and Dagny have memorized an enormous amount of what the characters say. Rowan established "Rowania"(her own country) after seeing Homestar establish "Homestaria."

Recently Jon and Rowan and Dagny decided to make a Homestar Runner chess set out of polymer clay. They've chosen different characters as king (Homestar), queen (Marzipan), pawns (The Cheat), and knights (Strongbad), and they've come up with a way to differentiate the two players' pieces. They enjoy playing chess together, and I'm sure this project will be a lot of fun for them.

Playing at homestarrunner.com has led us to conversations about soy products, music, the effects of caffeine, pronunciation, multiple choice questions, the evolution of computers, different styles of humor, the history of video games, Japanese animation, and children's television programs that are produced essentially as half hour commercials for action figures and toys. We've researched how the material on the site is made and how the person who does most of the voices uses various techniques to create voices that are so different from one another.

Another favorite site is www.neopets.com. It is a very complicated site to navigate. Dagny had no trouble learning her way around the site and finding hidden pages where she can get free things for her pets.

The Neopets site has a wide variety of games and an elaborate world where players can set up a bank account, keep track of interest, set up shops, maintain inventory, bid on and place items up for auction, and hunt for bargains. Players can also submit articles and stories to the site, follow news reports of events in Neopia, and play logic and math games.

My point is that, if your concern is that your son will not learn while playing on the computer, you have just not yet seen that there is learning to be found in anything and everything. Your son knows best what interests him. Trust that he is getting something he needs (whether it's learning or amusement or both) from what he chooses to do. If you limit his computer and video time, you will not only be telling him that you don't think he's capable of deciding what has value for him, you will actually be hindering his learning.

"Whenever people feel that they're not free to choose what they want to do, they are likely to resist, even if they see the purpose in what we are asking and would ordinarily do it." ~Marshall Rosenberg

Every day we struggle with trying to get our daughter to brush her teeth. Did you ever hold your children and brush their teeth when they didn't want you to?

No. Dagny and Rowan have always known their bodies are their own and that brushing their teeth is optional. They've also known a lot of people believe that not brushing your teeth can cause cavities and that their mouths taste better when they brush.

When they were younger, we asked them whether they'd like to brush their teeth, and most times they chose to. Every once in a while, if they were tired, they'd say no. Now that they are older they remember to do it on their own, although Rowan still likes me to set up her toothbrush for her. Sometimes they choose not to. Sometimes they go upstairs in the middle of the afternoon and brush their teeth just because they want to. There have been nights when I suggested they skip it because it was late, and they refused. Neither has ever had a cavity. Their hygienist comments that they don't leave her any work to do – all she can do is count their teeth.

Giving children a choice about whether or not to brush their teeth contributes to a relationship in which there is no reason for power struggles. Without the distraction of a power struggle, the child can look at teeth brushing in a rational way: My mouth doesn't taste good: I want to brush my teeth. I ate some sticky candy: I want to brush my teeth. They can choose to brush their teeth because it makes *sense* to do so. They have real life reasons for doing the things that they do.

People want to do things that make sense. They don't want to do things just because someone else tells them they have to. They don't want someone else to feel that they have the right to tell them what to do. A parent who chooses to give up control over her child's brushing gives the child the opportunity to take responsibility for her own teeth.

We've found that an electric toothbrush is more fun and also does a better job cleaning our teeth in a shorter amount of time. There are many toothpaste flavors available, and that helps to make brushing teeth more enjoyable too.

What a feeling of powerlessness the thought of being held and forced to do something conjures up for me! How can a child feel safe and secure in herself knowing that at any time another person can control her body simply because it is smaller and weaker? The chance of cavities can not be worth the damage to the child's self and to your relationship.

"Parents are often so busy with the physical rearing of children that they miss the glory of parenthood, just as the grandeur of the trees is lost when raking leaves." ~Marcelene Cox

If I've told my son ten times to come get ready for a bath and he ignores me, there is a point where I have to go and pick him up and take him, don't you agree? I set up his bath before his bedtime. He needs to go to bed, and he needs to take his bath first. Would you just skip the bath? What about the fact that he's ignoring his mother?

You say you 'have to' pick him up and take him. I like to question my have to-s, especially when they are leading to unhappiness for my children. What would happen if you didn't pick him up and take him? What would happen if he didn't take a bath that night? What message is he getting from being picked up and put somewhere he doesn't want to be? Is it truly more important that he take a bath than it is for the two of you to build a respectful relationship?

In our house baths have always been optional. When (and whether) they happen is up to the kids. Generally Dagny likes to shower in the morning and Rowan bathes in the evening, but not too close to when she wants to go to bed. She likes to know she has time to play afterwards.

When Dagny was younger, one of us would ask whether she wanted us to run a bath today. If she said yes, we'd ask whether she'd like it in the morning or later. If she said no, we just said ok. These days she takes a shower without discussing it with us.

We still ask Rowan. We ask her every other day, because she's not interested in doing it any more often than that. Sometimes she asks to take one, either to play, to get clean, or both. Overall she's not a big fan of taking baths. She'd rather be doing something else. We try to make it more enjoyable for her by having lots of bath toys, water tints, tub paints, and colored foaming soap available. We're happy to set up a portable DVD player so she can watch a movie while playing in the tub and to hang out in the bathroom to keep her company if she'd like.

If we know that we're going to a party the next day, we'll mention that to the kids so they can factor it into their decisions. I think people imagine that if you don't make your kids take a bath, they never will; that has not been our experience. Nor does it seem a very positive way to look at our children. There *are* times when one or the other has gone longer than I would choose to go without bathing. In the end I can't see any way in which that matters.

I can't remember a time when either of them has ignored me. I don't ever demand anything of them (i.e., come take a bath now), so we're not in situations where they would feel a need to. I think that ignoring me would be a way of trying to exert some control. The dynamics of our relationships don't create a need for power plays. If they were to ignore me, I would take that as a sign that something in our relationship needed examining.

We also do not have a set bedtime. We do not decide for them when they should go to sleep. They go to bed when they feel sleepy, just as I do. So, again, I would question the 'have to.' What might happen if you don't make your son go to bed at 'bedtime?' You can change the dynamic in your family by focusing more on joy and freedom and respect, and less on getting your child to do things on your schedule.

"A man can not say Yes to something with all his heart unless he has an equal right to say No." ~John Holt

We've tried chore charts, punishment for not picking up after yourself, and having the kids pick what chores they want to do and agreeing to do them every day. Nothing works. They're lazy and they just don't want to clean. Any suggestions?

I believe that what we think about our children affects what they think about themselves, even if we never vocalize it to them. I would be concerned about what messages your children are getting from you if you think of them as lazy. I recommend looking for the good in them right this minute and keeping that in your thoughts. I recommend looking at them through positive eyes instead of negative, and I recommend really thinking about what you are contributing to your relationships with them by thinking of them as lazy.

In our house we don't have 'chores.' Yes, of course, there is housework to be done. But we try not to think of it negatively, and no one is responsible for any particular task. Jon and I do the majority of the housework. We do it because we want our family to have a comfortable, healthy place to live, with easy accessibility to craft supplies, toys, food, books, movies, and other fun and necessary things.

We do not want our children to see housework as drudgery, and we do not want to see it that way ourselves. I found that shifting my perspective from 'have to' to 'choose to' made an enormous difference in my everyday happiness. When I had to rake the leaves, I wanted to get it over with. When I choose to rake the leaves, I love the way they smell and the sound they make and the fresh air and the time spent with others if they choose to rake leaves too. When I had to do the laundry, I got bored and wished someone else would do it. When I choose to do the laundry, I love the way the warm clothes feel coming out of the dryer, and the time spent sorting clothes is very meditative for me.

We do ask our children to help us sometimes. We ask; by which I mean they can say no. There is no power struggle, no reward or punishment, no guilt involved. Help that comes freely from a child who wants to lighten your load is a gift of love.

I remember very vividly the day that Rowan, who was four at the time, had a fever of 103 and was recovering from having stitches taken out (very traumatically) the night before. She was resting in the living room, and I began to unload the dishwasher in the kitchen. She got up off the couch and started unloading with me. I told her she was very sweet but that she should go lie down if she wanted to. She said no thanks, continued to clean, and then said, "See, didn't that go faster?" Moments like those do not *feel* like chores.

Just today I was raking and picking up sticks in the yard and Dagny decided to help me. We worked for most of the day. At one point I was raking near her garden, and she asked me whether I'd help her clean it out sometime. I raked it out with her help, and when we were done she said, "We're so different than other families." I said I had been thinking that too, thinking about how in some other families the kids have to do yard work as a chore, and how nice it was that she did it because she wanted to. I was glad the time we were spending together was not filled with resentment on her part, but rather happiness and companionship. She said, "I was thinking you just stopped what you had to do to help me." I was thinking about how nice she was to be helping me, and she was thinking the same of me. Neither of us was doing a chore.

When our children were toddlers, they loved to help us sort laundry and wash dishes. I've always enjoyed doing household tasks with my kids, and I try to make it enjoyable for them too. We've had some wonderful conversations while passing wet clothes from the washer to the person loading the dryer. As they've grown, they've begun to take the initiative. At some point Dagny began to clean her own room. How much cleaning she does varies from day to day, but she is developing a sense of responsibility for her things. It's not important to me how long it takes for that sense of responsibility to take root. She is on her own schedule, and I'll support her along the way. If, now, I go into her room and see the bed is not made, I'll make it if she'd like me to. If there's some laundry on the floor, I'll ask her if she'd like me to take it downstairs.

When there's a lot of housework to be done, I sometimes make a general announcement, asking whether anyone has time and feels like doing some cleaning with me. Sometimes they say yes; sometimes they say no. They often make a general announcement asking whether someone has time and feels like playing a game. Sometimes I say yes; sometimes I say no. We are four people who love each other and who live in a house together, so we're inclined to want to help each other and do things for each other – but not always. Accepting 'no' graciously goes a long way towards others accepting a 'no' from you, and an even longer way towards developing a helpful and caring relationship.

I have no interest in making my kids do things that they don't want to do. I have no interest in hurrying them along their way as they learn. I have faith that they will learn – whether it is math, reading, or housework, and I'm willing to help them out for as long as they need and want me to.

"If you want others to be happy, practice compassion. If you want to be happy, practice compassion." ~Dalai Lama

When my two year old spills her drink, I have her clean it up. Would you just leave it there until she figures out that it's her responsibility? How will she learn to clean up her own messes? Sometimes when she is angry, she makes a mess on purpose, and she has to clean it up. I don't want her to expect that someone's always going to pick up after her, so I have to teach her a lesson.

I would not leave the spilled drink. In our family, if a two year old (or three or four...) spills something, an older person gets some towels. We first dry the child off and make sure she's not stressed out about it, then start cleaning up the spill — with no discussion of whose mess it is. We might say something like, "That's a slippery cup, huh?" or "Did that surprise you?" or "Sometimes I get frustrated when I drop something." or "Look at the cool design that milk made on the floor. Did you ever finger paint with milk?" or "I told that milk to stay in the cup. Did it jump out and try to run away?"

Sometimes the little one will ask for a towel too. Sometimes she won't. In either case we are sharing a peaceful moment, not a stressful one. Our focus is on helping the child to feel ok (or even better, amused) about what has happened. Drinks spill. It's not something we need to get upset about. We can clean it up and move on.

We've never assigned ownership to messes. Dagny cleans up things Rowan's been using; I clean up things Dagny's been using; Rowan cleans up things Jon's been using; Jon cleans up things I've been using.

I know that when I say, "I don't tell my kids to clean up their messes," people sometimes 'hear' that my kids don't clean anything. They do — more and more as they get older. They do it because they want to help out or because they want the mess cleaned up. They do it for internal reasons that will be there when I'm not.

72

In my opinion making your daughter clean up can only end in a power struggle and sets up an adversarial relationship. I don't understand how you *can* make her clean up when she doesn't want to. Are you physically placing things in her hand? Threatening her with punishment if she does not comply? Either of these options will leave a child feeling out of control of her own body and, if anything, only add to her feelings of anger and humiliation.

Can you talk to her and try to come up with a different way to deal with her frustration? Maybe she could throw a pillow, take some deep breaths with you, or 'stomp out her grumpies' as a three year old friend of mine does. Dealing with strong feelings is not easy for anyone, but it is particularly hard for a young child. I think it's important to help her find ways to share how she's feeling and to let her know that it's ok to be mad.

What is it that she is so angry and frustrated about? I don't just mean on the surface, I mean deep down. If there's a pattern of her getting frustrated in certain situations, what is the common thread? Is she feeling out of control of some aspect of her life/self? It is much more important to deal with the root of the emotions than with trying to change her behavior. Trying to control her behavior will most likely cause more problems than it solves in any case.

As for what she'll learn from your cleaning up, maybe she'll learn that when someone is feeling upset it's nice to help them out. Maybe she will learn compassion and understanding. If my kids are going to 'learn a lesson' from me, I hope it will be that they are worth being treated with kindness.

73

"In life, you must try and be the type of person that your dog thinks you are." ~Anonymous

My kids (who are 8 and 5) asked for a dog and now they won't take care of it. I've told them if they don't we'll give it away. Do your kids take care of their pets?

We have three dogs, a fish, and two hamsters right now. The oldest dog has been with us since before Dagny was born, but the rest of the pets came after, most at the kids' requests.

We do not take a pet into the house unless the adults are willing to feed him, walk him, help him learn to live with people, and give him a clean place to live. Young children may at first be eager to take on the responsibilities for a pet, but to expect them to care for it regularly is not realistic.

A live being should not be used as a tool to help children learn responsibility and should not be treated as something disposable.

I kept thinking that I should have more to say on this subject, but for me it's simple: If parents commit to taking an animal into their home, they must be willing to provide for the animal's needs. Anything else is inhumane.

"Millions saw the apple fall, but Newton asked why." ~Bernard Baruch

My daughter is going through the 'why?' stage. She asks it over and over, about everything. How did you handle this stage?

While riding in the car one day with a three year old Dagny and our adult friend Laura, I answered approximately 2,467,893 questions consisting of the one word, "Why?" I answered the questions with lots of thought to how to help Dagny understand what it was she wanted to understand and with little thought to the fact that I was heading on a good twenty minutes of back and forth on why. I'd love to remember what it was Dagny was so interested in that day, but instead I remember a childless Laura turning to me in amazement and saying, "You're really good at this!"

I never thought of answering the never-ending whys as a skill. I suppose it could be, but to be honest I love to spend as much time as possible with a child when she's going through the why phase. For one thing, it's a great opportunity to see how another human being takes little bits of information and transforms them into a whole with meaning and value.

Playing "why" also gives the questioner an idea of some of the many things I *don't* know. Too often adults encourage the illusion that we are all-knowing. There's a temptation to bask in the glory, however little deserved, that comes with the hero worship that a child can send your way.

Many whys have no answers. These are wonderful because they give us a chance to share values, ideas, dreams, and visions. What better way to connect with a child?

I also enjoy the why stage because it's just plain fun. It's fun for the kids to try to drive me a little crazy. It's fun for me to see what variety of answers I can come up with, not only for the child, but for myself.

I believe that the average unschooling family asks why much more often than a mainstream family does. Often, asking why is what

75

brings a family to unschooling to begin with. Why should a child be separated from her parents every day? Why should thirteen years of her one and only life on earth be spent lining up, sitting down, and thinking on command?

Why leads us to conversations about emotions, human (and humane) behavior, and thoughts bigger than the universe. Why picks us up, shakes us around, and plops us back down facing a new direction. That's an awful lot of power for a three letter word.

"No legacy is so rich as honesty." ~William Shakespeare

I'm not comfortable with being 100% honest with my kids. There are some things they don't need to know. Do you keep anything from your children?

We choose not to keep anything from Rowan and Dagny. We believe that without complete honesty, there is very little chance of developing relationships in which we truly know each other. The honesty that exists between me and my children is perhaps the biggest rock in the foundation of our relationships. I don't want to do anything that creates distance between me and the people I love.

Often I find that thinking about telling them something difficult is much more uncomfortable than actually doing it. They continually surprise me with an understanding that seems beyond their years. We talk openly about war and death and sex and love and personal problems and anger and all of the other subjects that parents and children (and people in general) are sometimes uncomfortable discussing.

I'm so grateful for the open-ness of our relationships. I know that I have some part in making them so, but I am grateful that Dagny and Rowan choose to share their inner selves with me.

I also know that keeping things from children, even with the best of intentions, can have some negative effects on them. Children know when 'something' is going on, and often their guesses are much worse than the reality. It can be a relief for them to finally hear the truth. There is also a lack of trust implied in keeping things from them. Do my parents think I'm too young or too stupid to understand? Do they hide other things from me too?

A child who grows up knowing that her parents will always tell her the truth is secure in herself and in her world, and she knows that her parents respect her as an equal person. She's also more likely to meet the world openly and honestly, which in my experience makes for a much happier life.

There is no surer way to encourage your children to hide things from you (or from others in their lives) than to hide things from them yourself. The way we treat our children forms the basis for our future relationships with them, and if the goal is a trusting, honest, connected relationship, keeping things from them will do nothing to support that goal.

"My father didn't tell me how to live; he lived, and let me watch him do it." ~Clarence B. Kelland

My son likes to play with dolls, and my husband gives him a hard time about it. I don't think it hurts him any. He's very much a boy.

And your husband is very much a father. Does he change diapers, snuggle, bathe, kiss, and feed your child? Doesn't it seem reasonable that your son would want to play at nurturing a child too?

Why paint babies' rooms pink or blue and fill them with Barbies or Tonkas depending on their gender? If we continue to tell our boys to be brave and not to cry like a girl, as men they will bottle up their feelings. If we tell our girls that boys are different and they can never understand them, they never will. If we model in our marriages that only mothers are nurturing, caring, and domestic and fathers are bread winners, brave, and unable to plan a holiday, that is the kind of relationship they will look for as adults.

I once read somewhere that 50% of girls are 'tomboys.' What a nonsensical little statistic that is! If we can assert that half of girls like 'boy' things, obviously they're not really 'boy' things to begin with.

When we tell our boys they shouldn't be interested in something because of their gender we can cause them to question the validity of their feelings and can make them wonder whether they are missing some sort of natural inclination toward only 'boy' things. That could leave them feeling that there must be something wrong with them, when in fact there is something wrong with the whole idea of separating us into pink and blue categories.

I would encourage your husband to worry less about whether your son is 'very much a boy' and to focus more on helping him to be whatever he wants to be. Whether boys 'should' or 'shouldn't' be interested in dolls doesn't matter a bit. There's no need to look to others to see what is right for your child. Just look at him.

79

"Honest disagreement is often a good sign of progress." ~Mahatma Gandhi

My kids argue a lot and call each other names. I usually separate them by sending them to their rooms. I wonder whether they'd get along better if they were in school. Do you have your kids work it out on their own when they argue?

I went to school, and I certainly argued with my brothers and sisters. I think arguing is a perfectly normal part of life. Arguing is one of the ways we learn what we believe, how to incorporate others' beliefs into our lives, and how to get along with the people we love.

On the other hand, I think there are some things that we can do as parents that might increase the likelihood that our children will have an argumentative relationship and other things we can do that will decrease that likelihood. If the parents argue often, with each other or with the children, the kids are likely to argue as well. If the parents strive to listen to each other and to their children, the kids are likely to listen to others as well. When children live in an environment where their feelings and wants are taken seriously, they are more likely to take each other's feelings and wants seriously.

The idea of sending kids to their rooms is taken for granted by most parents. I have a few problems with it. One, I don't believe it is my right to send another person anywhere. Two, a person's bedroom should be a sanctuary, not a holding cell. Three, isolating someone who is upset and could probably benefit by some togetherness doesn't seem a very kind thing to do. And finally, separating the two people who are having the problem does nothing to help them resolve it.

I have found that, when they are upset and needing time alone, Rowan and Dagny will naturally seek it out, whether in their rooms, outside, or in a currently empty room elsewhere in the house. If they don't choose to do so, I can assume that they do not want to be alone.

Dagny and Rowan have their share of arguments. When they are arguing and one of them calls the other a name, I talk the problem through with them. I remind them that we want a happy, peaceful home where each of us feels safe and that name-calling does not encourage that. It sometimes takes a while to help them come to an understanding, but in the majority of cases they are able to do so.

I'm not a fan of the theory that says parents should tell their kids to work it out for themselves. For us, it seems to be better to have me or Jon there to hear complaints, help them 'hear' each other, give empathy, and help come up with solutions. Learning to communicate effectively and work through problems can be a life-long process. Expecting our kids to have it all figured out is unrealistic.

"Good manners have much to do with emotions. To make them ring true, one must feel them, not merely exhibit them." ~Amy Vanderbilt

Do you make your kids say please and thank you and send thank you notes when they receive presents? What about saying, "I'm sorry," when they do something wrong, like upsetting a friend? How are they learning manners?

We do not make our kids say please and thank you. We've all heard adults ask children, "What's the magic word?" In truth there is nothing magical about the word please. A person can very easily ask kindly and respectfully for something without using the word. Likewise, it is not necessary to say thank you in order to show appreciation. Of course, please and thank you can be positive additions to our vocabularies, but they've become more about control than about feelings in many families.

Coercing a child to say please or thank you does not model manners. It makes more sense to me to let my children hear me speak kindly to them and to the people around us. When a young child asks for something in a less than pleasant way, it's important that our response is respectful. Reacting by requiring him to say please would only model unkind behavior.

A thank you note can be a nice gesture. It can also be a mini-torture for a child forced to fill out twenty of them after his birthday party. Thank you notes written under those circumstances are totally devoid of any thankfulness. They're more about the parent wanting to look like she's doing a good job teaching her child manners than anything else.

Thank you notes are traditional, but they're not the only option. Ask your child how he would like to express his gratitude. You could send a picture of him using the gift or a drawing he would like the person to have. You could type out a letter, and he could sign it or decorate the envelope.

When I give a child a present in person, I'd rather the parent did not focus on whether or not the child thanks me. Any person I like enough to want to give a present is a person I want to have an honest relationship with. The child's authentic reaction to receiving the gift is fine, whatever form it takes (and whether it's a pleased reaction or not). Interrupting to instruct the child to thank me only takes away from the moment we are sharing.

I don't make Rowan or Dagny say "I'm sorry." It's not my place to tell them what their feelings are. If they feel sorry, they will express that in the way that feels right to them. A forced apology is meaningless. Saying you're sorry because you have to does not mean that you actually feel remorse. In addition, forcing an apology embarrasses a child who is probably not feeling very good about herself already. It adds one more thing for her to worry about as she tries to decide how best to resolve her problem.

What I've tried to do for Dagny and Rowan at times when they seem to want to apologize but feel embarrassed is to ask whether they'd like me to say anything to the other person for them. This usually opens up communication between the two people having the problem and makes it easier for them to work things out.

Often adults may feel that they've settled a situation by getting one of the children to apologize, but the children are left with an unresolved issue between them. Better to deal with the underlying problem than to train children to parrot a stock phrase.

"We've had bad luck with our kids — they've all grown up."
~Christopher Morley

My seven year old asks me to do things for him that I know he can do himself. Why should I make him a sandwich or tie his shoes? He's not behaving the way a seven year old should.

If you ask your husband to bring you a glass of water, should he tell you to do it yourself? Or do you hope that he will happily do it for you, if he can, because he loves you?

Seven is not very big. Every once in a while I see Rowan or Dagny from a certain angle and it suddenly occurs to me that they are really *little*. In so many ways they seem so grown up, but they're not. They still need me just as much, and sometimes in just as time-consuming a way, as they did when they were newborns. That's what I'm here to give them — whatever they need from me, whenever they need it.

I remember being a kid very vividly. I remember that no other peanut butter toast tastes as good as my mom's does. It may have been the exact shade of golden brown-ness that I liked, or the perfect, not too thin, not too thick layer of melted peanut butter, or the way she cut it into special shapes for me and put it on a tray. But really it's that all those things made me feel loved and special.

When my kids ask me to do something that they 'can' do for themselves, I know that it is not only a glass of chocolate milk they want. It's me, putting it in a special cup with a special straw and delivering it to them with a kiss. It's my love for them wrapped up in a glass. It brings me joy to love my children and to take care of them in the ways that they want me to.

One of my favorite mottos is 'love is a verb.' It's how we treat each other, what we do for each other, how we speak to each other, and how we are thoughtful of each other in big and little ways. Treating my children thoughtfully and kindly will not make them spoiled. It will allow them to experience good feelings that they are going to want to share with the people they love.

At seven, how should your son behave? Just the way he does. There are no shoulds in our house, only realities. I've found that accepting (and loving) people as they *are* makes for a much happier relationship than wishing they were the way I think they 'should' be.

Too soon your seven year old will no longer be asking you to do things for him. If you can find joy in helping him today, you will both look back on this time with happiness.

"Punishment doesn't even teach what not to do, much less the reason not to do it: what it really teaches is the desire to avoid punishment."
~Alfie Kohn

How do you feel about punishment? We recently decided not to punish our kids, but no one around us seems to understand the way we live. They think we're being judgmental of the way they parent.

I do believe so strongly in some things that I consider it wrong to do otherwise. I'm comfortable with that. We have to make judgments in our lives if we're going to live mindfully, honestly, and passionately; I don't want to live any other way. I can accept that other people make different choices, and can continue to love and support friends and family who make different choices, without agreeing with them.

We do not punish our children. While society gives us the right to do so, my own moral code does not. While they are less experienced than I am, they are not subordinate to me. I do not believe that it is ethical to exercise power over another human being, and particularly not over a child who depends upon me to meet her needs.

Given the number of books and articles written on the subject of punishment, I'm sure there are many people who believe it is not possible to parent a child without using some form. The use of time outs, withdrawal of 'privileges', taking away possessions, and grounding are all commonly accepted. In many places spanking is also commonplace. The idea that children are second class citizens is so pervasive in our society that it is not often even recognized by adults. I'm amazed that people can so easily forget or rationalize the feeling of powerlessness that goes along with being a child in mainstream society. I strive to do nothing to contribute to that feeling in my own children.

When I ask myself what kind of relationships I want to have with my children, I know that all of the components of my answer require as a foundation that we be able to deal with each other openly, honestly, and respectfully, as equals. Creating an environment in which I am in charge and they fear what I will do if their behavior doesn't meet my standards does nothing to contribute to that foundation. Using punishments almost guarantees a relationship in which the children will find dishonesty a better option than being caught.

Parents use punishment in an attempt to turn their children into the people they want them to be. I want to support Dagny and Rowan as the people they are and to support their efforts to learn to navigate through life. Living without punishment is definitely more time-consuming and can require a lot more thought, but the benefits are enormous. Accepting your children as whole people leads to relationships that are mutually respectful and caring and connected in a way that many people could never imagine.

"Him that I love, I wish to be free — even from me." ~Anne Morrow Lindbergh

Do you just let your kids do whatever they want? What if one of them broke something that belonged to someone else – you wouldn't punish her? Would you let her drive at thirteen or let her curse? You can't be your child's parent and her friend. If we don't give them discipline they'll think we don't love them enough to do it. Haven't you noticed that in recent years children are impatient and seem to be under the impression that the world revolves around them?

I've certainly not noticed impatience or self-centeredness in my own children or in the other unschooled children I know who are not punished in any way. They are treated with respect and, in turn, are respectful of others. They are listened to and, in turn, listen to others. They are treated with kindness and, in turn, are kind to others.

I do see a lot of unhappy children around us. They invariably are children who are disconnected from their families and who live with the knowledge that they are not in control of their minds or bodies.

When interacting with my kids, I focus on our relationships and their emotional cores. Punishing them would put distance between us and damage their senses of self. Giving them respect rather than discipline allows us to have honest relationships and keeps them whole. Rowan and Dagny have wonderful self-discipline. They've been given an opportunity to develop it. Jon and I talk with them, tell them what we think, answer their questions, and talk about their feelings and the feelings of the people around them. Not using discipline to control a child's behavior does not equate to being an uninvolved parent or having inconsiderate children. In fact, quite the opposite is true.

Neither of my kids has ever broken something on purpose. I'd imagine that, if it did happen, she must be very upset about something and would probably regret doing it pretty quickly. I know that's how I feel when I do something in anger. I'd console the person whose item was broken, replace the item if possible, and try to find out what's really bothering my child so I could help her to feel better. I can't imagine what punishing her would accomplish.

Both kids have broken things accidentally. When that happens I focus on the child, not the object. I make sure she understands I don't value the broken item anywhere near as much as I value her.

If Dagny or Rowan wanted to drive a car, I would ask her whether she wanted me to bring her to an empty parking lot or cemetery where she could drive safely, or sit on my lap and drive if she couldn't reach the pedals. I'd find a place with go carts she could drive, show her how to drive the ride-on mower, and brainstorm other ways she could do what she wanted to do. While it wouldn't be possible for her to drive on roads (real life limitation) I would do everything I could think of to get her close to doing what she wanted.

My parents did not allow me to curse. I cursed and still do. You cannot truly control another person. You may be able to control what she does when she's around you, but you can't control what she thinks or believes. You can share your values and opinions with her, but in the end she will form her own. I want to know my kids for who they really are. I don't want them to feel they have to hide parts of themselves from me.

To me, cursing and being hurtful with words are two separate issues. Rowan and Dagny have always used whatever words they want. I encourage them to be kind and do what I can to help them resolve situations in which they might feel a desire to be hurtful in peaceable ways. The word peanut can be used to hurt someone (What do you have? A peanut for a brain?), and for me the words in our vocabularies are nowhere near as important as how we use them.

Patience is learned through experience and over time and may well have more to do with personality than anything else. We no more need to teach our children to be patient than we need to teach them to read. If patience is important to you and something you hope your children will develop, focus on your own level of patience. Your children are watching how you behave as much as, or more than, they are hearing what you say.

Dagny and Rowan are two of my closest friends. They probably know me better than anyone else does. We share every day and extraordinary experiences. The relationships Jon and I have with them almost require a whole different vocabulary than the average parent/child relationship. For me, this is the most wonderful benefit of living an unschooled life. Our lives are intertwined and connected. I can guarantee you that they feel loved, because that is the number one priority in our family.

.

"I really believe unschooling works best when parents trust a child's personhood, his intelligence, his instincts, his potential to be mature and calm." ~Sandra Dodd, unschooling mom of Marty, Holly, and Kirby

What about the idea that we should remember who the parent is in our relationships with our kids? Shouldn't our children obey us? There are some rules kids have to obey, like not running out into the street or swimming without an adult at the pool. Children need limits, or they will push you. Can't we unschool but still enforce bedtimes, impose consequences, and have our children do chores? Why shouldn't I be the authority figure in our home?

Why should you be? I'm not being flip; it's a serious question.

Do you believe that your child will make bad choices? Do you believe that you always know better than he what is right for him? Do you believe that you have the right to control another human being?

I cannot reconcile my belief that my children and I are of equal worth with the idea of being in charge of them. Yes, they are less experienced. They need my help and look to me for guidance, and I give them what they ask of me. To give them more than that would be to rob them of their autonomy.

I don't expect (or want) my kids to 'obey' me and, in fact, would never think of giving them an order to obey in the first place.

One of the many things that I hope for Rowan and Dagny is that they continue to know in their hearts that they belong only to themselves. That knowledge seems to me to be an innate part of being human; unfortunately it is something that can be taught out of a child. The benefits of understanding that you are responsible for yourself are two-fold: you secure a feeling of freedom as well as the knowledge that no one other than yourself can assure that you live an honest, compassionate, responsible life. We do everything in our power to nurture that understanding.

People often say they need to teach their children self-discipline. It seems obvious to me that self-discipline is not something that can be taught. If it does not come from within the person, it is not *self-discipline*. It is when we interfere with its natural development that children lose the capability and desire to govern themselves.

No human being wants to be told what to do. I certainly don't. Moreover, it is not necessary that the parent/child relationship be an adversarial one. So much energy is wasted in trying to control children. That energy could be much better spent in trying to connect with them and to fill your relationships with respect and understanding – on the part of both parent and child.

It is usually assumed that children who aren't made to obey their parents will grow to be unruly, disrespectful, and 'out of control.' Nothing could be further from the truth. Children who are treated with respect are respectful of others. Children who are listened to as equals listen to others as equals. Children whose opinions are valued value others' opinions. A family where parents and children are allies is a peaceful family.

There are many ways to live with children without controlling them. The first step is to stop thinking of them as a separate group than adults, and start thinking of them as whole human beings with the same range of emotions and right to respect that an adult has. Starting from that point, it is inconceivable to think of making them obey you.

We have a pool. Instead of making rules like 'no swimming without an adult,' we sat down together (kids and parents) and talked about what we should do so that all four of us felt safe in and around the pool. One person thought the most important thing was that no one make anyone else uncomfortable in the water. Another person wanted to be sure we had a life saving hook. Another said it would be a good idea if there were always a strong swimmer around when a beginning swimmer went in the pool.

We ask that no one makes another person uncomfortable (which is a principle we live by in all aspects of our lives), we got a hook, and there's always a competent swimmer available when the pool is open.

No rules, just things we all agreed would make us feel safe, so there is no need to enforce anything. We make our decisions together.

Before my kids ever got to an age where they would be tempted to run into the street, we began a habit of holding hands whenever we walked out the door. Not a rule. No punishment if they didn't do it. We like holding hands.

Rules can make a family look as if it is operating very smoothly, but looks can be deceiving. In reality rules can make a child feel resentful and can cause him to find any possible opportunity to break the rules when out of his parents' sight. Rules, like punishment, affect only outward behavior – not the inner needs of a child. Demanding obedience from a child leaves little room for honesty in your relationship. Without that honesty the chances of having a connected relationship with your child are greatly diminished.

It is not true that children will push if you do not set limits. When you work together to keep your family functioning and happy, there is nothing to push against.

I have read online of people who unschool but still parent more traditionally, although I don't know any personally. The problem I have with this idea is, where is the line? If your children can learn to read without external pressures or timetables, can't they learn to do dishes the same way? Can you trust them to develop an understanding of mathematics but not trust them to understand and listen to their own bodies? If you're still separating life into academics and 'not,' it seems to me you are missing a piece of the big picture. If you pick and choose when you will treat your children with respect and trust, their relationships with learning (and with you) will be affected.

Is it important to remember who the parent is? Well, there *are* times when I try to remember who the parent is. When Dagny and I are both cranky and feeling bickery, I try to remember that I'm the parent and that I have more of a reserve of patience than she does. I'm the parent, so I can step back and change how I'm acting more easily than she can. When Rowan wants me to get up for the hundredth time to get her something in the kitchen, I remember that I'm the parent and that she can't do everything she wants to without asking for help. I can make her feel good or bad about that. I'm the parent, and I can choose to happily help her when she wants me to. When either one of them wants me to drop what I'm doing to do something with her, I remember that I'm the parent of two kids who won't be kids forever, and I remember that I don't want to miss one minute of being their parent.

"Freedom is not merely the opportunity to do as one pleases; neither is it merely the opportunity to choose between set alternatives. Freedom is, first of all, the chance to formulate the available choices, to argue over them – and then, the opportunity to choose." ~C. Wright Mills

You can't possibly offer your children unlimited choices. The fact is that sometimes the choice is *this* or *nothing*, and no child is going to choose to do things like go to the doctor. Isn't it a parent's duty to make choices for her child?

Of course no one is always going to be thrilled with the options at hand. The point is to have a choice of all the *available* options and not to arbitrarily limit the options based on what the parent thinks is best.

Children who know that they are truly free to make their own decisions make responsible, carefully considered choices. The belief that children won't choose to do what's best for themselves creates a self-fulfilling prophecy: controlling children may indeed lead to children who won't choose to do what's best for themselves, as their decision making will be tainted by their reactions to the loss of autonomy.

We do not make Rowan and Dagny go to the doctor. They choose to go to the doctor when they don't feel well and want help to feel better, just as I do. They choose to do things that make sense.

A real life example is that Rowan had a very traumatic experience with an unsympathetic doctor who gave her stitches with too little anesthesia when she was four years old. She had not been to a doctor since then, when she hurt herself running a year and a half later. Her ankle swelled up and was very painful. She did not want to go to the doctor. However, she knew that there was something really wrong with her body. She was very upset and scared.

We talked about some ways to make the experience less scary, and she made some decisions about what she's like us to do if she was not happy with something the doctor wanted to do to her. We made it very clear that, if she wanted to leave the hospital at any time, we would leave. We did not leave our house until she was ready to go. When we brought her to the hospital, she felt in control of the situation. She definitely would not have felt in control if we'd picked her up and said, "You're going."

The assumption that children will not choose what's best for them is disparaging. Given the opportunity, that's exactly what they will choose for themselves: what's best for them. It may not always be the choice the parent would have made, but they deserve the opportunity to make their own decisions.

What is a parent's duty? My duty is to my children's emotional cores – their inner selves. I try to make as few choices for them as possible. In fact, I can't remember the last time I made a choice for them. Certainly it was before they were verbal. I support them, explain things to them, help them when they want me to, make sure they know all of their options, and encourage them to do what feels right. They are whole human beings and more than capable of looking within themselves for their own answers.

"Whining is anger through a small opening." ~Stuart Smalley

My child whines too much. How do you handle whining?

Whining is not a pleasant sound to listen to, but it is sometimes the only way a child knows to express what she is feeling and can't necessarily put into words.

I have heard various advice on this subject: ignore her, whine back, tape the child so she can hear how it sounds. None of these ideas seem very kind to me, and it's important to me to treat my children with kindness.

What I have done if Dagny or Rowan whined is to try to solve the problem she is having without making an issue of the whining. Becoming frustrated only escalates the situation. It adds the stress of mom being upset with her to whatever stress the child is already feeling that's causing her to whine in the first place. If you just can't stand the sound of it, by all means tell her so, but do it calmly and gently, and not at the time that you are having the problem. It may not be something she can stop very easily, but maybe she'll try; hopefully your focusing on the problem instead of the noise will help you to deal with it in the meantime.

As unschooling mom Joyce Fetteroll once wrote, "Behavior is an expression of needs. The needs don't go away because the behavior goes away. The needs often get expressed in other ways or turned inward." Children do not do things for no reason. In the same way that, when a baby cries, parents think: Hungry? Wet? Tired? and respond to whichever need they think is most likely, when an older child whines, I go through a mental checklist: Hungry? Tired? Feeling put upon or ignored?

If one of my kids were to start whining consistently about something, I would think about what I could do to solve the root problem, not to change the child. Is there a pattern to the whining? Is something going on in the child's life that would lead her to feel out of control, not listened to, or frustrated?

As they get older children learn other ways to deal with frustration or unhappiness and develop the skills to communicate what they are feeling. To try to rush them through that learning will only make it more difficult for them and does nothing to make the present a happier time for either of you.

"They may forget what you said, but they will never forget how you made them feel." ~Anonymous

How do you handle temper tantrums? What about when one child doesn't want to go somewhere and you have to go?

Well, to begin with, I don't think of them as tantrums, which to me is a word with a heavily negative connotation. Instead I think of them as times when my child is expressing how she feels in the best way she knows how. By assuming that my children are always doing the best they are able to at any given time, I am able to approach each situation as their ally.

I believe that there is always a reason behind a person's behavior, and often a 'tantrum' comes about because the child's needs were not considered in advance by her parent. Rather than getting angry or frustrated with my child, I think about what I may have overlooked. Is she hungry or thirsty? Was she too tired for this errand? Am I not paying enough attention to her? More importantly, if I consider her needs ahead of time, we can avoid the problem altogether. No child *wants* to have a meltdown. It's our job as parents to meet and anticipate our children's needs and to make doing so a priority.

In *Teach Your Own,* John Holt wrote, "I would insist that much of the seemingly irrational and excessive anger of little children---'tantrums' ---is in fact not only caused by things that happen to them or that are said and done to them, but that these things would make us angry if they happened or were said and done to us." I'm careful not to treat my children in ways I would not want to be treated.

Many times parents become embarrassed at their child's behavior and focus on stopping her from acting the way she is acting as quickly as possible, rather than on helping her to feel better. I consciously remove myself mentally from whatever environment I am in, blocking out my relative watching me or the cashier waiting for me to 'take control,' and focus on finding out what is bothering my child and making it better for her. I show her that my attention is on her and that I'm not worried about what anyone else thinks about what is happening. Quite often if I quietly say, "Remember that I'm on your side and that I'm going to help you with whatever the problem is," it is enough to calm her.

A common reaction to a child's 'tantrum' is anger on the part of the adult. How can we, who sometimes have trouble dealing with our own feelings even with many more years of experience, expect a child of only a few years of age to have perfect control over her emotions? Is controlling feelings and not expressing anger and frustration something that we should be encouraging in the first place?

What messages is a child receiving when told to be quiet or stop crying? That it's not ok to convey emotion? That her feelings are not important to you? What message do you want to give? I want my children to know that how they feel is of utmost importance to me. I want them to know that expressing emotion is one of the things that makes us human and helps our relationships to grow.

Common wisdom these days says that the best way to deal with a tantrum is to ignore the child. I vehemently disagree. A person who is upset needs to feel love and connection, not desertion.

As far as the specific scenario you mentioned, we talk over our plans ahead of time so that, if Rowan or Dagny doesn't want to go somewhere, we can figure out another option for her. If she's agreed to go and doesn't want to when the time comes, I first determine whether there's any way for her not to have to go. If there's no way out of it, I've said I'm really sorry but it's too late now to change this. I've said that next time we can make a backup plan. But today we just need to go, and I hope we can try to make the best of it and enjoy each other's company. I'll offer to do something she'd like to do after the required activity. We often bring a game in the car if she's in the middle of playing with it or think of something that will make the car ride fun and not seem like such a letdown from what she was doing.

Dagny and Rowan are pretty understanding in these situations. By the time they were two or three, they knew that I didn't want to make them do things they didn't want to do and that I try to be sure I never say we 'have' to when it's simply that I want to. I believe that, if you treat your child respectfully and take her wishes seriously while she is a baby and toddler, you will develop a relationship in which you will both feel that you are working together to find solutions to the problems that arise.

"If we are to attain real peace in this world, we will have to begin with the children." ~Mahatma Gandhi

What about episodes of rage? Do you let your kids know their behavior is wrong? What if it is directed at you (i.e. calling names or hitting)? Do you have set consequences for this kind of bad behavior? We generally send our children to their rooms until they can control themselves.

When one of my children lashes out in anger, I let her know that I'm on her side and that I want to help her feel better. I try to address how she is feeling rather than labeling the behavior itself. If someone I love is angry, I *want* her to tell me. Sharing our emotions and working things through together is a huge part of what relationships are all about.

I do tell them if they are doing something that makes me uncomfortable, and I explain that I need to feel safe too (from both physical and verbal 'attacks'). We have freedom to do what we like, but not license to infringe on others' peace and safety.

We realized some time ago that often a problem with anger is simply a result of low blood sugar. Keeping a plate of finger foods readily available is in many cases enough of a preventative measure. For those times when it is not, though, I try to help Rowan and Dagny come up with ideas for other ways to express their anger – like stomping or throwing a pillow at the wall – and help them find things that calm them, such as deep breathing, working on a puzzle, or listening to music. We come up with these ideas when they are happy, not in the heat of the moment.

Over time they've each developed their own strategies for dealing with a rush of anger. Rowan will tell me to just leave her alone for a while, and she'll go to a quiet room until she feels better, or she will climb up on my lap, and remind me to 'sit quietly' (something she came up with for when she wants to be with me but doesn't want me to talk or try to make her feel better). Dagny generally goes to her room to read or listen to loud music for a while.

Dealing with strong emotions is not easy for anyone, but it's particularly hard for someone who's had so little experience with it. Learning to live peacefully with others takes time. Feeling the rush of adrenaline and reacting internally (stopping to think, breathe, remove yourself from the situation for a minute) instead of lashing outward is a learned skill. I see myself as a support system for my children as they learn, and while they do so, I model the ways in which I deal with anger myself.

I don't think of my kids' behavior as *bad* or *good*. I assume that they are doing the best that they are able at any given moment. As for consequences, I'm sure they're not always happy with what comes out of their mouths and feel bad sometimes. I know I sometimes say things I regret. I also think such a strong rush of emotion can be a scary feeling. There's no need for me to impose an artificial consequence on top of the naturally occurring ones, even if I were willing to do so.

I try to handle these situations in a way that keeps us connected. I don't want my kids to control themselves. I want them to be at peace with themselves and with the people around them.

"Kindness in thought leads to wisdom. Kindness in speech leads to eloquence. Kindness in action leads to love." ~Lao-Tsu

We use natural consequences with our children. My three year old never wants to wear a coat in the winter. If we're going somewhere and he refuses, I leave it at home. When my ten year old leaves his roller blades outside, I leave them there so he will see that they can be damaged by the weather and learn to take better care of his things. When I play a game with him and he gets mad, the natural consequence is that I put the game away. How do you handle these kinds of situations?

If Dagny or Rowan wanted to go outside without a coat in the cold, I would tell her to let me know if she changed her mind and send her out with a kiss. Both of my kids do go out in much less clothing than I would be comfortable in and are perfectly comfortable. I can't feel their bodies. They can.

I would not leave a child's coat at home if we were going somewhere. I used to ask the kids whether they'd like to wear coats. If they said no, I would throw some in the car in case they wanted them later. Now I just keep a bag in the back of the car with sweaters and jackets, so there's always one available if someone wants it. The way I see it, it is my responsibility to meet their needs – clothe them when they are cold, feed them when they are hungry, comfort them when they are sad. The fact that they're not cold now does not mean that they won't be cold later, and it's easy enough to plan for that contingency. Learning to plan for future possibilities is something that comes with time. Until Rowan and Dagny take on that responsibility for themselves, I will happily do it for them.

Being cold because your mother decided not to bring a coat for you so you'd learn a lesson is not a natural consequence. It is a punishment. The thing about natural consequences is that you don't make them happen. They are the consequences that happen naturally. Any time a parent plans for something unpleasant to happen to her child so that she will learn a lesson, it is a punishment.

If you want to have an egalitarian relationship with your children, it is necessary to examine your language very closely. Many times people use euphemisms (particularly for punishment) without even realizing it, and 'natural consequences' seems to be a popular one these days.

If my child left something outside that would be better off indoors, I would bring it in for her. The natural consequence of that is that my children feel loved.

If you do things for your children out of love, they learn to do the same. When Dagny forgets to put her bike away, Jon does it. When Jon left a drink on the counter because he got distracted from getting his dinner, Dagny put it in the refrigerator. Treating children thoughtfully lets them experience good feelings that they're going to want to share with the people they love.

Putting the game away is a consequence you decided on, not a natural consequence. It's a punishment designed to get him to behave in the way you want him to behave.

I like my kids to tell me when they're mad or upset (or happy, or scared, or...). Rowan gets frustrated playing games sometimes. We usually just end up changing the rules to make it more fun – maybe make it a cooperative game instead of a competitive one, or make up something silly to do while we roll the dice. Often she makes up her own rules, and I'm just along for the ride. After all, the point of our playing together is enjoyment. If we're not having fun, something needs to change, and it's not the child.

Instead of focusing on teaching kids a lesson, parents can focus on making their children's lives comfortable and joyful.

"Society chooses to disregard the mistreatment of children, judging it to be altogether normal because it is so commonplace." ~Alice Miller

We don't punish our kids very often, but we do give them a swat on the bottom when it comes to things like running out into the street or touching a hot stove – safety concerns. I'd rather see them spanked than dead. You can't reason with a one year old.

Neither can you expect a one year old to be responsible for keeping himself safe.

What does hitting a person tell him about the danger of fast cars or hot burners? That if the cars or heat don't hurt him his parents will? In *Punished By Rewards*, Alfie Kohn writes, "Regardless of what we are trying to get across by spanking, paddling, or slapping them, the messages that actually come through are these: 'Violence is an acceptable way of expressing anger' and 'If you are powerful enough you can get away with hurting someone.'" These are not messages I want my children to hear.

It is the parents' job to ensure the child's safety. A young child cannot be expected to understand that a) the stove is hot and b) the heat will hurt them. A preverbal child cannot be expected to understand that a) a car is coming and b) the driver might not stop in time and c) the car could hit him and d) getting hit by a car hurts. How does a 'swat on the bottom' explain any of that?

I am the one person in the world my child should feel most invulnerable with. The thought of instilling fear that I might hurt them into my children repulses me.

Children do not want to hurt themselves. If mine are about to do so and don't know it, I am there to keep them safe. If my child tried to touch a hot stove, I'd get an oven mitt, talk about why we use them, maybe show her the steam coming off a pot and how it felt cooler up high but as we went lower it got hot, and talk about how hot it must be in the pot. I would support her in her explorations while keeping her safe.

Spanked or dead are not the only two choices. There are so many other things you can do to protect a child from being hurt that don't damage either your relationship with the child or the child's inner self (not to mention his backside).

"I think that too often we fail to feel situations 'from the child's point of view,' and that failure leads us to teach our children other than what we think we're teaching them." ~Astrid Lindgren

I was raised in a house where spanking was a daily occurrence, and I didn't want that for my kids. Now I've spanked my daughter, and I don't know how to change our relationship or make a different kind of relationship with her younger brother.

I would apologize to your daughter for spanking her, and talk with her about what your childhood was like for you. As you were spanked yourself, you should be able to empathize with each other. It might be helpful for you to spend some time thinking about your childhood and the feelings that accompanied your spankings.

I would ask her what she feels about having been spanked (and be open to letting her share anger/frustration with you). Any major change to your relationship is going to take time and your willingness to allow her to vent her feelings.

Assume that your kids are doing the best they know how to do, and approach problems as their ally. Make yourselves a team working to make your family a peaceful, happy one. Show them that they are worthy of respect and kindness and a safe and loving family.

Take the time to see things from their perspectives. If we look at things from our kids' points of view, seeing them as whole people with real, very big feelings, a lot of what most parents do doesn't make any sense and isn't fair or right. If you keep your goal of a happy, healthy relationship in mind when you are interacting with your kids, you can make it a reality.

A wonderful resource for parents who want to learn non-punitive ways of living with their children is an email group established by unschooling mom Pam Sorooshian. It can be found under 'NoMoreSpanking' at www.yahoogroups.com. Another great resource is www.neverhitachild.org.

"...for many of us, parenting has been filled with struggle. There is a better way. You don't have to learn it. You already know it. You only have to trust it." ~William Martin

We want to parent more peacefully. How do we begin? I'm realizing that, while I thought I was a very relaxed parent, I actually controlled my kids in a number of little ways. I've also realized that I don't take the time to see things from their perspectives. At this point we don't seem to talk very nicely to each other, but I want to change that. When they're acting up I hear my mother's voice telling me to take control. Will I ever be the parent I want to be?

We can't stop people from making comments about our parenting, but we can decide they aren't allowed to talk in our heads. Focusing on how you and your children feel instead of on how some uninvolved person feels will make the transition to a new relationship with your children an easier one.

I would begin by looking at your children as your partners rather than your adversaries. Think about whether or not you can say yes (and be willing to put effort into making a yes possible) when your knee jerk reaction is to say no. Remember that they are doing the best they know how at any given moment and that the only person you can truly control is yourself.

Parents will say things to their children that they would never think of saying to a co-worker or friend. Try to be aware of what you're saying and what message your words are conveying. Does what you are doing and saying affirm the belief that children are whole people? Or does it reinforce the idea that children are 'less than' adults and therefore can be treated differently? Does it show your children that you value them for who they are? Or does it give them the impression that you wish they were different in some way?

Try to remember what it felt like to be a child. Some of my most defining moments from childhood are things that my parents may have long forgotten as insignificant. Every moment of childhood – of life – is a potential memory. I want my children's memories of me to be happy ones. I want them to know that I am on their side, here to help them do/get/be whatever they want. My job is not to shape them, but to give them the room and the time and whatever else they need to be who they already are and to show them with my words and actions that they are exactly whom I would like them to be.

Make your children your partners in your effort to change your parenting. You could ask them to remind you to take a deep breath if they don't like the way you are treating them. Encourage them to be honest with you when they feel you are being controlling or not seeing things from their points of view. Be open to their complaints. Let them know that you are working hard at what you are doing because you want a better relationship with them.

Don't be in a rush to react to a situation. Give yourself the time to look through your children's eyes. People often think that a slow-paced life is less full; but, in truth, when you take things slowly and thoughtfully, you are living each moment to its fullest.

Author Marshall Rosenberg wrote of making the transition to communicating non-violently with his children: "On the day I am thinking of, my oldest son and I were having a conflict, and it was taking me quite awhile to communicate it in the way that I was choosing to, rather than the way that had become habitual. Almost everything that came into my mind originally was some coercive statement in the form of a judgment of him for saying what he did. So I had to stop and take a deep breath, and think of how to get more in touch with my needs, and how to get more in touch with his needs. And this was taking me awhile. And he was getting frustrated because he had a friend waiting for him outside, and he said, 'Daddy, it's taking you so long to talk.' And I said, 'Let me tell you what I can say quickly: Do it my way or I'll kick your butt.' He said, 'Take your time, Dad. Take your time.'"

If you find yourself treating your children disrespectfully because you feel they are not respecting you, remember that they are watching how you behave in order to learn how they should behave. Respond to disrespect in a respectful way and give them time to feel and see the difference in how they are being treated. To change the dynamic in your relationship *you* have to be the one willing to make changes to yourself. Given your example they will learn more effective ways of communicating in time.

You can be the kind of parent you want to be. We make ourselves who we are every day – every moment. Life is full of little choices that can make a big difference. Paying attention to the choices you are making, living mindfully, will help you to get where you want to go.

"Have patience with all things, but first of all with yourself."
~St. Francis de Sales

Don't you ever have one of those days where you mess up completely with your kids and say something awful? Or days when no matter what you do your kids are miserable and cranky?

When I read that question, I immediately pictured a few not so great moments. Of course I mess up. I know very well the feeling of hearing things come out of my mouth as if someone else is saying them and I have no power to stop them. All the while I'm thinking, "What a terrible thing to say!" I have actually yelled at my children because I was frustrated with their yelling at each other. The kids and I have times when we are overtired or sick or just plain grumpy. Unschooling does not make us more than human. Striving to be a peaceful parent does not make me a perfect parent.

I am not by nature a patient person. When Dagny was born, I realized that I had to develop patience if I were going to be the mom I wanted to be. Eleven years later I still have to work at it, although not as consciously as a few years ago. The greatest tool I've learned for helping me to remain calm is to take three deep breaths before reacting in any way. But, of course, I don't always remember to do it.

The best I can do when I lose my patience is to own up to my mistakes and to remember that a bad moment does not have to ruin the whole day. When I haven't lived up to my own expectations with the kids, I make sure to talk to them about it. I want to be sure we're not left feeling disconnected in any way. It's important to me that Rowan and Dagny know that they can be honest with me about how they feel about what I did, and it's important to me that they know how I feel about it too. Luckily for me they are not under the illusion that I'm a superhero (well, Rowan did tell me that holding things is my super-power!) and can forgive me my mistakes.

I've found that often my mood sets the tone for the day. If I notice that I am being unpleasant and change my attitude, the atmosphere in the house seems to lift. The way I usually go about changing my mood is to go into my room for a few minutes and read. Distracting myself for even a short time helps me to start fresh.

Reading and writing at www.unschooling.info and at the UnschoolingDiscussion, unschoolingbasics, AlwaysLearning, and AlwaysUnschooled e-mail lists at http://groups.yahoo.com/ helps to keep me focused on being the kind of parent I want to be. Talking about my beliefs with others who share them and being questioned about why I treat my children the way I do reinforces my commitment to respectful parenting. Reading about how other parents live with their children helps me to see solutions to problems I might be struggling with.

"When we think we possess people there is a tendency to run their lives for them, and out of this develops extremely inharmonious situations. Only when we realize that we do not possess them, that they must live in accordance with their own inner motivations, do we stop trying to run their lives for them, and then we discover that we are able to live in harmony with them." ~Peace Pilgrim

We're talking about MY children. I've done a lot of reading about parenting, and I know what's best for them. Do unschoolers have any expectations for their kids, academically or otherwise? At the very least you must expect your kids to read or write a certain amount each week.

My children are only 'mine' in as much as they choose to be.

Each of us has an inner voice that, given the chance, will bring us to joy. I cannot hear my children's inner voices. They sometimes choose to share them with me, but where their hearts lead them is something I cannot (and would not want to) control. I don't want anyone to decide what's 'best' for me, and I won't take away my children's freedom to make decisions for themselves.

Our expectations for the kids (and ourselves) are that we treat each other kindly and with respect and are honest with each other. We've found that living with our children in freedom has resulted in responsible, thoughtful, kind, helpful kids. People are often shocked to hear that we don't use punishments or have the kids do chores along with not doing lessons. They imagine a messy house and horrid children. That's not our reality. We treat them respectfully, and they return the favor. We're thoughtful of their needs and wants, and they are thoughtful of ours. So while we don't have the same expectations that most people have for their kids, we don't have unruly kids who run our lives. They have freedom, not license, as A.S. Neill writes about in *Summerhill*. We're a team, and we work together to make each other's lives happy.

When I hear people say that if we don't control what our kids learn/do/wear/eat/etc. that things will fall apart, I can't help but think that they don't have a very high opinion of children. Why would a child want to be less than her best self? A person who has expectations for herself wants to live up to those expectations. A person who knows others have expectations for her feels those expectations as a weight that binds her to a path she may have no desire to be on.

I'm not in any way in charge of what Dagny and Rowan do with their time. They make their own choices. At this point Dagny spends a lot of time reading (books like *Tuck Everlasting*, *Holes*, and this week *Romeo and Juliet*), using the computer, watching TV and movies, writing poetry, music, and stories, swimming, playing guitar, talking to her friends, and hanging out with her friends and family.

Rowan likes to play board games, watch TV, and play on the computer. She loves to be read to. Dagny and I read to her during the day, and Jon reads books with her and Dagny at night – not every night, just when they all want to.

Her days are mostly spent playing dress-up, making things out of boxes or paper or craft supplies, painting, playing with friends, drawing, swimming, playing with dolls/cars/blocks, cooking, playing with the dogs, talking to us, playing outside, making presents for people, playing video games, and all the million other things kids come up with to do.

I try to keep a lot of fun things around and add new things to do and places to go pretty regularly – always as options, not requirements. I keep my eyes and ears open for things one of us might be interested in.

I don't think there's a magic number of minutes a person should write (or read, or anything) a week. How would you come up with that number? It makes more sense to me to trust the kids to write when something needs to be written. I don't want them to write for arbitrary reasons (i.e., because I think they should). I want them to do things for reasons that make sense to them, and for reasons that make them feel happy or challenged or interested. I want them to write because they have something to say, or need a list, or want to communicate with a friend. Real life reasons.

What works for us is to let the kids show us what's best for them. They know. We could only guess.

Reading parenting books can be helpful. You can come across new ideas, learn to see children in a different way, and learn things from people you may never meet, but who share your values and principles. However, giving the advice in parenting books (including this one!) more weight than your children's opinions and needs and wants won't do anything positive for you or them.

"The major purpose of a standardized test is to allow reliable and valid comparisons to be made among students taking the test." ~The National Education Association Website

How do you know that your children are learning? Do they take standardized tests?

I don't quiz my kids. They've never taken a test, and the only tests they will ever take will be of their own choosing. As long as Dagny and Rowan are living full and happy lives, I know that they are doing just fine. It is not important that anyone else feels pleased with what my kids know. It is only important that they do.

I don't believe it's possible to get through a day without learning anything. I doubt it's possible to get through an hour without learning anything. I don't need my kids to take a test to prove that to me. Of course I do sometimes know when they have learned something. Our days are spent in connection with each other. Often we learn things together. Just as I knew when Dagny had learned to walk, or when Rowan had said her first word, I know when Dagny learned what a golden orb spider looks like and when Rowan learned how to count by fives. I simply do not purposefully seek to find out what they know.

People tend to see standardized tests as a way to ascertain whether or not teachers are doing a good job. The idea is to hold the schools accountable. Rowan and Dagny are accountable only to themselves.

While the NEA believes it's important to compare children to each other, I believe that it is damaging and unkind. It causes embarrassment, shame, and feelings of deficiency and superiority. It is interesting to see how differently a child who has never taken a test views herself. My children do not compare themselves to anyone but their own best selves. They learn because they are interested, and their learning has value for them in a way that a child brought up in the 'will this be on the test?' atmosphere of schools would find difficult to understand.

117

When Rowan was six, a friend used the word 'fail' when talking to her. She turned to me and said, "What does fail mean?" As I explained it, I realized that failure is something that has little meaning to a person who has not had her knowledge scrutinized and judged. I can't help but think that she'll be all the happier for never having experienced it.

"Live together, as well as you can; enjoy life together, as much as you can. Ask questions to find out something about the world itself, not to find out whether or not someone knows it." ~John Holt

My father likes to quiz our kids whenever he sees them. He asks them math questions and geography questions. It makes the kids uncomfortable, but I'm not sure what to do. I don't think he'll ever understand unschooling.

I believe that what is inside a person's head is private. There is a reason we can't hear each other's thoughts. Our thoughts and knowledge make up a big part of who we are, and we should have the right to share ourselves or not as we choose.

Whenever one person asks another person a question that he already knows the answer to, his agenda is not honest; he is not dealing with the other person as an equal. Quizzing a child is intrusive and demeaning. I consider it my responsibility to protect Dagny and Rowan from anyone who is not treating them respectfully. I usually try to deal with the situation by using humor, quizzing the quizzer or saying, "If they wanted to take tests they'd go to school," in a lighthearted way. If the person persists, I am quite willing to lose the humor and simply make it very clear that he is not to continue with what he is doing.

Many people take quizzing kids for granted and haven't put much thought into it. Sometimes one comment is enough to get them thinking, and they come to the understanding pretty quickly that it's not a nice thing to do. Other people see it as something that kids just have to put up with or are sincerely concerned that your child isn't learning 'enough.' In either of those cases I defend my child's right to not be put on the spot. It is no one's business what she knows, and there is no list of things that she should know at any given time.

Whether or not the person I'm dealing with can ever understand that isn't really the issue. The issue is whether he can understand that, if he wants to spend time with Rowan and Dagny, he will have to treat them with respect. As with so many other things in our lives, the question I ask myself is: what message are my children getting from the way I respond to this situation? If I don't back up our beliefs with actions, the message could very well be that they're not my beliefs after all.

"I am enough of an artist to draw freely upon my imagination. Imagination is more important than knowledge. Knowledge is limited. Imagination encircles the world." ~Albert Einstein

Aren't you afraid there will be gaps in your kids' knowledge? Really, what could be more important than for a child to learn math, science, history and English? What happens if my child reaches age eighteen and still doesn't know what she wants to do with her life? I'm afraid she'll want to live at home forever and mooch.

It's more important that they develop open and connected relationships, that they have the freedom to be who they are, and that they find joy in their lives, among other things.

In reality, though, unschooled kids *do* learn math, science, history, and English. The difference is that those 'subjects' are not only explored at designated times, for a designated period. The difference is that they learn about them for real life reasons. The difference is that they *want* to learn.

How can there be a gap in something that has no predetermined shape? As unschoolers, Rowan and Dagny are free to determine for themselves what the shape of their internal models will be. I'm confident that they will fill all the pieces of their own particular puzzles.

Kids who go to school are told regularly what they are lacking in through tests, grades, and progress reports. Every bad grade is a blow to their self-esteem. Every test gives the message that what's important is what they don't know, not who they are. I went to school. I was taught history, science, English, and math. There are lots and lots of things I do not know about those subjects. Does that mean there are gaps in my knowledge? Or does it just mean that no one can know everything there is to know?

I haven't known a lot of eighteen year olds who *do* know what they want to do with their lives. There's a societal expectation that they will, but reality seldom matches that expectation. People do not stop growing at age eighteen. What a person wants to do with her life when she is fifteen will most likely be different than what she wants to do when she's twenty-one, thirty-five, fifty-six, or eighty-two. Life is not static.

If my children wanted to live here forever, I would be thrilled. I want to share as much of my life with them as they are happy with. I don't see living at home as the equivalent of 'mooching.' Just as Dagny and Rowan contribute to our home and family life now, I'm confident that they would do so as adults.

"You cannot teach a man anything. You can only help him discover it within himself." ~Galileo

School teaches a child so many topics that she wouldn't be exposed to otherwise. How can this hurt a child? If our children don't go to school and get exposed to different subjects, how will they figure out what they want to do with their lives?

As unschoolers, we believe that learning comes from within. I do not teach my children; they learn. They do learn from me, but they also learn from talking to other people, watching television and movies, reading, playing, planning parties, taking trips, shopping, camping, and taking care of their pets. They learn by living.

How much of the learning that happens in a school setting stays with a person? How much is forgotten as soon as the test is taken or the paper written? What an unschooled child learns she learns for herself. She owns her knowledge, and it becomes a part of her.

What I believe hurts the child is the idea that there is a list of things that every person must know, and that anything that is not on that list, no matter how interesting to her, is unimportant and a waste of time.

What I believe hurts the child is the belief that she cannot learn something unless it is taught.

What I believe hurts the child is the loss of freedom, privacy, and self-determination that comes with institutional living.

What I believe hurts the child is the loss of ownership of her body and mind.

The assumption that, if a child is not in school, he will not be exposed to a variety of subjects is false. An unschooled child is exposed to *life*. Life is not divided neatly into categories labeled 'science' and 'math,' but it certainly encompasses those subjects and more – all of them in fact!

Think about the people you know. Are most of them finding joy in doing something they learned in school? Are they even looking for joy? Traditionally, figuring out what we want to do with our lives means figuring out what career we want to work in. Without school, the meaning broadens.

"School was the unhappiest time of my life and the worst trick it ever played on me was to pretend that it was the world in miniature. For it hindered me from discovering how lovely and delightful and kind the world can be, and how much of it is intelligible." ~E.M. Forester

Don't you worry that your kids will be unprepared when the time comes for them to leave the nest? What about college? I don't see how my kids will be prepared for the real world if they don't go to school, and I can't imagine dealing with a teenager at home all the time.

Our goal is that there will not be a particular moment when our children must suddenly be pushed from the nest. Our hope is that, by allowing our children to seek out and take responsibility in their own time with our guidance and support, but not pressure, they will experience a smoother transition into adulthood and will think of us as a safety net rather than an obstacle.

The problems of a typical teen/parent relationship are created in large part by the dynamics inherent in a system that separates parents and children from the time the child turns five years old (or often earlier). It is very difficult to retain a connected relationship when the amount of time spent together is so minimal and is so often spent in preparation for the next day's tasks. Add to that the fact that a mainstream teenager has little to no control over her own life or time, has little opportunity to pursue what interests her, is dealing with the flood of emotions that hormones bring, is put on a schedule that does not permit her the sleep her body needs, and lives in a society that encourages her to pull away from her parents at a certain age whether she wants to or not, and you have a recipe for unhappiness.

Our society has choreographed a 'typical' progression from child to adult, and expects all teenagers to travel the same path. A person who doesn't feel comfortable on that path is a rebel or a delinquent. A child who is not ready to move on as quickly as another child might be is perceived as immature or spoiled or 'slow.' A child who is

125

ready to move on more quickly than others has no opportunity to do so. Unschooling gives each child the time and the room to follow her own path and to travel that path with the loving support and companionship of her family.

The groundwork we lay with our kids when they are young is vitally important to our future relationships. The relationships I have with Dagny and Rowan are open, honest, and respectful. We have our difficult moments, just as anyone in a relationship does, but overall it's a pleasure to spend time with them. I have no reason to believe that will change at any particular 'teen' age. We will ride the swells of hormones and growing pains together, and each of them will leave the nest in her own time and way.

I do not worry that they will be unprepared, because I trust that they will know when the time is right. They will have spent a lifetime making their own decisions about what they are capable of. Just as they knew when they were ready to tie their shoes, take off their training wheels, or watch a scary movie, they will know when they are ready to fly. They aren't in preparation for anything. They live in the real world right now, and it is a wonderful, amazing, challenging, beautiful, extraordinary place.

In *Teach Your Own*, John Holt wrote, "I used to say, and say now, that a college degree isn't a magic passkey that opens every door in town. It opens only a few, and before you spend a lot of time and money getting one of those keys, it's a good idea to find out what doors it opens (if any), and what's on the other side of those doors, and to decide whether you like what's on the other side, and if you do, whether there may not be an easier way to get there." Rowan and Dagny will decide for themselves whether college is the way to get where they want to go.

When people say that school prepares children for the real world, what's implied is that it is the difficult parts of school (doing things you don't want to do, forced interaction with peers, following rules that you don't believe in) that are important. What's implied is that the real world is going to be an unhappy place and that being treated unfairly by people is a part of life.

It may be a part of life in school, but it is not a part of our lives. School is as far away from the real world as possible. In school we

126

learn that we cannot control our own destinies and that it is acceptable to let others govern our lives. In the real world we can take responsibility for choosing our own paths and governing our own lives. The real world is what we make it. As unschoolers we can choose to make it fascinating and loving and peaceful, and we can immerse ourselves in it every day.

I believe that having your time regulated by bells, eating on a schedule, having very little privacy or opportunity for self-determination, having to ask permission to perform bodily functions, and having to think on command, causes nothing but a feeling of fear when you are finally let loose into the world. It does nothing to help you to live a joyful life.

No adult is forced to sit when she wants to run, listen when she wants to sing, draw when she wants to read, or be inside when she wants to be outside. The real lessons that children learn in school do nothing to improve their lives as adults and do much to hinder a joyful childhood. In *The Six-Lesson Schoolteacher*, John Taylor Gatto (New York City Teacher of the Year in 1990) lists the six lessons he believes are really taught in school:

"The first lesson I teach is: 'Stay in the class where you belong.' I don't know who decides that my kids belong there but that's not my business."

"The second lesson I teach kids is to turn on and off like a light switch."

"The third lesson I teach you is to surrender your will to a predestined chain of command. Rights may be granted or withheld, by authority, without appeal. As a schoolteacher I intervene in many personal decisions, issuing a Pass for those I deem legitimate, or initiating a disciplinary confrontation for behavior that threatens my control."

"The fourth lesson I teach is that only I determine what curriculum you will study. (Rather, I enforce decisions transmitted by the people who pay me.)"

"In lesson five I teach that your self-respect should depend on an observer's measure of your worth. My kids are constantly evaluated and judged."

"In lesson six I teach children that they are being watched. I keep each student under constant surveillance and so do my colleagues. There are no private spaces for children; there is no private time."

These are lessons that an unschooled child never learns, and not one of them will help a child live in joy or contribute to her growing up to be a happy and autonomous adult.

"What does education often do? It makes a straight-cut ditch of a free, meandering brook." ~Henry David Thoreau

I've read that there's a window of opportunity for a child to learn to read, and if they don't learn by the time they're five, it will be much more difficult for them to learn. How do unschooled children learn to read?

The idea that all children should be able to read by a certain age is one of the things that causes the most problems for children in school. Pushing reading onto a child before she is ready and interested is of no benefit to her and, in fact, can be very detrimental. Why then is the idea that it is necessary so pervasive?

For one thing, our society places a huge importance on reading. Not many activities are considered as valuable, much to the disservice of people more interested in mechanics or art or any number of other things. Secondly, a classroom full of children who know how to read is much easier for a teacher to manage than a classroom in which some know how and some don't.

Just as families' lives are scheduled around what is convenient for the school system rather than what is best for the family, the idea that children must learn to read by a certain age has much more to do with the school's operation than it does with what is actually in the best interest of the children. This system of education has led to children's being labeled and drugged when they do not learn to read at the age that the schools' administrators feel is ideal. It has led to children who feel shame and frustration instead of excitement at learning something new.

Unschooled children show every day that, given a nurturing environment with someone available to answer questions and read stories as well as to provide interesting things to read and look at, each child will come to reading in her own time.

The other night Rowan and I were watching television, and we saw a *Hooked On Phonics* commercial. We started talking about what it is they're selling and whether there are kids who really need that

129

program. Rowan thought for a minute and said, "As long as you're unschooling your mind's bubbling up with how to spell and how to read." I love the image of bubbling up. It's active and happy and full. If Rowan's mind is bubbling up, I don't want to do anything to take the air out of those bubbles.

When we look at learning to read as a short term goal, we miss out on the big picture. What is it we really want for our children? We want Rowan and Dagny to enjoy experiencing the world throughout their lives, including experiencing learning about new things. There is no surer way to squash a love of learning than to make learning mandatory.

As an example, a month or so ago Dagny showed a schooled friend one of her magazines, *Kids Discover*. She told the friend that she really liked the magazine because it was fun and interesting and also because she learned a lot from it. Her friend, who was on summer vacation, responded, "Don't show it to me then! I don't have to learn during the summer." Such a thing would never occur to my children. They love to learn. They seek out knowledge and soak it in. A child who was forced to do phonics lessons when she wanted to play is not likely to feel that way about learning to read or learning anything else.

Unschooled children learn to read in many different ways. The general pattern for Dagny and Rowan seems first to be interested in books and magazines as objects. Next they noticed letters, learned what letters are in their names, and learned to draw them. Soon they found that there were patterns involved. Suddenly one day words became interesting, and they realized that letters put together in a certain order can be read and understood by other people. With this realization came the understanding that the letters make different sounds and that, if they can remember the sounds, they can read and spell. Rowan made that discovery within the past year and is now able to read many things. She happily realized the other night that she can read "in her head."

Dagny is at a different stage of learning. She is a proficient reader and has recently become interested in spelling and punctuation. Because of this interest, her understanding is growing at an amazing rate. She reads very often, and writes poetry, plays, and music, as well as a family magazine. When she was nine and not very interested in spelling or punctuation, it would have done her no good, and some harm, for me to push her to learn about them.

What we as parents do to support our kids in this adventure is to provide a rich environment and to be available when the kids want or need us. Our house is filled with books, the four of us have many magazine subscriptions, and reading together is something we all enjoy. We do not pressure them to read or to value reading above everything else. Reading is just like any other aspect of our unschooled lives – done for enjoyment's sake, when the time is right.

"I am always ready to learn, but I do not always like being taught."
~Winston Churchill

When my son is reading, he sometimes asks me what a word says. I have him sound it out so that he will become a better reader. He is struggling with beginner books, and I expected he'd learn to read by now. What do you do when your kids ask you how to read something? Maybe I should teach him phonics. I'm also not sure when I should correct him while he's reading. He doesn't like me to do it, but how else will he learn?

I think of learning to read as a process that spans years, rather than as something that is over and done within a month or a year. At thirty-six years old I am still learning new words and developing new understandings of what I read.

I'm not a huge fan of most beginner books. Often they're pointless and boring. I'm not saying I wouldn't ever buy them (and in fact we have a lot of them), but I don't think they're necessarily something that every child is going to be interested in. Rowan's much more interested in reading things she comes across in daily life – signs, e-mails, letters, words on TV, catalogs and magazines – and things that are seemingly beyond her – my books, for example, or longer books that we've been reading aloud, such as *Harry Potter.* She does sometimes pull out a beginner book, but not very often.

I also don't think that being able to read a beginner book is the beginning and end of learning to read. Babies' playing with books as objects, two-year-olds' singing the alphabet song, four-year-olds' writing their names over and over and making books full of stories that only the author can read, children's asking parents to read the same book again and again until they have it memorized – all of these stages are parts of learning to read, and come from the desire of the child to understand the world around her. Given the opportunity, she will continue to pursue that desire without any need for coercion on her parents' parts.

I have been amazed at watching Rowan's journey from tearing up catalogs as a favorite activity at six months old to being able to read things on her own. Her wonder and pride at figuring out what she seems to see as an interesting puzzle have inspired me to enjoy learning new things in a way that I never did before I had children.

She asks me a lot of questions about letters and words such as, "Why does the 'A' make different sounds, but the 'D' doesn't?" I never told her that the 'A' makes different sounds. We've not done phonics lessons. Words are all around us, and she is naturally making connections just as she does when figuring out so many other interesting things in life.

I am careful to do nothing that would diminish her sense of ownership in any way. If I insisted that she sound out a difficult word herself, I would be interfering with her process and trying to get her to learn on my terms. If I sat her down for a phonics lesson, I would be doing the same thing, with the added disadvantages of boring her completely and convincing her that maybe asking mom a question isn't such a good idea. I could also be giving her the message that I think she can't learn without being taught.

Instead, when she or Dagny asks me how to say a word, I just say the word. It seems unkind not to, and I don't see what purpose it serves to make them sound it out. I do not believe that having to sound things out is the only (or best) road to reading, and I think it's important to answer their questions if I know the answer. I'm a resource for them, just as a dictionary or an encyclopedia can be a resource. They know that, when they want to know something, they have many options for how to go about finding their answers. One of their options is to ask me. I sometimes come across a word I haven't seen before and am unsure of how to pronounce it. I am just as likely to ask someone as I am to look it up. Neither is a better way to find the answer. The important thing is to find the answers you want – the process is irrelevant.

Being made to sound things out can also be a source of frustration for a child and can make him feel embarrassed by his lack of knowledge. If your goal is to encourage his love of reading, why

133

not do everything you can to add joy instead of roadblocks to his experience?

I would suggest you only correct your son when he asks you to. If he doesn't like it, I wouldn't do it at all. When Dagny is reading aloud, she'll sometimes say the beginning of a word and look at me, waiting for me to tell her what it is. At this point it's only words like 'entourage' (that one came up last night when she was reading me *Politically Correct Bedtime Stories* as my bedtime story). She loves to read and has a huge vocabulary, and I wouldn't think of correcting her when she didn't ask me to.

You say that you expected he would know how to read by now. You can let go of those expectations and accept him as he is. He is as he should be.

"What rewards do, and what they do with devastating effectiveness, is smother people's enthusiasm for activities they might otherwise enjoy."
~Alfie Kohn

What do you think of reading incentive programs? A local restaurant is offering a free lunch for any child who reads ten books. My son is learning to read, and my mother makes it a point to tell him she is proud of him. He has started to avoid reading when she is around, and it's made me think that maybe using external motivation to get my son to read isn't a good idea. On the other hand we use a token system to get him to obey us, and that seems to be working. He can earn rewards like extra time with dad if he's good, and if he's bad we take tokens away from him.

I think "I'm so proud of you" is one of those expressions that people use without really thinking about what they are saying. The fact that your son no longer wants to read around his grandmother is enough to show that he doesn't like hearing that she's proud of him.

Your son's reading is his. It has nothing to do with his grandmother. He doesn't do it for her, he does it for himself. He might feel as if she wants him to perform for her, and that, if she can feel proud of him, she might also feel disappointed in him if he does not do as well as usual one day.

When we have a situation like this I talk with Rowan or Dagny. I find out how she feels about it, and ask whether she wants me to talk to the adult. Sometimes she's happy to leave the situation as it is. Other times she says she does want me to talk to the adult; we discuss what she'd like me to say. Or she may decide to talk to the adult directly.

I have quite a few concerns about reading incentive programs, and in particular those sponsored by restaurants. When food is used as a reward, it can cause all sorts physical and mental health issues. That in itself is enough of a reason not to participate, but there are many other reasons as well.

The actual goal of these incentive programs is to get the business that will come along with the child – parents and siblings who will need to eat too. The restaurant does not have your son's best interest at heart. You do. So consider: is a $5 pizza worth risking your child's love of reading?

The very idea that you should earn something for reading implies that reading is not worthwhile or enjoyable in its own right. Reading has been turned into a chore for many children who might otherwise enjoy it. School does enough of that. I don't think parents should contribute to it too.

A wonderful resource for parents who want to learn more about the problems that rewards can cause for their children is the book *Punished By Rewards*, by Alfie Kohn. He explains very compellingly that, while rewards may help to attain a short term goal, they are quite harmful in the long term.

The biggest problem I have with token reward systems is that they set up an adversarial relationship, when what I want with my children is the opposite. They put the adult in a position of power over the child. This disparity does nothing to contribute to a healthy relationship.

I stay away from labeling their behavior as 'good' or 'bad,' but Dagny and Rowan are 'good' for reasons internal to them – reasons that exist whether I'm with them or not.

Reward systems may motivate a child to change his behavior, but they create a tension between how he acts when he knows you're watching and who he really is. The chances are that there will be no beneficial long-term effects on behavior from using a token system. When the tokens stop, the change in behavior will stop. In the meantime your use of tokens as tools to control your child cannot be adding anything positive to your relationship with him. Trying to control our children leads to discord. Letting go of trying to control them and mold their behavior gives them the freedom and the desire to become their best selves for intrinsic reasons.

The specific example you gave of doling out time with dad depending on behavior seems like a very bad idea to me. I'm sure your husband enjoys spending time with your son. Making your son earn it seems to imply that he has to earn his father's love and

136

attention. While that may not be the message you are hoping to convey, it just may be the message your son hears.

"A censor is a man who knows more than he thinks you ought to."
~Laurence J. Peter

Do you censor what your kids read? What about movies? What about watching the same movie over and over?

Rowan's recently begun to read on her own, and Dagny reads quite a lot. We do not censor what they read. Just as they choose what television shows they want to watch based on what's interesting and comfortable for them, they choose what they want to read. Dagny will sometimes, if she's not sure about a book, ask me to read it first to see whether I think there's anything in it that would be disturbing for her. I'll tell her a bit about any parts I think she might not like. In the end she makes her own decision. If she begins it and finds she's not comfortable with it after all, she has no problem with just not reading any further. A child who hasn't been free to make her own choices might be more likely to plow through the book without listening to her own reactions to it just to grab that piece of forbidden fruit. Without those external limitations, Dagny can comfortably choose to do what is right for her.

Dagny and I talk a lot about the books each of us is reading. We talk about story lines, characters, things we came across that we didn't know before, whether the story is well written, and whether we think the other person would enjoy reading it. She has inherited my love of reading and of books – their feel, their weight, their smell, their histories, and their ability to leave our bodies on the couch while transporting us to places far away. Dagny will choose what places she wants to travel to in her life and knows that I'll be there when she comes home.

I think censoring is damaging to the relationship between the parent and child. It implies a lack of trust in the child's judgment. I know that Rowan and Dagny would find the idea that I didn't think they were capable of making their own decisions a lot more damaging than anything they could ever read.

We try to get as much information as possible about a movie before we see it if the kids aren't sure it's going to be something they'll enjoy. For the most part the only thing they both actively want to avoid is being scared, although that's become less of a problem as they've gotten older. Rowan also prefers not to see realistic violence. We generally ask someone who has already seen the movie for her opinion and read about the movie on various websites. Again, if partway through the movie one of the kids decides she doesn't like it, she will just stop watching. We're willing to leave a movie theatre with one of them if she wants to. When Rowan saw the first *Harry Potter* movie, she had us bring her out during the parts she found scary but watched most of the movie. With videos we can fast forward through anything they don't want to see.

When parents censor their children's input – whether it's from reading, TV, movies, or the computer – there has to be some basis of fear in their decision. I don't fear that my children will read about violence and think it sounds like a good idea. I don't fear that they will read about sex and decide to try it out today. I trust that they will see violence for what it is, and see sex as something that they will come to when the time is right. I trust that, if they come across something that is confusing or upsetting, they will come to me to help them sort it out.

Rowan has a great affinity for voices. For her, watching a movie over and over allows her to analyze why and how the actors use a certain intonation or volume to convey emotion or humor. After seeing *Shrek 2* she explained to me the difference between the way Donkey says, "You really need some tic-tacs or something cuz your breath stinks" in the first movie and the way he says, "The position of annoying talking animal has already been taken" in the second movie. She talked about the level of anger Eddie Murphy put into each sentence and the differences in volume and drama he put into them. It's easy to see in Rowan's case what one of the appeals of watching a movie again and again is. It may not be so easy to see in another child, but that does not mean there is not a reason he is drawn to it. Trust your child to know what he needs, and help him get it in any way you can.

"'Go look it up' tends to mean 'I don't know' or 'I know but I'm not going to tell you.' What's the advantage of that?" ~Sandra Dodd

When my daughter asks me how to spell something, should I tell her to look it up?

If my husband asks me how to spell something I tell him. Why wouldn't I extend the same courtesy to my children? I think it is unkind not to answer any question asked of me if I know the answer. I wouldn't do it to my husband, and I won't do it to my children.

There are a number of other reasons I don't believe in telling a child to 'look it up.' Many times stopping to look something up would interrupt the flow of creativity. I know that when I'm writing, my consciousness is sometimes focused in a way that would be disturbed by having to stop and get a dictionary. When my kids are writing, their focus is on what they want to say and how they want to say it. It would be inconsiderate of me to attempt to redirect their focus, and it could also give them the message that I do not value what they are saying as much as how they are saying it and whether or not they know how to use a dictionary.

My priority is not to make sure my kids learn how to use a dictionary. My priority is to make sure that I help them accomplish whatever they want to accomplish and to be helpful in the way *they* want me to be. Unschooling parents are an important resource for their children. Denying them the resource they choose to use is antithetical to the spirit of unschooling.

I don't believe that looking a word up helps a child learn to spell any more effectively than just telling them how to spell it. How would it? In either case the child is able to visually see the word. In fact, if the parent spells it aloud for her, she can hear it as well.

We have quite a few dictionaries around our house. They're easy to get to and are used pretty often. Occasionally Dagny likes to 'read' the dictionary, looking for words she doesn't know. Other times she uses it to look up a word's meaning or spelling. Somewhere along the line she gained an understanding of alphabetization, partly from asking questions and partly from observing the layout of the dictionary.

If your concern is that your children will never learn to use a dictionary, ask yourself this question: If your child manages to reach adulthood without ever touching a dictionary, in what way could it possibly have been important for her to do so?

Like anything else in an unschooled child's life, if a dictionary is available, the child will make as much or as little use of it as is necessary and valuable to her.

"Human nature is not a machine to be built after a model, and set to do exactly the work prescribed for it, but a tree, which requires to grow and develop itself on all sides, according to the tendency of the inward forces which make it a living thing." ~John Stuart Mill

I see reading as mandatory to a happy childhood. It's one of the things I remember most fondly about my own childhood. I also love to write, and find it a great asset in my life to be able to write well. Shouldn't I give my children the same advantage?

I see freedom as mandatory to a happy childhood.

I think it's wonderful to approach parenting with the goal of helping our children to make happy memories. What is not so wonderful is deciding for them what those memories should be.

It sounds as if you were given the opportunity to determine for yourself what you loved to do and given the space and time to do it. That it happened to be reading you loved doesn't mean that reading is what will bring each of your children joy and be something they look back on fondly. On the contrary, if you decide for your child that reading is mandatory for her happy childhood you could very well be sabotaging your own goal. A child who is made to read and to feel that she should enjoy it when in fact she'd rather be outside throwing baseballs is not likely to develop a joyful relationship with reading.

You can be an example to your children of a person who follows her passion. You can share the joy it brings you. What you can't do is make reading or writing something they are passionate about if they're just not.

I love to write. I also love to make jewelry, can fruit, take photographs, cook, organize, read, learn about how our brains work, and design rooms and shelving. All of those interests have been an asset to me at one time or another. Rowan and Dagny share some of my interests, and I enjoy that connection; but I also enjoy sharing in and supporting them in what they enjoy.

Give your children the advantage of being able to decide for themselves what is of value to them. Give them the freedom to develop their own assets. In doing so you'll be giving them a chance to look back fondly not only at the time spent doing things they enjoyed, but on a mother who took their interests seriously and appreciated them for who they are.

"Where did we ever get the crazy idea that in order to make children do better, first we have to make them feel worse?" ~Jane Nelson

My child's handwriting is atrocious. She doesn't seem to care, but it's embarrassing for me when she has to sign something in front of other people, and I've told her she's got to improve it. How will she take notes or write papers in college?

In order to feel embarrassment over your child's handwriting, you must in some way feel that she is a reflection of you. I think it is valuable to recognize our children as separate, whole people who are not the handiwork of their parents.

I would imagine that your embarrassment is causing your daughter some discomfort. I don't think making her feel bad about it will help her to develop better handwriting. Accepting her handwriting as part of who she is would be a more loving response.

If your daughter decides to go to college, presumably it will be because there is something there of value to her. In that situation she will most likely do whatever is necessary in order to get what she wants from the experience. If that means learning to take notes, she will do so; or she will find another way to record information, perhaps using a tape recorder or laptop. The ready availability of computers has done away with much of the need to write by hand, so passing in legible papers shouldn't be an issue.

Many people, people who went to school for years, have less than perfect handwriting. My own handwriting is very erratic. It has never caused me any problems. I went to college. I took notes. It may have been difficult for anyone else to read them. But I could read them, and that was what mattered. I typed my papers (and made some money typing papers for others in my dorm as well). Now, as a person whose handwriting seems to be getting progressively worse, with a house to maintain, bills to be paid, two kids who have at times wanted me to help them learn cursive, and a book to be written, I am still not finding my handwriting to be a barrier between me and anything I want to do.

144

Some people can effortlessly copy Italic Cursive and adopt it as their own style. Others see handwriting as more of an art form with which they can express themselves. Then there are those who see writing as a way to get what's in their head out in order to remember it or share it with others. Your daughter may find at some point that she is interested in handwriting as an art. She may become interested in handwriting analysis or the origins of handwriting styles. Or she may just be one of those people who see writing as a tool, and that's ok. If at some point she wants to improve her handwriting, you can help her find ways to do so. In the meantime it is much more important to see your daughter in a positive light than it is to worry about what others might think of her handwriting.

"It is among the commonplaces of education that we often first cut off the living root and then try to replace its natural functions by artificial means." ~Alice Duer Miller

When we go shopping I ask the kids to estimate how much change we got back. Then I have them count it to see whether they were right. It feels a little contrived, and I'm not sure if it meshes with the unschooling philosophy. I'm thinking instead that, when I don't feel like they're doing enough math, I'll just play games that involve math with them. Can you suggest any good math games?

I think it's unnecessary to create situations or ask questions that you don't need the answer to in order for your children to learn. It feels contrived because it is; you are only asking the question in order to get your kids to do math.

Schooled parents have so many preconceived ideas about how math should be learned, and it can be very difficult to let go of those ideas. However, in order to reap the benefits of an unschooling life, it is necessary to let them go. If you continue to think of math as something that they can only learn through artificial means, your children might come to think of math as disconnected from real life and to think of themselves as unable to learn without being taught.

Math is all around us – not just in change or recipes or games. Trust your kids to see it and internalize it in the ways that make sense to them. In school children are often taught mathematical language before they've developed an understanding of the meaning behind it. A child who has been given time to build up a knowledge base can more easily grasp the significance of symbols and formulas when she comes to them in her own time. She can make connections between what she has observed and the ways in which we use the language of mathematics.

I could name lots of games that require math to play. We have a large collection of games, and probably a majority of them do. Many of our favorite games are listed at the end of this book. However, when we play games with our kids, we do it purely for the enjoyment of playing and spending time together. I feel it would be dishonest to have a hidden agenda when my children thought I was just enjoying their company.

When I say that I believe people learn what they need to know in their own time and way, I mean that the parents do not need to assess what their kids are 'lacking' and try to fill the gaps. We have never done anything specifically for the purpose of making sure our kids learn something. We don't think in terms of math or science or history. Separating things into subjects may work for schools (or does it?), but in life things swirl together and take off in a million different directions, often forming the base for future connections. If we try to look at one little piece, we miss out on all of the other wonderful things that are happening around us.

Your children will learn the math they want and need to learn. They may learn some from games, some from conversations, some from playing on the see-saw, some from TV, some from reading, some from playing with blocks, some from listening to music, and some from observing nature. How they learn it is not nearly as important as being able to trust that, when you want to play a game with them, you do not have an ulterior motive.

Moving away from school-think is not easy for many people. After all, we spent at least thirteen years thinking in terms of subjects and linear learning, with a person in charge spoon feeding us the information that was chosen as important for us to know. To think that none of it is necessary for our own children can be frightening; it can also be invalidating. Did we waste a good portion of our lives? Whether we did or not, we can give our children the gift of never having to wonder the same thing.

"If I am given a formula and I am ignorant of its meaning, it cannot teach me anything, but if I already know it what does the formula teach me?" ~Saint Augustine

Do unschooled children ever learn the multiplication table?

Some children may never choose to memorize the multiplication table. Most of us were taught in school that memorizing the table was an important part of our educations. Unschooled children are proving that it is not necessarily true.

Our goal is not that our children memorize the table; it is that they develop as much of an understanding of multiplication as is useful in their lives. The table is a tool that can make computation quicker. It is not a necessary part of understanding multiplication itself. Rowan, who has no interest in the table yet, does have a basic understanding of multiplication. When she was six, she asked me how to write forty. When I answered, "4-0" she replied with a very excited, "But that's tendy-four!" She is making the connections that form the basis for understanding multiplication. Whether or not she ever decides to memorize the table, she will be able to use multiplication if she wants to.

Many children who do not memorize the table actually come up with very quick ways to do multiplication (and other mathematical operations). Dagny is very amused that I have to write problems down in order to complete them. To her that's an added, unnecessary step in many cases. The way an unschooled child does math may not look familiar to you, as she will come up with her own systems and formulas. I find it fascinating to get a glimpse of the ways my kids compute. It always makes perfect sense and is something I would never have thought of myself, as successfully schooled as I have been.

Of course, some children do memorize the table, and some others, like Dagny, like to fill in the table as a form of entertainment. When she one day needed to figure out quite a few multiplication problems, she asked me whether there was a faster way to get the answers. I drew a table and told her we could fill it in. Then she could refer to it when she needed an answer. Within a few days she was asking people whether they wanted to play a new game she had learned. The traditionally schooled recipient of the question invariably looked confused, amused, and finally intrigued when he realized that this 'game' was actually the multiplication table.

Interestingly, when she draws a table she doesn't stop at 10 or 12 as we were taught to do in school. She puts in as many numbers as she can fit. For her it isn't about memorizing a table; it is about understanding what the numbers mean, their patterns, and how they work together. I don't think she has memorized all of the standard multiplication table as of yet, but she certainly knows how to get the answers. More importantly, she understands what both the question and answer represent.

"How could youths better learn to live than by at once trying the experiment of living?" ~Henry David Thoreau

How do your children learn to be responsible with money? Do they get an allowance?

From the time Rowan and Dagny were very little, I sat near them while I paid the bills. They've always been interested in what I was doing. It sometimes makes it hard to concentrate, but it's given them an understanding of how much money we have and where it goes. They like to stamp the envelopes and play with the receipts (setting up banks and stores) and ask many questions. At this point they know a lot about our budget and how Jon and I feel about money, borrowing, shopping, saving, and generosity.

The best way to learn to be responsible with money is to be given the opportunity to use it and to make decisions about it. Dagny and Rowan have their own money and equal access to any money the family has. We asked them how much money they needed each month, and that's what they get. If their needs change, that amount will change too, within our means. I hesitate to call it an allowance, because it is not in the traditional sense of the word. It is not tied to anything. They are not required to spend it on certain things; if they want to save it all they're free to spend money from the family budget instead if it's available. They're part of our family, and they get part of the family's money.

We generally only go shopping when there are specific things that we need. We don't do a lot of impulse buying. If we are at a store and one of the kids sees something she likes, we talk about how much it costs and whether it's something she thinks she'd like to buy. Sometimes she ends up saying that she doesn't think it's worth the price. If she tells me she wants it that day and we can afford it, we buy it. Neither of them has ever gotten upset about not being able to buy something right away. They know their wants are important to us, and we do our best to meet them.

When the kids were toddlers, if they wanted to look at something, we would stop and look at it. I would say, "That is pretty (or looks fun, or what is it? etc.)." It didn't, and still doesn't, always turn into a conversation about buying it. It can be enough just to enjoy it for a few minutes in the store or to talk about someone it reminds us of or think about whether we could make something like it ourselves. Each of them did go through a short phase of being more interested in buying things. I imagine they were working through an understanding of some kind.

We try to share with them a feeling of abundance. We as a society have so much. I think it's important to show in your own shopping behavior that the buybuybuy way of life that is all around us does not bring happiness.

Dagny often checks with me to make sure that what *I'm* spending is 'in the budget.' She feels a responsibility for how our money is spent. I get some strange looks from people who hear me 'answering to' my child, but you get used to strange looks when you're an unschooler.

"Knowledge which is acquired under compulsion obtains no hold on the mind." ~Plato

A friend sent my son some pictures of snakes that were in his yard. I told my son to get some information together about the snakes to email to our friend. That way he could cover science, writing, typing, and research. He didn't want to do it and we ended up having an argument. What would you do differently as an unschooler?

If someone sent Dagny some pictures of snakes, there are lots of possible outcomes: She might say, "That's nice, thanks," and go about her business. It might be something that grabs her interest, inspiring her to look for more information or ask me to find more. It might spark a memory, in which case she might tell me about a show she watched on snakes last week where she learned _____. I might see it and say, "That's cool, what kind of snake is that, do you know?" (because I want to know, not to find out whether she knows) or "Oh, I saw a snake like that on the Discovery channel. Did you know they _____?" It could be that she's mildly interested and later makes connections with other things she learns about snakes. In any case, it's a joyful experience, not one that sets up a power struggle between us or makes learning a chore.

When Dagny writes to a friend, she does it for real life reasons. She wants to thank him for thinking of her, or has something she wants to share with him. Her writing may very well cover science, writing, typing, and research, but for us that is just the side effect of connecting with someone, not the purpose.

When we choose to remove our children from school, we can continue to view our lives through school's narrow focus, or we can open up to the limitless being that life can be. Forget subjects. Forget tests and 'have to-s' and science labs and term papers. Forget cafeteria food and February Vacation and bells that tell you where to go. Forget gym class and reading groups. School is not a part of your life anymore, and it doesn't have to be a part of your child's.

"Learning CAN only happen when a child is interested. If he's not interested it's like throwing marshmallows at his head and calling it eating." ~Katrina Gutleben, unschooling mom of Kathrynn and Aiden

My son wanted to learn to play the saxophone. We spent a lot of money on an instrument and signed him up for lessons. Now he doesn't want to go anymore, and we've already paid for four months in advance. If we let him quit, we'll be out a lot of money, and we're afraid he'll never learn to follow through on things. I think he'd learn a lot if he'd just stick with it. I'm afraid he's quitting just because he thinks it's hard.

I try not to base my decisions on money or fear. Instead, I look for joy. Is your son finding joy in his lessons? Will he find joy without them? Which decision will bring joy to your relationship?

However, in our family this is not a decision that would be mine to make. Dagny and Rowan decide for themselves how they want to spend their time. When they have a hard time choosing, I help them and tell them what I might do, but they know that I'll support whatever decision they make and that I'm not emotionally invested in whether or not they continue with an activity. I also remind them that, if they decide to stop doing something today, it doesn't mean they can't pick it up again next week, or next year, or even when they're old like me. They know, too, that they can continue to learn without continuing a class. Choosing to leave a class does not have to mean leaving the interest behind. It can mean deciding to pursue the interest in a different way.

It's very difficult to know whether you're going to enjoy something until you've given it a try. That sometimes means spending some money on the effort (although that can often be minimized by taking a trial class, getting together with a friend who is involved in the interest, renting or borrowing an instrument, or taking a trip to the library). When we spend money on something the kids want to try, we do so with no strings or expectations attached. We encourage them to try something if it appeals to them. Maybe they will love it and realize that they have found their life's calling. Maybe they will enjoy it and do it for a while, but then it will lose its appeal. Maybe it will be something they dabble in for years. Maybe they will immediately hate it and choose to drop it as quickly as possible. It is our responsibility to open up as many opportunities for them as we possibly can, but it is not their responsibility to embrace every one of them.

Looking at the big picture, why should we follow through on things that are unpleasant? Our lives are finite. Why spend a moment doing something unnecessary that you would rather not do? There are more things to see and do in this world than we will ever know. I wouldn't want my children to waste their time unhappily playing the saxophone when they could be discovering something that truly brings them happiness.

Dagny's learning to play the electric guitar. It can be very challenging. One time when she seemed frustrated I thought she was going to stop her lessons. When I asked her about it, she said she hadn't even thought of stopping. It's worth the struggle to her. Given the freedom to make up their own minds kids *will* choose to do things that are difficult for them – if it's something they feel passionate about.

If your son is no longer interested in the saxophone, he won't be learning just because you keep bringing him to class. You can let him decide for himself which hurdles he wants to get over and which ones he wants to go around. Who knows what he might find while he's taking the scenic route?

I'm always amazed at how many things my kids are interested in. One day it's the violin, the next day it's explosions, the next week it's how cars work – or flowers or dogs or electricity. Because they are following their interests, the things they learn become a part of them. I see myself as the person who walks beside them, along with Jon, making sure the path is clear so that they can get wherever they want to go. Making them continue with something they don't want to do would be like saying, "No don't go that way, I want you to go this way instead," and I believe they have the right to choose their own paths.

Money spent on helping your children to explore the world is never wasted. If what your child ends up learning is not what you thought you were paying for, does that make it any less valuable?

"Children do not need to be made to learn about the world, or shown how. They want to, and they know how." ~John Holt

Our children understand unschooling in a way we never can because for them it is simply life. I asked Dagny and Rowan whether they'd be willing to answer some questions too. Here's what they had to say:

Rue: Why do you think that unschooling is a better way for you to live?

Dagny: I think that being free is a better way to live, and that's what unschooling is. I think the only rule should be to live life how you want to live it. If you can't do that, then you can't unschool.

Rue: What do you wish people knew about unschooling?

Dagny: That it's not bad for your kids. That they would see other people, and that they will learn!

Rue: How did you learn to read?

Dagny: I don't really know, but I remember that one day I picked up a book, and read it, without really understanding how I did it!

Rue: Have you ever thought you might like to go to school?

Dagny: No way.

Rue: What do you like about unschooling?

Rowan: I like that I can play whenever I want and no one's telling me, "You have to do this now." I have a lot of time to do things that kids who go to school can't do.

Rue: How did you learn to read?

Rowan: Well I look at the book, and I just figure out what the word says. If I've heard a book a lot of times, I memorize it and then I know what the words say.

Rue: Have you ever thought you might like to go to school?

Rowan: NO!! Because school seems like a prison for kids. They're told what to do. You have to bring someone with you to go to the bathroom. They can't leave if they want to. You're far away from your family. It's not right.

Rue: How do you feel about being in a book about unschooling?

Rowan: (arms up in the air, shouting and giggling): Free the children! Free the children!

"Children are people we should be spending a lot of time talking to, listening to and helping because they're new here. Instead it's standard operating procedure to be short with them, shush them and limit them. We make them small." ~Deb Lewis, unschooling mom of Dylan

Fifteen things I wish adults would not say to children:

1) Do you want a spanking?
2) 1, 2, 3…
3) You're ok.
4) Don't cry.
5) You always _____.
6) Good drawing/running/sharing/eating/etc.
7) I'm disappointed in you.
8) I don't want to hear another word from you.
9) Come now, or we're leaving without you.
10) Sit still.
11) It's for your own good.
12) You have to eat your dinner, or you can't have dessert.
13) You have to put that away before you take out something else.
14) Don't be a baby.
15) If you're not good, we're not coming back here ever again.

Fifteen things I wish adults would not imply to children:

1) I don't trust you.
2) You don't try hard enough.
3) I can boss you around because I'm bigger.
4) Adults know everything.
5) You don't know what you're capable of.
6) Possessions are more important to me than you are.
7) You should believe what I believe.
8) Your feelings are not important.
9) It's ok to ignore kids.
10) I don't have time for you.
11) You have to earn my love.
12) I want to change you.
13) You owe me respect.
14) I know what's best for you.
15) You're not a whole person.

One thing I wish parents would say more often:

1) Yes.

Some favorite games and resources:

Set
Mancala
Origami supplies
Guess Who?
Monopoly Jr.
Magazines
Books – including some in other languages
Books on CD
Bingo
Pillows
Blankets
Office supplies
Clue Jr.
Television/cable
Musical instruments
Trouble
Life
Scrabble
Sewing, knitting, and crochet supplies
Rush Hour
An indoor swing
Electronic components
Archery set
Stack
Trampoline
Zip line
Play kitchen
Sand table full of beans with beakers, measuring cups, etc.
Vehicles
Sandbox
Lego
Magnetic words, shapes, sticks and balls, and letters
Battleship
Doctor supplies
Chess

Mirrors
Balls
Computer/Internet
Easy Bake Oven
Tea set
Magnifying Glass
Binoculars
Thinking Sticks (http://sandradodd.com/thinkingsticks)
Telescope
Calculator
Woodworking supplies
Costumes/masks/wigs/hats/gloves/makeup/shoes
Geoboards
Stopwatch
Adding machine
Timer
Herd Your Horses
Bikes
Air Hockey table
Scooters
Stilts
Blocks
Dolls, pretend animals, and people
Pixter
Puzzles
Mazes
Video and computer games
Printer
Scanner
Marbles
Mastermind
Yahtzee
Puppets
Backgammon
Stratego
Things to take apart, such as phones, keyboards, timers, etc.
Movies

CDs
Operation
Dice
MadLibs
Color Train
Globe
Maps
Twister
Play dough
Balloons
Dominoes
Rokenbok
Kid Kinex
Toobers and Zots
Polymer clay
Camera and video camera
Worst Case Scenario
Chinese checkers
Checkers
Kite
Sports equipment
Microphone
Seesaw
Memory
Othello
Apples to Apples
Cash register
Old checkbook and register
Tub toys: tints/tub paint/shaving cream/foam letters/boats/water wheel/plastic cups
Body crayons
Connect 4
Don't Make Me Laugh, Jr.
Cranium
Calendar
Trains
Playing cards

Uncle Wiggly
Creepy Crawlers
Husker Du
The Touch
Pizza Pileup
Hula hoops
Mighty Beans
Marble Run
Temporary tattoos
Step On It
Zoom Out
Photosensitive paper
Gardening supplies
Microscope
Radio
Ello
Candy Land
Dollhouse
Tent
Henna

Craft supplies:

Different kinds of tape
Paper of various sorts and sizes
Crayons
Markers
Spin Art
Modeling sand
Colored pens and pencils
Elastics
Silk flowers
Bubble wrap
Paint chips
Crepe paper

Poster board
Pipe cleaners
Eye droppers
Feathers
Fabric/ribbons/lace
Paints
Brushes made of different materials
Canvases
Buttons
Googly eyes
Stickers
Hole punch
Safety pins
Tacks
Beads
Wire
String
Cardboard
Tin foil
Rope
Bags – paper, colored, zipper, gift
Paper plates and cups
Toothpicks
Popsicle sticks
Paper clips
Wallpaper
Carpet remnants
Chalk
Recycled jars/papers/tubes/containers/packaging
Sequins
Glitter
Candles
Glue
Stapler
Balloons
Old magazines and catalogs
Clothespins

Straws
Pompoms
Things from nature (pinecones, rocks, leaves, twigs, flowers)
Good scissors
Old photos
Boxes
Stamps
Styrofoam
Contact paper
Ribbon
Felt
Stencils
Tissue paper
Cooking supplies
Space to make a mess

Many thanks to Kelly Lovejoy for the huge amount of time, thought, and effort she put into helping me edit this book, and for her tireless efforts to explain the proper use of the much abused comma.

Thanks also to Ren Allen, Sandra Dodd, and Anne Ohman for their input and encouragement.

Finally, thanks to Valerie Fitzenreiter for too many things to name, and for her unshakable belief that I could write something longer than 1,000 words.

~Rue

Praise for *One Thousand Wells*

"Original, perceptive, and compelling . . . In an astonishingly honest voice, Jena Lee Nardella reflects on the questions we ask ourselves when the odds are overwhelmingly against us—why hope that seems foolish is still necessary."

—Amy Tan, bestselling author of *The Joy Luck Club*

"Very few people can write a book about how they have already changed the world before they're even thirty. Jena is one of those rare gifts from God. Her story, her heart, and her journey of bringing clean, fresh, life-giving water to the people in Africa is one you will never forget. Read *One Thousand Wells* and then help her dig some more."

—Kathie Lee Gifford, *Today*

"Buckle up, you're about to meet one of love's heroes."

—Bob Goff, honorary consul, Republic of Uganda and author of *Love Does*

"An authentic and inspiring read for those who want to make a difference in the world."

—Tony Hale, Emmy Award–winning actor from *Arrested Development* and *Veep*

"This is a story of idealism maturing, step by step, into lasting love—and it's a story every idealist, and every almost-cynic, must read."

—Andy Crouch, executive editor, *Christianity Today*

"Jena Lee Nardella lives her life with honesty and humility—always learning and always adventurous. In *One Thousand Wells*, her indomitable spirit shows through! A delightful read that shows what can happen when you love others with your whole life, pursue passion with reckless abandon, and allow yourself to be changed along the way."

—Gary A. Haugen, author of *The Locust Effect*

"Jena's passionate, reflective and uncompromising journey has inspired me and the team at charity: water for years. Her leadership has not only directly impacted the lives of so many with clean water but inspired countless others to break from apathy and follow their passions to give and serve."

—Scott Harrison, founder of charity: water

"Oliver Wendell Holmes put it best, 'Give me the simplicity on the other side of complexity.' That, in a phrase, describes where many social entrepreneurs stall out. They run up against complexity and are overwhelmed by it. Jena Lee Nardella is one of the very few who not only made it through that obstacle but now has the wisdom and skills to be a guide for others."

—Fred Smith, president of The Gathering

"*One Thousand Wells* is the journey of a calling, from start to finish. It's for the ones of us that always felt the call to something 'big' in our bones. What's refreshing about Jena's story is that it isn't too massive for us—it gives us hope that the world can be shifted through persistence, a dedication to one's cause, and baby steps. If each of us lived with the plain love and bold obedience of Jena, there'd be a thousand more tales of loving the world—instead of saving it—out there. It is so evident—the world needs more stories like this one."

—Hannah Brencher, author of *If You Find This Letter*

One Thousand Wells

How an Audacious Goal Taught Me to
Love the World Instead of Save It

Jena Lee Nardella
Foreword by Donald Miller

HOWARD BOOKS
AN IMPRINT OF SIMON & SCHUSTER, INC.

New York   Nashville   London   Toronto   Sydney   New Delhi

Howard Books
An Imprint of Simon & Schuster, Inc.
1230 Avenue of the Americas
New York, NY 10020

First Howard Books trade paperback edition June 2016

HOWARD and colophon are trademarks of Simon & Schuster, Inc.

For information about special discounts for bulk purchases, please contact Simon & Schuster Special Sales at 1-866-506-1949 or business@simonandschuster.com.

The Simon & Schuster Speakers Bureau can bring authors to your live event. For more information or to book an event, contact the Simon & Schuster Speakers Bureau at 1-866-248-3049 or visit our website at www.simonspeakers.com.

Interior design by Robert E. Ettlin

Manufactured in the United States of America

1   3   5   7   9   10   8   6   4   2

The Library of Congress has cataloged the hardcover edition as follows:

Nardella, Jena Lee.
One thousand wells : how an audacious goal taught me to love the world instead of save it/ Jena Lee Nardella.
pages cm
Includes bibliographical references.
1. Nardella, Jena Lee. 2. Humanitarianism—Religious aspects—Christianity. 3. AIDS (Disease)—Africa. 4. HIV-positive persons—Africa—Services for. 5. Water security—Africa. 6. Community development—Religious aspects—Christianity. 7. Community development—Africa. 8. Christian women—United States—Biography. I. Title.
BV4403.N37 2015
277.3'083092—dc23
[B]
2015008454

ISBN 978-1-5011-0743-6
ISBN 978-1-5011-1019-1 (pbk)
ISBN 978-1-5011-0744-3 (ebook)

For the thirsty and the satiated.
May water be our bridge.

"We know from history that massive human failure is possible. It is foolish to assume that we will save ourselves from any fate that we have made possible, simply because we have the conceit to call ourselves homo sapiens . . . on the other hand, we want to be hopeful, and hope is one of our duties. A part of our obligation to our own being and to our descendants is to study our life and own condition, searching always for the authentic underpinnings of hope. And if we look, these underpinnings can still be found."

—*Wendell Berry*

Contents

Foreword by Donald Miller   xi

Prologue   xiii

Part One: The World Opens Out   1

1   Union Square   3

2   She Breathes the Air and Flies Away   9

3   Taking on a Mountain   13

4   Finding Shelter   17

5   The Day I Met Bill   23

6   A Culture of Whatever   35

7   The Boy Who Was Dusk   39

8   The Risk of Yes   47

9   Something Better   53

10   Sailboat, Sailboat, Sailboat   61

11   "There's a *Girl* on the Bus?"   67

12   Promising Not to Promise   81

Contents

13 Secrets of Change   93

14 The Six Flags Miracle   105

Part Two: Coming Together   113

15 Fundraising by *Harambee*   115

16 A Bridge of Water   131

17 Image Bearers   145

18 Daughter of Lwala   159

19 The View from the Clouds   167

20 Learning What Love Requires   183

Part Three: Slowly by Slowly   195

21 We Cannot Bring the Rain   199

22 A Hero Can Be Hard to Find   211

23 Fool's Errand   221

24 The Third Way   233

25 All the Good That You Will Do   243

26 One Thousand Wells   251

Epilogue   255

Acknowledgments   257

Notes   267

Foreword

A good story needs a lead character who is humble and at the same time has a good ambition, something that actually matters. Good stories have to be risky. And the best stories are the ones where the protagonist risks something in an uncertain pursuit, and if she fails, she may lose her life, or be left alone, or be terrified, or ridiculed. My friend Jena Lee Nardella has been living out one of these great stories, a story that you will not want to miss.

Over the last ten years, I have been witness to Jena's singular pursuit of an audacious goal to build a thousand wells in Africa, literally saving lives all over the continent. This was risky. This was the sort of thing that might fail. But nobody wants to read a story about wanting to be as safe as possible. We need some suspense questions that drive us to keep watching or reading. Will Romeo get to marry Juliet? Will the *Apollo 13* astronauts survive? Will the Hoosiers win the state championship? These questions propel us and keep us on our toes. Jena's is a story you want to root for, a protagonist you want to believe in.

You can also tell a great story and a great protagonist by this little test: if the protagonist in the story dies, what dreams die with the protagonist? If the lead character gets hit by a bus, what doesn't happen? I remember three years into Jena's effort, we were together on her twenty-fifth birthday. I was at her party thinking, "What would happen, God forbid, if Jena just walked out of this restaurant and got run over by a bus?" Hundreds of thousands of people would go without water and some may even die. People would die if Jena's story does not get resolved. That's a good story. That's a really, really good story. As we read Jena's story, we are challenged to listen to our own lives and to ask the question, "If I am hit by a bus, what doesn't happen?"

In these pages, Jena not only shares her ambition to bring water to Africa, taking you through villages, mountain ranges, and tour buses. She also brings to life, with as much honesty as she can, the doubts and failures she faced on the way to doing a good thing. She brings you into the drama of closed doors and uncertainties of trying to live out a good story. And though the work she does is serious business, she never takes herself too seriously. She invites you into her world like an old friend; there are no facades.

We are each telling a story with our lives. And sometimes I think God is asking us if the stories we're telling are good ones. Not all of us will devote ourselves to Africa, nor should we. But we all must find a suspense question that will drive us. We must start with the knowledge that life itself will end, and that by living our stories we are setting the compasses of the people around us through example. And Jena's is an example that will inspire you to go out and live a great story.

—Donald Miller, bestselling author of *Blue Like Jazz*

Prologue

I could smell my breath against the bandanna. I had tied it over my mouth to protect myself from the dust-filled air, but my throat was still sore from breathing it. Soil caked my hair and eyebrows; my eyes felt dry as paper. A United Nations Land Cruiser, with its radio antennae wagging into the limitless sky, overtook us on the right and kicked up a plume of dust from the dirt road. I rolled up the last crack in the window, but dust continued to blow through the vents. Baboons watched us curiously from the roadside.

Three of us sat crammed in the backseat of a double cab pickup. Our sweaty backs stuck to the vinyl bench as we drove over a bridge across the rushing Nile River toward a place called Lira. We were on the final stretch of what felt like an endless journey from Nashville, Tennessee, through Kampala, Uganda, and then north for five hours through a region marked by a generation of violence and fear. It was 2005, almost twenty years since the Lord's Resistance Army (LRA) had begun waging guerrilla warfare in northern Uganda—raiding villages, capturing children, and raping women.

Brakes. Brakes. Brakes!

Men in military uniforms appeared on the road ahead, guns pointed at our truck. As we slid to a stop, a soldier approached the driver's window, and three other men with AK-47s surrounded the car. They were angry, and they asked our driver something we could not understand. His response was apparently unsatisfying to them. They gestured for him to get out of the vehicle.

"Not today," our friend Vincent responded from the passenger seat. "We have visitors."

Looking inside the window, the armed men saw Edward, our Ugandan colleague, and my friend Joel and me, white Americans in our early twenties.

I don't know how I got here, I thought, *but I know I made a mistake.* I closed my eyes against a rising nausea.

More talking. Angry negotiating. Then I felt us start to move again. I opened my eyes and I looked out the back window to see the soldiers waving, laughing at us.

"What did they want?" I asked, breathing the dusty air again.

"A bribe," said Edward. "They thought if they could scare us enough, we would pay them off."

"But we would do no such thing," Vincent added. "They are the cowards."

As we continued on in the dust and the heat, military personnel still lining the roads, I felt like a coward, too.

Joel and I were there to visit the small town of Lira, where more than a thousand people lived in an internally displaced persons camp. Our fledgling organization, Blood:Water Mission, had sent funds to Edward and Vincent's well-drilling operation so they could build ten clean water wells in Lira as a pilot project. This was our opportunity to see what had already been done and visit the camps where more progress was needed.

We finally reached the outskirts of Lira, where makeshift shelters packed both sides of the road—hastily constructed huts with mud and sticks for walls, thatch and tarps for roofs. The instant we turned into the camp itself, crowds surrounded our vehicle. Joel and I got out amid a rush of children, chickens, and goats.

As Julius, one of the camp's leaders showed us around, I felt like I was walking through news footage of a natural disaster, only this disaster was man-made. Families—as many as seven people to a hut—lived in shelters smaller than most American walk-in closets. A barbed-wire fence surrounded the camp, although it was unclear if it was keeping the LRA out or refugees in. Plastic Port-a-Johns overflowed with excrement. Some of the children had no clothing, everyone was coughing severely, and teenagers stood around with nothing to do because they had no access to school. As we'd been told, the camp had no drinking water, because the well pump was broken. Food was scarce, fear was high, and hope was far away.

Most of the people we talked to had been at the camp for at least three years. This was not their home any more than it was mine, but staying here was safer than living in an isolated village that was vulnerable to the LRA's rampages. The day before we arrived, the LRA had killed five women who had gone back to their village to tend their fields. An entire generation was waiting for the war to end, though they had never known life without it.

A little boy in shorts and a torn, unbuttoned shirt met my eyes. He was playing with a piece of wire. His stomach was bloated—the ironic sign of severe malnutrition.

I remembered how my mom used to correct me when I was a child and told her I was starving. "Jena, sweetie," she would say. "You don't know what starving means. You are hungry, but you are not starving."

Looking around the camp that day, I saw what starving looks like: It looks like blank stares from children who have never lived outside a barbed wire. It looks like parents in anguish because they cannot save the lives of those they love the most. It looks both helpless and ferocious. It looks like the absence of a good God.

I had been traveling through East Africa for the past three weeks, but these communities were still new to me. In the face of such brokenness,

I ached to close my eyes and wish it all away, to get back in that dusty truck and curl up with my doubts and fears. The safety of my childhood had not prepared me for war zones or beaten landscapes. My faith had once felt unshakable. Places like this were deflating almost every conviction I held.

But I had decided early in my life that, whether or not I had faith, I could do something. So I smiled at the boy, the truly starving child. He hid behind his mother. Then I looked at Joel, and we began to follow Julius toward the camp's broken well. Toward the reason we were there.

• • •

It was two years earlier, when I was twenty-one, that a vision for something extraordinary came to me. It came not as a gentle suggestion, but as an overpowering desire for change. It came from the convergence of a global health emergency, a collection of young musicians, and a personal need to live out a promise I had made to a homeless man twelve years before.

The vision included serving African villages where women and children walk several miles a day to find water to keep them alive. It included advocating for families whose immune systems were so weak from HIV that diseases in that water caused mothers to bury their babies and children to bury their parents. It included providing clean water for one thousand of those African communities.

And it included the consistent urge to walk away.

In Kenya, the people say *pole pole,* or "slowly by slowly." In Zambia, they say *panono panono,* or "brick by brick." These phrases refer not just to speed, but also to the uneven, up and down, three-steps-forward-two-steps-back nature of life.

If you look at the time it takes for corn to grow in western Kenya, or for a girl to walk with her bucket to the nearest watering hole in the hills of Rwanda, you see why the pace of life follows the growth of the land. If you witness a community coming together to build its own well, only to see its destruction through a senseless war, you begin to expect an uneven path in all things. And if I look at my own life, I see that the only way to reach an audacious goal is slowly by slowly.

When I was in high school, my classmates voted me Most Likely to Devote My Life to a Lost Cause. I took it as a compliment. But the thing about lost causes is that they're only lost if you leave them behind. If you stay in there, if you keep hoping in action, if not in feeling, if you listen to how circumstances are shaping your calling, you may discover they are not lost after all. You may discover they are the most beautiful, extravagant examples of abundance in your life. You may start keeping your eyes open to causes that seem the most lost of all—whether they are in your backyard or in a small community in Lira, Uganda.

My story of cofounding an organization to address the HIV/AIDS and water crises in Africa is not really mine. It is more a story about forming relationships in villages, tour buses, and living rooms with people who act every day, trying to make a better life for others. They have names and faces and families who love them fiercely. They have that same passion for change that began in me as a child. My dreams, like theirs, have matured in the dust of dry African summers when rain didn't come. In the deceit of broken relationships and lost money. In the rhythm of children dancing.

I don't believe in as much as I used to. I don't believe in ending global poverty. I don't believe that people will always make choices based on the good of others. And I don't believe the world is mine to save.

But what I do believe in, I believe in more. I believe that to love well, we must choose love every day. I believe that the point of life is community: letting others transform us. I believe that our grief over wrongs can become a passion to make things right. And I believe that God is good.

As I stood in that displacement camp among a weary crowd of men, women, and children, I recognized that even in their hopelessness, they had the will to survive. They had a longing, just as I did, to flourish.

I began walking to the well because I was in too deep to turn away. I was too certain that, as long as there are still people in the world who face unbearable obstacles, we cannot give up. I was too convinced that I was right where I belonged.

Part One

The World Opens Out

"A kind of light spread out from her. And everything changed color. And the world opened out."

—John Steinbeck, *East of Eden*

1

Union Square

My parents had experienced a thing or two in the world by the time I arrived. That might explain why security—and fear—were such a part of my early childhood.

My father was the first American-born member of his Chinese immigrant family. Even though he lost his mother at age five, endured beatings from bullies in San Francisco's Panhandle, and weathered the abuse of a stepmother who refused to feed him, Dad made something of himself as a prosecutor who put bad guys in jail. My mother survived martini-mixing socialite parents from the Midwest and became a psychiatric nurse with compassion deeper than the bottomless drinks of her father.

Mom and Dad fell in love on a blind date one San Francisco Christmas Eve and married soon after. They lost their first daughter to a congenital heart defect when she was eleven months old. As their next child, I was fiercely protected—my parents set out to ensure that I would know little want, fear, or loss. When my brother arrived nearly three years later, their circle of protection enclosed him as well.

We grew up with alarm systems in our home, emergency whistles on our backpacks, and lunch pails filled with food too healthy to be traded in the cafeteria. On the first day of kindergarten, my dad drove behind the school bus to make sure the driver made good use of turn signals. If my parents had occasion to fly, they took separate airplanes so that, should one plane go down, they would not orphan us as their parents metaphorically had.

Restaurants were complicated for us. If the nonsmoking section smelled at all like the smoking section, we walked away. If the nonsmoking section passed the first test, Dad still wanted to sit facing the door.

We had an earthquake plan, a fire plan, and a Y2K plan. "Be prepared" was our motto. And so I went to day care with a Cabbage Patch Kid in one hand and Caution in the other. I refused to risk slides on playgrounds, salt on my food, or the deep end of the swimming pool. I lived for rules, seat belts, and year-round SPF 50 sunscreen.

My dad had logical reasons for all this protection: he made legal enemies through his work. My mom had research-based reasons: she knew the data; she knew about all possible threats to children. They both had intuitive reasons: the world had been a dangerous place thus far.

· · ·

When I was nine, our family moved to Burlingame, a small suburb in the San Francisco Peninsula. Known for its affluence and Victorian neighborhoods, Burlingame hosted a Pottery Barn, United Colors of Benetton, and one of Starbucks's first non-Seattle shops.

Our new house was tucked securely into the neighborhood cul-de-sac. Brick stairs lined with honeysuckle climbed from the street to our front door. A towering row of eucalyptus trees shaded the nearby boulevard of El Camino Real. My existence fit into a four-mile radius and was filled with all the right activities for a Bay Area third grader: piano lessons, ballet, T-ball, and Kumon, an after-school speed math program that was popular among Asian students. Burlingame, like my childhood, was beautiful, safe, and smelled like peppermint patties.

At that point, it hadn't occurred to me that my life was privileged and protected. Our family lived and looked like our neighbors. I enjoyed riding my pink Huffy bike around the block, going to sleepovers, and watching *Full House* on Friday nights.

But on a crowded San Francisco street, my world opened out.

Mom and I were walking to a bistro near Union Square. People crowded the streets—hurried men in suits, tourists in matching t-shirts with cameras around their necks, an old woman pulling a shopping bag on wheels. I treaded carefully on the gum-stained sidewalk, over grates and cigarette butts. Graffiti defaced the parking meters. Chinese characters embellished the awnings of restaurants. The air smelled like the concrete public bathroom we avoided at the farmers' market on Saturdays.

I felt small and uncertain.

Then, walking up Geary Street, I saw him. He was a tall black man with sunken eyes, standing on the edge of the sidewalk. He balanced himself on the balls of his feet, calling out to passersby. Calling out to me.

"I'm hungry," he said.

I looked around to see if anyone else was listening. The outside world scurried forward. My world stopped. I paused to listen to him. He sounded defeated, like something had broken him.

"I'm hungry," he repeated. His face was sad. It seemed that every person who ignored him hurt him more. I felt a pain in my body—something wasn't right. Then Mom called from farther down the sidewalk, and I shuffled to join her.

At lunch, my hamburger sat on my plate untouched. I fiddled with the paper wrapper of my straw. As a third grader, I had already learned a lot about the world. I had learned that pickles and cucumbers are the same thing and that the earth orbits the sun, not the other way around. I had learned that we have to say goodbye to friends sometimes and that Christmas presents can be disappointing. But it was inside that bistro, with a plate full of food, that I learned that there were people in the world whose lives were very different than mine.

For a moment, I forgot that I was a shy, accommodating child. That hamburger didn't belong to me, and I knew it. Mom knew it, too, when I asked for a to-go box. I whispered a request to find the man.

"We can try," she whispered back.

We traced our steps from the restaurant to the parked car, my patent-leather shoes tapping along the sidewalks. *He won't be hungry anymore*, I thought. *He'll know I heard him.*

We arrived at the block where the man had stood, but he was no longer there. The streets were less crowded, and the summer sun was creeping its way behind the cityscape. It hadn't occurred to me that he wouldn't be there. I had his hamburger, after all.

Mom and I walked a few more blocks, circling Union Square in search of him, but we both knew he was gone.

Mom's caution was rising as the sun sank.

"We need to go home, sweetie," she said. "It's not safe for us to be here."

The Styrofoam container I held suddenly felt heavy with disappointment. Not just disappointment that we couldn't find the man, but disappointment that streets existed where grown-ups could walk by a hungry man's pleas for help. In my child's mind I wondered: *What did they believe that made them capable of ignoring a person in need? Did they think this man deserved to be hungry? Did they feel they had permission to walk past him?*

As I stood silently on Geary Street with a hamburger in my hands, I knew that what happened to that man on the street was wrong. I knew that no human being deserves to be hungry or ignored or forgotten. Though I could not express it at the time, I knew that every person is worthy of dignity—no matter what.

. . .

What is it about childhood perception that makes us able to see right and wrong for what they are? What is it that makes such awareness slippery in our adult minds?

Since that San Francisco day, I have seen a thousand wrongs in this world: Mothers with no option but to give their children dirty water. Men abusing power. Death so common in a community that funerals are held nearly every weekend. But I see through worldly eyes.

When I try to see Kenya or my Nashville neighborhood as I saw the streets of San Francisco as a child, experience gets in the way. The wrongs in this world do not hurt me the way they did once. The injustices don't seem as shattering. But whether or not I *feel* the ache that I knew as a child, I want to act on those young convictions.

Because if we believe that we are not better than a hungry man on the sidewalk, if we believe that the death of someone else's child is not different than the death of our own, if we believe that sensitivity to injustice is imperative, then we should be outraged when we look at the world. Our outrage doesn't need to lead to helplessness or, worse, cynicism. It can be the impetus that opens the world out.

I never found the man whose voice called to me, whose eyes chase me down the alleyway of my memory.

In more ways than I can count, I am still looking for him.

2

She Breathes the Air and Flies Away

My awareness of others would one day define my calling. But as a heartsick third grader on a San Francisco street, and then as a shy preadolescent, my sensitivities seemed more a burden than a gift. My days of consciousness began to include extreme self-consciousness. And a preoccupation with all things Shana Glick.

Shana Glick was the most popular girl in the fifth grade. She wore her thick, wavy hair in braids, dressed in coordinated outfits, and was Jewish. As Shana's most avid follower, I wanted to be like her—which meant trying to become Jewish, too.

I learned songs in Hebrew, lit a menorah for the eight nights of Hanukkah, and searched for the hidden matzo on Passover. I went to Jewish camp and attended temple with Shana's family several times. I loved the rituals of the Jewish tradition. I loved the rhythm and poetry of Hebrew—a language that seemed beautiful enough, sacred enough, to communicate with a God who might be both majestic and near.

I had carried questions about the universe and my small place in it since the day the homeless man opened my world out. Was there a Being out there who cared about that man? Who cared about me? As I tried to be like Shana, my curiosity about God grew. I wanted to communicate with him—or her—or it. Whatever the case, I longed to be heard.

At the time, my parents were on their own journey of faith and began taking my brother and me to a Presbyterian church. The new community of friends there was good for our family, but I still preferred the serious devotion of Jewish practices over Sunday school arts and crafts. I began to believe that if I lit candles and recited Jewish prayers, perhaps this God of Israel would speak to me, just as he had to people thousands of years ago. Even more important, just as he did to Shana Glick.

I found comfort in following Shana and receiving the benefit of grade school popularity by association. I had no idea how good I had it socially until my parents told us we were leaving California for Colorado. At my new school, girls my age huddled together like flies, out to swarm whatever vulnerable specimen they could find—which, unfortunately, happened to be me.

It didn't help that I was "slow to develop," as my mom said, referring not just to social reticence, but also to my chest size. When an eighth grader called me "Kansas" and I said, "No, I'm from California," it seemed the whole school was laughing. Not for the first or last time, I retreated into the bathroom to cry.

I began to wear a training bra, though I had no need for it. (I still don't have a need for it, despite years of training.) Wondering if I was simply a late bloomer, I asked Mom how old she was when she developed. She replied, *"Not until I had them surgically augmented, sweetie."*

I was doomed.

I considered my options: submit myself to the insecurity of chasing boys with a pack of thirteen-year-old girls or disqualify myself from the entire junior high game. The answer was easy. I decided to stop trying to be pretty for the boys and acceptable for the girls. I would be a tomboy instead—a wimpy tomboy, but at least I would have a place in my school's social structure.

Thanks to my dad's obsession with the 49ers, I was good with a football and knew a lot about the game. I also played on softball, basketball, and soccer teams—though I was never the best player. At the height of my tomboy phase, I subscribed to *Sports Illustrated,* decorated my bedroom walls in sports posters, and dressed up as Steve Young (the 49ers quarterback) for Halloween.

Years later, my comfort level with being "one of the guys" would come in handy while traveling the country in a bus with a bunch of men. My love of sports would make for easy conversation with wealthy businessmen over beers and burgers. In junior high, my tomboy phase meant that girls didn't mind me because I wasn't competing with them for attention, and I could be with boys without worrying about getting kissed.

I avoided the discomfort of any dance, social event, or non-sports-related after-school activity. Instead, I retreated to my bedroom, where I lay on the carpeted floor and stared at the ceiling for hours. Sometimes I doodled in my journals, penned questions to God, or wrote poetry. *I am a sensitive girl who wants to understand life,* I wrote. *I hear the cry from every suffering heart. I see my hopes and dreams in the millions of stars. I want everything to be okay.*

I lit candles and recited my Jewish prayers: *"Baruch ata Adonai, elohaynu melech ha'olam asher kidshanu bemitzvotav vetzivanu l'hadlik ner shel Shabbat."* (Praised are You, Adonai our God, Sovereign of the Universe, who makes us holy with *mitsvot* and instructs us to kindle the lights of Shabbat.) I didn't know what *mitsvot* or *the lights of Shabbat* were, but I prayed the words anyway, with fervor. My room was my temple. My prayers were smoke signals to a God I wanted to believe in, a God who might even be real.

Could it be, I wondered, *that the God of the Universe cared about everyone? Even me, no matter what others thought of me?* There, in my basement bedroom, I started asking the questions that would one day shape themselves into faith.

In my isolation, the popular musicians of the mid-nineties kept me company. I put socks in my training bra and danced in front of the mirror, lip-synching to "Dreamlover" in my best Mariah Carey impression. I hammered through my schoolwork while listening to R.E.M.'s "Nightswimming."

But the music that resonated with me the most was a self-titled album by a band called Jars of Clay. I spent many nights lying on the carpet with the CD on loop as I flipped through the album booklet. *In open fields of wild flowers,* one song began, *she breathes the air and flies away.* I imagined the words referred to me. *In no simple language, someday she'll understand the meaning of it all.* They made me wonder if perhaps, beyond junior high, I might encounter people whose questions and prayers were similar to mine.

I felt I had company in the lyrics of the album, just as I did through the words of the Jewish prayers. But these words were about Jesus—about a love that heals pain. *They say that love can heal the broken, they say that hope can make you see, they say that faith can find a Savior, if you would follow and believe.* I wanted to believe.

I didn't know then that my introspection gave me a head start in cultivating a moral seriousness that would become part of my life's vocation. I did hope that in some way my devotion would grant me greater understanding of life, beyond the walls of my bedroom. In the meantime, I lit my candles, recited my prayers, and allowed a rock band's CD to serve as the hymnbook of my adolescence.

3

Taking on a Mountain

One summer in junior high I learned my scrawny legs held the power to climb mountains—literally. It happened when my grandparents paid for me to attend Cheley Colorado Camps, a monthlong residential outdoor adventure camp at the base of Rocky Mountain National Park. Cheley's Outward Bound–style programming took suburban kids like me away from television, air-conditioning, and summer idleness and placed them on a mountain trail, class IV rapids, or a western saddle. It was where my mother had spent summers when she was a girl. And where I did not want to go.

Despite my protests, that July I found myself unpacking my socks and underwear (carefully labeled with my first initial and last name) into wooden drawers next to rows of bunk beds. I worried about getting stuck with a top bunk. What if I needed to go to the bathroom in the night? What if I fell off?

On the first weekend of camp, all sixty girls in our unit gathered to create the Code of Living—a collective set of values we would agree to live by for the month. The Code of Living was a sacred practice that created common ground among all of us outside the influence of peers at home. I remember my first summer's Code of Living even now. It included compassion, teamwork, carpe diem, and sense of humor.

To my relief, that rookie summer I not only got a bottom bunk but I

13

also discovered an "adventure" that was just my style: I spent the first three weeks at the archery range. Most campers resorted to archery when they were sick or injured. But caution preceded me, and I chose day in and day out to shoot arrows at a bale of hay. I was branded the "Archery Girl" as I mastered a sport that I could just as easily have done at the archery range less than a quarter mile from my backyard.

On the final week of camp, I looked at my activity sheet and saw that my request for archery had been denied. Instead, I had been signed up for a three-day backpacking trek that included climbing a 13,000-foot mountain. I pointed the mistake out to my counselor, who kindly suggested I begin packing my backpack. I believe her response included the words "push yourself a bit more." I cried all night.

The next day, I found myself standing at the trailhead with nine other girls, our backpacks at our feet. As I struggled to hoist the backpack up on my own, two of the girls offered to help. Once the girls and I managed to secure the pack, my knobby knees began to shake from its weight.

I stayed in the back of the single-file line, feeling slightly less alone than I had one hour earlier. I counted my steps as I walked, and a rhythm began to inform the journey. We played word games. We told embarrassing stories. We sang songs, sounding like mountain hippies as we belted out James Taylor and Joni Mitchell. We guessed at the names of wildflowers and pines and stopped to look at them. The weight of our packs was overwhelming, the trail steep at times, and the air thin as we gained altitude. But no one complained, not even me. We were in this together, each carrying some part of what we needed for the days to come.

Years after that first hike, I would climb the hills of Rwanda with women and girls who carried buckets of water for survival instead of backpacks for recreation. They, too, would sing, tell stories, and play games as they walked. But they were not at an adventure camp, they were on a quest to live that day. They would teach me just how heavy a weight could be.

Our campsite that night sat at ten thousand feet, tucked at the base of South Arapaho, the mountain towering three thousand feet above us that we were going to climb the next day.

Early the following morning, we unzipped our tired bodies out of our sleeping bags, and with gloves, hats, and fleece sweaters, we assembled, shivering, outside our tents. We gathered water and began boiling it on our stoves to make oatmeal and hot chocolate.

I had never climbed a mountain before. I didn't have the slightest idea of what would be required. As we began to walk, South Arapaho looked very far away and very high. I kept my eyes on the ground and tried not to think too hard about what I was doing. The air was cold as the sun began to rise.

Several hours into the hike, the rocks became scattered boulders. I climbed up on all fours, not trusting my feet or my ability to balance. The air was becoming thinner, and each step from one boulder to another cost more oxygen than I could take in. The other girls moved ahead quickly. The triumph I had felt the day before dissipated, and my insecurity and fear returned.

I crawled, sweating and fighting tears. I wanted to quit. I wanted to negotiate with God and figure out if there was any way I could get out of this terrible place and time. I didn't want to climb this mountain. I'd *never* wanted to climb a mountain. I stopped moving.

A girl named Ali sat next to me on the rock, pulling my water bottle out of my pack and handing it to me.

"You're doing an amazing job, Jena. You can't stop now. We're so close to the top."

Another girl named Victoria descended from the rocks above me. Her backtracking humbled me.

"I can't do it," I admitted to them.

"Look at how far you've already come! We totally believe in you." *Where did these people come from?* "Teamwork, remember? We all peak together or we don't peak at all. Let's go!"

We began to climb. The counselors and other girls cheered me on from about one hundred feet shy of the peak, waiting for me. When Ali, Victoria, and I reached them, we all grabbed one another's hands and took our final steps to the top together.

White beauty surrounded us. Everything was both still and alive at the same time. We donned warmer clothes and huddled in a circle, our arms around one another's shoulders. Carpe diem.

As I stood 13,400 feet above sea level on that rocky peak in the company of an intrepid group of girls, something inside me shifted. I could do this. I could take risks. I could be part of a community. And we could reach the summit together.

I returned to Cheley for the next six summers, learning physical and relational skills that would one day carry me through the deserts of Africa and the rocky land of running a nonprofit organization. Those summers prepared me for a job that involved living in places with no water, toilets, or electricity. I learned how to get dirty and cook over a fire. I learned how to pace myself and travel light.

Most important, I learned that to take on immovable mountains, the first thing you have to do is move. You have to grow used to the weight of your pack, adjust your lungs to the quality of the air, and build muscle for the grade of the incline. You have to trust your boots on wobbly boulder fields, get up at three in the morning to beat the afternoon storms, and find people to climb with who share the same code of values. In other words, before you try to conquer something as big as a mountain, you have to change.

4

Finding Shelter

Back in Colorado that first summer, my parents had found a church for us, a landmark brick building in the center of downtown Colorado Springs. I liked it because it had a basketball court in the fellowship hall and because a janitor named Jim let the kids sneak into the bell tower. Beyond that, it was the place I had to be because my parents were there.

During the church service, I sat in the balcony with my youth group friends, passing notes. The rituals of singing hymns and drinking from tiny plastic cups of grape juice for Communion felt less sincere to me than temple, less poetic than the music I listened to. The view over the heads below was certainly dull compared to my mountain experience. I squirmed—physically and spiritually.

One January day when I was fourteen, I sneaked out during the sermon and walked to Arby's. There, I noticed a homeless man at the corner table. I pulled out my allowance money and bought him coffee. He looked up at me with squinty eyes, thanked me for the coffee, and told me his name was Frank. Then he returned to scribbling on a brown paper bag from a stack of bags in front of him. He mumbled words that were as unclear as the ones on the paper.

I liked Frank, and I liked being able to buy him coffee. I wanted to know him. So I continued to sneak out on Sundays and sit with him and his furious writing. I also began to sneak out on Wednesdays when Mom had Bible study at church. Frank wasn't anywhere to be found on Wednesdays, but I met other homeless people who congregated in the downtown park.

I must have been an unusual sight—a slight girl dressed like a skater with baggy pants and a low-hanging backpack, walking through Acacia Park to spend my allowance on Subway sandwiches for our city's homeless neighbors. But the stories of those who our city ignored intrigued me. The people behind the stories became my friends. It was a second chance to help that man in San Francisco. A do-over.

Many of the people I met downtown lived at the Red Cross shelter, just a mile from the park. Soon after I got my driver's license I drove myself to the shelter for the first time. A woman with frizzy hair, her belly sticking out from her shirt, walked out as I walked in. A few men in hoodies and baseball caps were smoking by the front door.

"I'd like to volunteer in the nursery," I told the tired woman behind the reception counter.

"We don't need any help there," she told me. "But how much time do you have today?"

"Um, I don't know," I said, disappointed.

"Come with me," she said. I followed her through a multipurpose room, where army-green cots lined the walls, separated with dividers. Women sat on the beds, some wrapped in wool blankets. Children ran around chasing one another. Piles of clothing and belongings crowded each cot. I tried not to stare as I walked through.

We entered an L-shaped room filled with cafeteria-style tables and metal chairs. The smaller part of the room had a counter and a sink.

"We need to feed one hundred fifty people by six o'clock," the woman told me, pointing to the food scattered across the counter. "That means three hundred sandwiches in the next hour and a half."

I soon stood alone next to a pile of day-old bread and lunch meat from the local grocery store. Determined not to disappoint, I put on oversize clear plastic gloves and began to assemble the bread, meat, and condiments, one at a time, over and over again.

As I worked, I thought about the children running around those cots. What would it be like to want something better for your kids but to feel powerless, a constant beneficiary? "Homeless" was as straightforward and brutal a truth as any, I decided. It was not what they had but what they lacked that defined them. Despite all my park conversations, that was the first time I really considered what it would mean to belong to no place in particular.

Working in the kitchen wasn't as romantic as I had thought playing with homeless children would be. But that afternoon I built an altar of sandwiches, an offering. As the residents lined up for their meal, I knew I was where I wanted to be. And it seemed to me that the God I heard about from my parents, the God that Jars of Clay sang about, would be in this kind of place, too.

I would return home to the comfort of my bedroom, journal about the people I'd met that evening, and pen questions to God about why there was such disparity within the bounds of my own city. I read over and over a passage from Matthew that I'd first heard in Sunday school. Jesus tells his followers that the Kingdom of God is for those who fed him when he was hungry, who gave him something to drink when he was thirsty, who clothed him when he was naked, and who offered shelter when he was a stranger. Jesus says that righteous people will ask when they saw him in such need. Jesus told them that when they did any of these actions for the least of these, they were doing them for him.[1]

This was exciting to me. Loving others, which brought me such purpose, was a way of loving Jesus. So I went back to the shelter again and again. A smile, a sandwich, and sympathy were all I had to offer, but those gifts were becoming my expression of what I believed to be true and right in the world.

A Vietnam vet from Sacramento named Mark was a resident at the shelter and became my partner in ensuring meals were assembled on time. Mark was in his sixties and wore a red-and-blue flannel shirt over his leathery skin.

Mark and I developed a routine. By the time I rushed downtown from school, he would have recruited four or five fellow residents to help us with dinner. The grocery store donations came by 3:00 every afternoon. The food was often an odd combination of day-old bagels, potato chips, bagged lettuce, and birthday cakes, but we always found a way to turn it into a meal.

After Mark and I consulted about what we should make from the smorgasbord, we directed the homeless volunteers in assembling the food. I remember that our help on one of the first days we worked together came from a thirty-year-old black man named Anthony, a red-headed woman named Ginger who had recently lost her twin daughters to the government, a mother-daughter pair named Lucy and Sarah, and a stuttering twenty-something named Stretch who was on crutches because he had jumped off a fence when he was drunk.

At six o'clock, the residents lined up for dinner. They were tired from long days of thankless work, and it was our joy to provide what sustenance we could. As soon as every resident was fed, Mark, the homeless volunteers, and I loaded our own plates and sat with the others at the tables. Many of the residents spoke Spanish, and they coached me through my faltering attempts to learn the language, laughing at the mistakes I made along the way.

After I'd served at the shelter for a few weeks, I officially joined the volunteers as the kitchen coordinator. Four days a week for the next two years, I hurried from school to the shelter to make sure that dinner was served. I loved the act of direct service, of looking people in the eye and offering them something tangible.

I began to involve friends from my high school. The idea caught on, and I started meeting with student council and volunteer clubs at other high schools and asking each one to adopt a day of the week to volunteer at the shelter. It invigorated me to see my peers, as well as the residents of the shelter, respond with such enthusiasm to this arrangement. I was unaware at the time that connecting an overlooked community to a community of resource would become the vocational pattern of my life. I simply loved being the bridge between two worlds that shared the same zip code and yet seemed so different.

Somewhere along the way I discovered that while many of the residents wanted a life like mine, the shelter was the place I yearned to belong the most. I cared more that this ragamuffin community loved me than I did about what my high school peers thought of me. I spent more evenings there than I did in my own house. Mismatched sandwiches sustained me more than Mom's brilliant cooking. It seemed the God I wanted to know, the God I wanted to know me, was there with me, too.

That room of cafeteria tables and rejected grocery store food was full of sunken stories and battered hopes. Bitter worldviews and incremental dreams. But amid the smells and the yelling, the 911 calls due to outbreaks of fighting, the unfathomable circumstances that even I knew would never have a happy ending—amid it all, the stories sang to me. That place, in all its brokenness, was sacred.

My prayers now encompassed more than ancient Hebrew words or sips of grape juice on a Sunday morning. My prayers were actions and interactions, my most earnest response to Jesus' invitation to feed the hungry and, in doing so, to feed him. I knelt my whole self before this world of want that I was just beginning to understand. I leaned my spirit toward people whose vulnerability taught me about the depravity and resilience of humanity. Expressing my budding faith meant I showed up, every day that I could.

Among the homeless, I had found my home.

5

The Day I Met Bill

By the time I neared high school graduation, my generation's grunge CDs lay dusty in our basements and Kurt Cobain was no longer with us. My classmates and I moved on to the more upbeat rock of Matchbox 20, Barenaked Ladies, and later, to everyone's regret, the Backstreet Boys and *NSYNC. We tempered the angst-driven hormones of early adolescence, pulled our skater pants up a little bit, and felt the new millennium arrive with a whimper.

Meanwhile, my interest in the life and sacrifice of Jesus developed into a more serious devotion to Christianity. I immersed myself in traditional Christian practices and beliefs and earnestly sought to serve God with my life. As a result, my church youth group became my social stage, along with a school Bible study and a Friday lunch worship group called Campus Club.

I still felt physically inadequate, scared of boys, and blushingly uncertain of adolescent protocol, so I appreciated the protection of Christianity. Church was a place of rules—which I loved to follow. I hung out with good kids who weren't trying alcohol or drugs, weren't allowed to watch *Friends*, and never even thought about kissing. My most extreme high school rebellion was when my best friend Amy and I spent the night at our friend Holly's house and watched *Dawson's Creek*.

This was the era of the ichthys fish, which Christians placed strategically on the back left corner of their minivans and in their yellow pages advertisements. As a teenager looking for shape to my growing faith, I consumed the Christian industry. I read Christian books, wore Christian t-shirts and jewelry, and sent Christian greeting cards.

And of course, I listened to Christian musicians, such as Jars of Clay. I remember discovering a store in the mall called Station 316 that sold only Christian music. It had signs that said things like, "Do you like the music of the Cranberries? Then you would like Sixpence None the Richer." That was exactly what I wanted to know! I had been taking a Sharpie to all the cuss words in my Green Day and Nirvana liner notes in case my mother saw them. Now I could just buy the Christian versions of these artists.

I felt proud of my niche identity. I felt I was standing up for Jesus by wearing/reading/eating gospel-driven materials. I felt safe. Without realizing it, I had become not only a believer in Christianity but also a believer in the Christian subculture—a culture that wanted crisp answers from its members about faith.

"What is God saying to you in your life right now?" my youth group leader asked each of us on Wednesday nights.

Like, actually saying? I wanted to clarify. I faked an answer when the question got to me, relying on words such as "patience," "obedience," and "trust," while others seemed to answer with conviction.

I didn't feel I had much to say as far as a testimony either. My friends and youth group leaders had powerful stories of living selfish lifestyles but then one day going to a Christian camp or coming face-to-face with their own depravity and surrendering their lives to Jesus. I had no conversion moment that showed I was a born-again Christian. My spiritual growth was mysterious and real, but it was an unsatisfying story. I also didn't know how to express, even to myself, that the place I felt closest to God was a homeless shelter in downtown Colorado Springs.

As I wrestled with this confusion, I saw that most of the Christian adults in my life seemed to want my peers and me to live in a safety zone, not step out into the world. This contradicted my belief that faith and action always went together—and it was the beginning of a tension between my convictions and American evangelical Christianity that I still feel today.

My beliefs merged with new questions and inklings of answers as I moved to Spokane, Washington, to attend Whitworth University in the fall of 2000. I was drawn to this small Presbyterian university because its mission statement reflected my personal mission: "To honor God, follow Christ and serve humanity." It was a gift not to know how hard following that creed would be.

. . .

When I checked the box next to "nursing" during freshman orientation in college, I imagined nursing to consist of holding a patient's hand during distress, cleaning a wound, or immunizing needy children. When I sat down in my first class, I realized that before I could care for a patient, I needed to master the science. Oh, and I needed to stop passing out at the sight of blood.

Within a few weeks, my notebooks filled with lectures and diagrams that appeared to belong to a comprehending student. The fact was, I was great at copying diagrams, but my science classes were a conceptual blur. Atoms and molecules may be the most real matter in all the world, but they were the least real to me.

I decided to find other ways to meet my need for human connection. I volunteered with the Red Cross to teach first aid and CPR classes on weekends. I also got an on-campus job as the go-to student for any health concerns in my two-hundred-person dormitory. I had the title of "medic," but I was more like a water girl passing out ice packs and Band-Aids and safely removing vomit from the carpet when students failed to make it to the bathroom on time.

My role as medic did make me responsible for driving students to the ER when needed. One time I rushed to the ER with an eighteen-year-old guy who was writhing and crying as he keeled over from pain in his side. As I was busy getting him water, making calls to his friends, and ensuring that all of his paperwork was filled out correctly, I sensed an unfamiliar discomfort in my own side. The feeling became disabling, a stabbing pain. I sat down and considered whether or not I needed to be admitted, too, but as he was taken into surgery for appendicitis, my pain lessened.

I went back to the ER when my friend Kelly had kidney stones. I had a similar experience of feeling the symptoms she was describing in my own body. It turns out my real problem was, as I came to call it, "overactive sympathy syndrome." Even today, watching others in physical pain is harder for me than experiencing pain myself.

These somewhat anxiety-producing experiences also gave me, and everyone around me, clarity that I was preparing for the wrong profession. I knew that nurses weren't supposed to become patients, but I didn't know what to do about it.

Ironically, learning about the immune system in my medical microbiology course would be my escape from medicine. I marveled as I saw how the human body is its own world, complete with a defense system against enemies. Dr. Frank Caccavo lectured on a particular virus that the immune system is unable to defeat: HIV, the human immunodeficiency virus. I learned that the essential players of the immune system are like generals in an army, deploying troops to fight off incoming disease. But HIV hijacks those generals, not only disarming the immune system but also repurposing the generals to work on behalf of the enemy.

After a person is infected, it can take up to ten years before any HIV symptoms appear, so by the time a person feels sick, the body is already overrun with the virus. When the immune system count is irreversibly depleted, the virus is then considered AIDS. People with AIDS do not die from the virus itself but from other infections that a wasted immune system can no longer defeat.

I was horrified. The very cells that were meant to protect became the vehicles of ruin. I was aware that the world was full of injustice from poverty, war, and other consequences of human behavior. But I had not considered that living organisms could develop such destructive intention. It hadn't occurred to me that the physical earth, in all its beauty, could hold such devastation. If I could apply morality at a microscopic level, it seemed to me that HIV was a work of evil against humanity.

I wanted to know more. Like most Americans, my only touch point for HIV at the time was Magic Johnson. I remembered as a ten-year-old watching Magic announce his early retirement from the Lakers because he was HIV positive. I remembered the panic of the media as people speculated about the causes and dangers of HIV and AIDS. Since then, Magic had become an example of someone who could live a relatively normal life with HIV treatment, but the flurry around his diagnosis had made more of an impact on me than the follow-up. In class I was learning more about that cellular process, but I still did not know anyone personally who was HIV positive.

That changed a few weeks later when Dr. Caccavo invited us to a campus forum in which residents of Spokane shared what it was like to be HIV positive. A forty-one-year-old man named Bill spoke openly with the twenty of us in the room. His cheeks were bright red, with surfacing veins across his face. Small crevices made his nose look like a boulder field. The tips of his right index and middle fingers were white, as if they had been dipped in chalk.

"I have been living with HIV for eighteen years," he began. The virus had only been known in America for about twenty years at that point, so he must have been one of our country's earliest cases.

"I got married in nineteen eighty-two, but divorced within the year. In the process of our divorce, we accidentally became parents, and I turned to alcohol to numb the pain. In the span of two years, I had about twenty-five sexual encounters. Some I didn't consent to. Others I paid for. Some of them, I don't even remember."

I felt foolish for assuming Bill was gay. Besides Magic Johnson's case, the news had rarely reported on heterosexual men with HIV.

Bill said he had been on eighty medications in the last two and a half months because his immune system was so weak. He listed the names of his ailments, adding commentary to them as if they were his children: enlarged liver ("So many meds for this"), systemic mitosis neuropathy ("I feel like my entire body is on fire"), Raynaud's disease ("Do you see my hands?"), rosacea ("I have had three operations on my nose to improve it"), and fibro-myalgia ("I can't walk sometimes. My body becomes paralyzed").

"I take medicine *all* of the time," he concluded. "I feel sick *all* of the time. People are afraid to touch me. Some won't even look at me."

As a young student at a cloistered liberal arts college, I had little context for what I was hearing. All I could think of were the scenes in *Ben-Hur* when the women with leprosy are shunned and sent to a colony. But here I was sitting in real time with a man who lived a few miles from my dorm.

Bill looked around the circle. "I used to be narrow-minded and judg-mental," he confessed. "But truly, you can love someone with the disease. That's what I've learned the most."

• • •

Since the day I heard Bill speak, I have listened to hundreds of AIDS testimonies in Africa. I have heard a group of Ugandan teenagers tell me about the shame of having HIV after being kidnapped as child brides. I have held the hand of a man dying of AIDS as he spoke of his wife and children.

Everyone with HIV has a narrative. Sometimes it comes across as medical history. Sometimes it sounds like a religious testimony. Sometimes it's more a list of answers to frequently asked questions.

Early on, when I would hear a story about HIV, I felt like a voyeur peering into secrets I should not know. Then I realized how healing listening can be. These are stories of vulnerability and horror. Many times they are also stories of deep gratitude, told by Lazaruses who were counted for dead but have been given a second or fifth or twelfth chance at life. Cradling someone's testimony of HIV is a sacred responsibility. I try not to break it as I receive it and carry it with me. And each story I hear reminds me of Bill.

In 2001, when I met Bill, there were 1,500 people with HIV and 450 more who had AIDS in Spokane, Washington. I learned that in other parts of the world, the statistics were much higher.

One article predicted that AIDS would claim 68 million lives in the next twenty years. It was a number beyond comprehension. Sixty-eight million men, women, and children who would each have a testimony of their own chronology of physical and emotional pain. Medicaid covered the costs of doctors' visits and medications for Bill, but who would cover the cost for those in poor countries? The infection rates were escalating in places where treatment was inaccessible and unaffordable. More than 20 million HIV cases were estimated in sub-Saharan Africa alone. I learned that the same communities where people were struggling to survive with HIV often lacked access to safe drinking water. That meant that people with compromised immune systems were drinking the very contaminants that threatened them.

I also learned that the virus was affecting people my age the most because those between eighteen and thirty-five were dating, marrying, and having children. The key generation in developing countries was dying. Just as HIV attacked essential cells that keep a body healthy, so it attacked the members of a society that keep villages and families fed. Injustice on a global scale was the echo of injustice on a molecular level.

I pasted news articles about HIV into a spiral-bound journal and tried to make sense of what I read. *Why aren't more people talking about this?* I wondered. *Did they even know? Did they care to know?* Despite my years at the shelter and the relationships I'd built with the community in Acacia Park, I was just beginning to grasp the magnitude of the world's imbalances. I thought of the homeless man in San Francisco and began to understand that our world is full of street corners where the disenfranchised stand alone, crying for help.

In light of such global destruction, political science classes suddenly seemed much more relevant to me than nursing classes. I found excuses for missing Anatomy, begging my lab partner to cover for me during the dissection unit.

Every paper I wrote or presentation I did for my nursing classes veered toward a discussion of justice, human rights, and HIV. I began to work with the Spokane hospice, volunteer at the local homeless ministry, and become involved in a social business for low-income women. I worked with the First Presbyterian Spokane youth group every week. And with a burst of conviction, I pinned a red ribbon over my heart and paraded through my small campus, soliciting signatures to petition Congress for universal access to treatment for HIV. Antiretroviral therapy was the newest and best medical option for HIV, but it was unavailable in the developing world. Magic Johnson could afford the treatment, but a woman in a rural African village could not. I decided that I would be the one to change that.

Bolstered by these new experiences, I charged my advisor's office in the science building with a change of major form in my hand.

"Are you sure about this?" my advisor asked. I had already completed three semesters of nursing courses, and it would be hard to graduate on time with a new major—political studies. On the other hand, even the smell of the science building nauseated me.

"I would be a horrible nurse," I said. She didn't argue.

I walked out of the building with the form in hand, relieved to know that my desire to help those who are sick in the world didn't mean I had to be a nurse. I didn't know exactly what it *did* mean, but I had the sense that it would involve work that brought me joy instead of pain or boredom.

Vocation is surprising like that. Sometimes we try to make it much more difficult than it is. We assume that we have to be martyrs, monks, or missionaries in order to be doing what God wants us to do. I hold fast to the words of novelist and theologian Frederick Buechner, who writes, "The place God calls you to is the place where your deep gladness and the world's deep hunger meet."[2] As a nurse, I could have served a need in the world, but not from my own deep gladness. There were other needs in the world that I would be glad to serve, I realized. I just needed to find them.

• • •

My new academic advisor in political studies, Dr. Julia Stronks, told me about a grassroots organization of student activists called the Student Global AIDS Campaign. I made a deal with her: if her department would pay for my flight to the SGAC annual conference in Boston, I'd return ready to launch a chapter on Whitworth's campus. She said yes, and I got on a plane.

Boston was a long way from Spokane, in more ways than geography. As I carried my backpack and sleeping bag across the historic Wellesley campus, I wondered what I had gotten myself into.

Students packed the seats and crowded the aisles of the theater-style lecture hall. It was a reunion for many of them. Most of the students had not traveled far, hailing from other prestigious universities on the east coast. Some were dressed as I had imagined Ivy League students would dress. Others were covered in piercings and tattoos. My clunky shoes and hoodie made their own statement.

An SGAC organizer introduced herself, shouting over the cackle of students, while a student scribbled a statement on the white board: *Fund the Fight, Treat the People, Drop the Debt, Stop the Spread.* Besides a couple of graduate students from the Harvard Kennedy School of Government, most of the organizers were my age.

Throughout the weekend, we received briefings on the key bills that were before Congress. I furiously took notes, not understanding half of what I wrote down—acronyms like WTO, TRIPS, AZT, NIH, USITC. I quickly got the sense that there were countless facets to the AIDS epidemic. It wasn't just a health crisis—it was a social, economic, and political crisis. And it was an emergency that needed more advocates to fuel the change.

I looked around, invigorated to be in a room of peers who also believed they could change the world. Every person in that room had a conviction, everyone believed in making a stand for justice. I felt alive with passion, at home with a group of people who saw the world for what it could be. It's a passion I've seen often in college students over the years, a fierce focus on social good that has a sad tendency to slip away when meeting the "real" world after graduation.

When I returned to Spokane, I fulfilled my commitment to Dr. Stronks and started an SGAC chapter on campus. I found it difficult, though, to generate urgency in other classmates. Most students signed my petitions with fake names and even faker emails. Most of the funds I raised came out of my own pocket just to save face. It was my first taste of the dilemma almost every fundraiser faces: how to inspire very compassionate but very busy people to care about what you believe is one of the most important things in the world.

In the end, my entire SGAC group consisted of me and five freshmen whom I lovingly referred to as the Freshmen Five. Later that year, the Freshmen Five and I attended a lecture a visiting professor was giving for interested students in the area. He spoke about how the students on his college campus in Illinois had begun a powerful movement in activism for HIV/AIDS.

Eager to discover the solution to the problem of student apathy, I raised my hand and asked what motivated the students on his campus to be so involved.

The professor answered, "One word: Bono."

This was the answer I was looking for! I waited for him to elaborate. When he didn't say anything else, I asked, "What's a bono and how can we get one on our campus?"

The student sitting next to me grabbed my sleeve and pulled me back into my seat.

"What?" I defended in a whisper.

Through Google later that afternoon, I discovered I was decades behind in pop culture. The protection of my youth group had kept me away from one of the most prophetic voices of our generation. All of a sudden, I began to see Bono everywhere. His music, his activism, his universal influence in the media. He transcended politics and culture and bodies of faith while speaking and singing about his own convictions. When he urged people to care, they responded with their whole hearts. Or at least they wrote enormous checks to help those they'd never met. As an artist and icon, Bono could take on the HIV/AIDS crisis with his gifts of music and poetry. He was as valuable to the global fight as the nurses and the doctors. And he expressed his faith in a way the whole world could understand. All I needed was to get a Bono to visit our school.

6

A Culture of Whatever

"What do you care about?" the white-bearded speaker asked the audience. "What do you *truly* care about?" He paused. "That is a question that almost everyone will take seriously if you ask them."

It was my senior year of college, and I was hooked on advocacy. My advisor, Dr. Stronks, continued to support my passion for changing the world. She asked me to join her and other faculty from the political studies department at a Faces of Justice Conference held on the campus of Grand Canyon University in Arizona. The speaker was a professor from Washington, D.C., named Dr. Steve Garber. I wrote down Dr. Garber's question in my journal and considered my answer.

What do I truly care about? HIV/AIDS and the people who are affected by it, I thought. *More broadly? People who are overlooked.*

"We have entered the Culture of Whatever," Garber continued. "Ironically, the more we know, the less we care. This info-glut age can make us dangerously numb." I scribbled his words down into my journal. "That's why we need to know what people care about and start caring about those things, too. The greatest challenge is to attach yourself to the cares of the world and still keep going. To know the world and love it still."

I didn't understand all that he was explaining, but I was intrigued.

At the end of the lecture, I went up to introduce myself to Dr. Garber. Here was a gentle man in his fifties with a soft voice and curly white hair who looked everyone in the eye with kindness. I should have known that he would be curious to hear my own answer to the question he asked the audience.

"You can call me Steve. It's fine," he assured me. "What is it that *you* care about?"

I told him I cared about the AIDS crisis. He seemed particularly interested in my answer, but I didn't know why. He gave me his business card and asked that I follow up with him later that week.

I called Steve a few days later from the duplex I shared with four other girls. My roommates' music from the living room made it difficult for me to hear his quiet voice, but he seemed to want to know about me. I was still unsure about the purpose of our conversation, but I talked about how I cared about overlooked people. I shared about the homeless man in San Francisco, working in the shelter, what I had learned about HIV, the fears I had for a world facing an epidemic that too few people were talking about, and the need for dignity and compassion and justice. I shared about the SGAC chapter I'd started, my clipboard of petitions, and my hope to bring my passions into the world when I graduated.

I stopped to wait for his response, but I heard only silence. *Maybe I talked too much*, I thought.

"Hello?" I asked into the phone.

"Are you familiar with Jars of Clay?" he said finally, his non sequitur response further confusing me about the nature of our conversation. I asked him to repeat his question.

"The rock band Jars of Clay," he said. "Have you heard of them?"

The band whose album I knew by heart? Whose lyrics kept me company through adolescence, proving to me that there were people who felt the same way about the world that I did? The ones whose songs I believed were written for me?

"Yes, of course," I answered.

"They are friends of mine," he began, "and they care about the same things that you care about." I had brought their music with me to college, but I knew little about their personal stories. "We've been talking about Africa recently and their desire to put their creative energies behind an effort to address its complex needs for clean blood and clean water. They care deeply about AIDS and clean water in Africa." He paused. "And so do you."

I put my hand over the phone and ran out to the hallway, gesturing to my roommates to turn the music down. I anxiously pointed to the phone as if the president were on the line.

Steve continued. "The guys called me last week from their tour bus on the west coast. They have an honest concern for Africa, but they don't know what to do about it, given their gifts and time. Their craft is playing guitars and keyboards." He paused again. I plugged my left ear to try to hear him better. "Well, they asked if I had any ideas. And you came to mind. They're playing a show on your campus next week and I suggested they meet you."

Now I was the quiet one. Had I heard him right? With a deep breath I told Steve I'd be glad to meet the band. I asked if they would be willing to meet with our SGAC chapter—all six of us. He said that they were touring college campuses to do just that: meet with students and talk about AIDS.

As soon as I hung up the phone, I dug through my CD binder to find my old Jars of Clay album. I hadn't listened to it in years, but as soon as I curled up with my headphones, the beginnings and endings of junior high returned to me. The lyrics were not just familiar words—they were truths I was living out. I wondered if my loneliness and questions five and ten years before were more than just phases I'd had to pass through. Maybe they'd been preparing me for something.

Then the fear set in. I would be hosting a Grammy Award–winning band that had toured with Sting, Sheryl Crow, and Matchbox 20.

I emerged from my room with a mix of anxiety and eagerness that would become familiar to me in the years ahead. Could Jars of Clay raise awareness for the causes I believed in? I felt encouraged for the first time in months—and totally unprepared.

7

The Boy Who Was Dusk

The Freshmen Five and I plastered posters on campus advertising that Jars of Clay was coming to speak about the AIDS crisis before their concert. We secured a lecture hall and rallied students to attend. Our recruitment numbers immediately increased as we applied the Bono phenomenon of associating a cause with a band.

When the tour bus rolled in, I stood in the parking lot to greet the band and escort them to the lecture hall.

"You must be Jena," the band's lead singer, Dan Haseltine, said as he walked down the stairs of the bus. He looked familiar to me from the booklet of the album, although his grunge look of the nineties had been buttoned up a bit. I shook Dan's hand and greeted the three other members: keyboardist Charlie Lowell, guitarist Matt Odmark, and guitarist/vocalist Stephen Mason.

We walked across the wooded campus in the crisp November air, my body shivering both from the cold and the anticipation of the day. The audience of about one hundred people was already seated and waiting, so I made a quick introduction, and Dan walked to the front of the room.

"I heard somewhere that AIDS would leave fourteen million orphans," he began. "Fourteen million," he said again. "I don't know about you, but I can't grasp that. So I'm going to tell you about a boy named Kevin."

Dan went on to describe his first trip to the country of Malawi in eastern Africa the year before. In Malawi, as in other African countries, entire generations of people ages fifteen to forty-nine were dying because of AIDS. In a Malawi village, he met an HIV/AIDS support group of about fifteen people who wanted to talk about the crisis.

"I scanned the room as each of our new friends introduced themselves," Dan told us. "My eyes stopped at a boy. He had a hollow glaze behind his eyes. He often rolled his eyes around as if it was hard to focus on anything. He looked down as he spoke about the way this group of people had helped him feel loved and supported.

"I learned that this young man's name was Kevin, and he was eleven years old. He had dreams of being a doctor, and he wanted to go to school. He wanted to help people the way this group helped people.

"Kevin's voice and story overwhelmed me. This boy's imagination, young and full of fire, did not line up with the sad truth of his reality. Even as he referred to his knowledge of his life expectancy, he also said things that suggested he thought he would grow old. He was both night *and* day. That was the gray hollow in his eyes. He was dusk."

The room was quiet as Dan paused. He had just made fourteen million orphans real to us.

Dan went on to tell us that the stigma of AIDS in Africa was killing more people than AIDS itself. Anyone thought to have AIDS lost their job, was driven from the community, became a disgrace to the family name, and was often left to die alone. Most people who had HIV/AIDS never talked about it; they would infect their partners rather than risk being found out.

As Dan spoke, I remembered the stigma among my homeless friends back in Acacia Park. Mark once told me that his family seeing him as a disgrace was more painful than the daily pangs of an empty stomach. To be left alone, to be ashamed, to be fearful—these are also life-threatening diseases.

Dan looked around the room. "All of us visiting that day felt rage that there were so many Kevins in the world—and that we in America have found ways to excuse ourselves from responding to them. In America, we spend a lot of time learning facts and making judgments about people rather than getting to know who they are."

As Dan spoke, I felt known without having said a word, the same way I'd felt in junior high when I heard Jars of Clay's lyrics. This time it was Dan's convictions about justice that sang to me. His words gave shape to my unfolding worldview.

"We want to heighten the conversation in this country about AIDS," Dan said in conclusion. "Far too few people are talking about it right now. Many people know the facts, but even if they want to help, they feel overwhelmed and paralyzed. We need to get to know the *people* of Africa. Then we can really love them."

What Dan understood implicitly, and what I would come to know in the years ahead, was that Americans are not in need of a scientific or political nudge toward caring about HIV/AIDS. They need a gut check. They need electricity to jump-start the heart. The call needs to be more than statistical. It has to be personal—and it has to inspire rather than shame.

I could tell Dan was a dreamer with grand ideas, and he wasn't afraid of trying to make them happen. That day I began to understand that we need doctors, researchers, and engineers to help solve the health crises around the world. We need politicians to get services to the poorest places on the planet. But to get to the heart of an issue, we need artists. Singers, writers, and storytellers know how to stir the moral imagination. Musicians ask us to seek with humility rather than to know with certainty. Poets respect the mysteries of our darkest questions and still call us to love. Artists speak not of blood cell counts but of Kevin.

When Dan finished his talk, he and his band mates shared more stories, fielded questions, and encouraged students to join our SGAC efforts on campus. The Freshmen Five and I looked at one another, elated that Jars of Clay had just endorsed us. Our campus still didn't have a Bono, but we finally had a voice affirming what my small petitions had been trying to say. We had someone who shared our dreams.

. . .

After the presentation, the band and I retreated to a campus dining room to talk about their vision for an organization they wanted to begin. They called it Blood:Water Mission, a name derived from two things Africa urgently needs: clean blood (blood free from HIV) and clean water (water free from disease).

When I asked about the water concern, I learned that many communities in Africa are several miles away from water sources like rivers and ponds. Even then, many of those water sources are not fit for human consumption, especially for people with weakened immune systems. Contaminated water is a common cause of death for those who are HIV positive. This was the first conversation of many when I discovered there was a lot more to the story of Jars of Clay than what I'd known in junior high.

Dan and three buddies had begun Jars in college, playing in coffeehouses in Greenville, Illinois. In 1994, the band won a contest in Nashville. Three of the four guys dropped out of college and moved to Nashville, picking up another guitarist along the way.

As the band's success grew, Dan saw his role as an advocate carry more potential—and more weight. Having grown up in the era of Live Aid concerts, he had a constant sense of the social responsibility of an artist. In 2001, he learned that a study showed that only 3 percent of American evangelical Christians would be willing to help a child who was orphaned by HIV/AIDS.[3] He was horrified. I, too, was dumbfounded when he told me. It seemed to me that Christians would have been the first to care for AIDS orphans. But I was also learning that fear can trump love in all of us, sometimes without our even realizing it.

At the time I met them, the band had earned multiple Grammys, sold more than 5 million records, and enjoyed long-term Billboard success from their breakout song, "Flood." I knew their music was sometimes played on "secular" radio, but their greatest fan base was recruited from the niche market of the Nashville-based gospel music industry. Their main listeners were American evangelicals—the ones who were the least interested in supporting a child affected by HIV/AIDS.

Dan observed that more than twenty years into the pandemic, fear, judgment, and stigma still surrounded those with AIDS. This was especially true in the American church, which was slow to address something that demanded an immediate and compassionate response.

Just as they had on my college campus, Jars of Clay was using their platform in concert halls, clubs, and churches across the United States to introduce the AIDS crisis in Africa. They spoke eloquently, and with conviction, and yet most of the responses they got reflected the 97 percent of evangelicals who were apathetic or even felt morally justified in their inaction—likely due to the connection AIDS has to the gay community or ideas about sexual promiscuity. In his frustration, Dan realized that he could no longer rely on statistics to move his audience. He needed to put a human face and story to the statistic. He decided to go to Africa and see for himself.

"On a cold December morning in 2002, just hours before I was supposed to fly to South Africa," Dan recalled, "I was invited to a living room conversation where Bono was meeting with Nashville-based artists."

I nodded enthusiastically to make sure Dan knew that I knew who Bono was.

"He was on a mission to recruit musicians to champion the AIDS crisis in Africa, and Bono reminded us that our responsibility as artists was to look at the world and describe it. He said we shouldn't have to look too hard to see that there was an emergency ensuing in Africa."

Dan told me that Bono called out the American church, accusing it of being the Sleeping Giant—true to Dan's own observations. Like many Nashville living rooms, this one had a guitar in the corner. Bono grabbed it, and he sang the hymn "They Will Know We Are Christians by Our Love."

After being commissioned by this modern-day prophet, Dan boarded the plane to Africa. There he saw for himself the impact a lack of clean water has on those who are HIV positive.

"Their immune systems were so weak that they were dying from waterborne illnesses," he told us. "Community members who could have helped the sick instead had to spend their days walking to find water. Water sources were often several miles away from their homes, and the water was full of bacteria."

Dan met a mother who was dying of AIDS who wanted the same health for her children as Dan wanted for his toddler son. He met people with great commitments to developing their communities. He realized how it takes so little to do so much, and he wanted to be a good steward of what he now knew.

I appreciated Dan's humility and respect in describing the people he had met in Malawi. Though I thought of him as a celebrity, he spoke like someone with a simple passion to help others. Most important, he spoke not as a hero helps a victim but as a friend helps a friend.

Dan shared from his personal experience what I had been learning through my studies: Africa needed holistic practices to combat the effects of AIDS, famine, and poverty. Civil war and greedy government decisions were hindering strong countries from flourishing. Many people knew how to farm and knew the skills of irrigation, but they were hungry because there was no rain.

But Dan's stories reminded me that I had little firsthand experience with the people who lived with these facts. In rural Zimbabwe, he saw preschool children singing their ABCs, radiant. He saw gratitude for porridge in a bowl. He saw African women and children dancing before God the way David danced before the Lord. He saw the sharp rocks of the desert cry out to God in their beauty.

I longed to know this land and these people, too.

"On my flight home," Dan continued, "I wrote in my journal, *Blood: Water Mission. Clean blood and clean water for Africa.* It's been a year now, and I can't stop thinking about it."

I could tell Dan couldn't stop thinking about it. It was all he talked about.

Dan looked over at his band mates, "I keep wondering if we as a band can create a conversation that mobilizes Americans to advocate for AIDS clinics and clean water wells in African communities."

"If we use our platform for this," Matt added, "we want to make sure we are doing it well, calling people to the right thing." These men were interested not in being rock stars with a cause but in bringing real help to the communities in Africa.

Over our paper plates of mass-produced pasta, I eased into the joy of finding people with a similar worldview who were ahead of me on the path. Our conversation together was natural, as if this wasn't the first time we had met. I wished I had more time with them to understand their ideas and opportunities, but they needed to do a sound check for the concert that evening. We exchanged email addresses and said we would stay in touch.

"We are looking for someone to help us turn this vision into a reality," Dan told me as he climbed the stairs of the tour bus.

Was he inviting me to be that someone?

I loved the imagery of blood and water. It seemed so simple and straight-forward. Walking back to my duplex, I thought of Dan's final words before we wrapped up our conversation: "We know that Christ gave himself fully as both blood and water poured from his side as he died on the cross. We know that the people of Africa are in peril over those two life-giving substances: Clean blood, blood free of HIV. Clean water, water to quench thirst forever. What I am asking now is, *What part will I play? What will my worship of service look like? What part of blood and water will I be for the people of Africa?*"

Before I walked through my front door, those questions had become my own.

8

The Risk of Yes

Back in my room, my imagination ran free with the possibility of real-world impact. The four guys I just met had passion—and they had a platform.

I had nearly a year of college left, but I was ready to leave the classroom and put what I believed into action. And I wanted to partner with the band to do it.

I called Dad to tell him about my ideas.

"That's terrific, Jena Roo. So what are you going to do about it?"

"Huh?" I replied.

"You have a vision for this. Don't you think the band should know about it?"

"Dad! They're grown-ups! They don't need advice from a college student." My dad's suggestion seemed absurd to me—but it did give me pause.

Growing up, I had an abundance of ideas, but they weren't practical because I was too young. I made lists of places to travel, movements to start, and passions to realize. The dreams spun and danced in my mind and in my journals, visions of What Ought to Be in This World. I had neither the maturity nor the means to realize them.

But this time, I hung up the phone and let youth be my strength. I wrote down every idea, question, and possibility that came to my mind about Dan's vision for clean blood and clean water in Africa. I constructed a plan for how the band could influence its audience to take on the cares of the poor and overlooked. The plan included practical ways to engage college students across the United States in fundraising and advocacy. It included brainstorms about how Blood:Water could provide direct, lifesaving support to HIV clinics in Africa. And it included a set of core values, like Cheley's Code of Living, by which Blood:Water could operate.

I felt like I was breathing life into an unformed being that had been growing inside me since childhood. I felt like I was praying.

It occurred to me that I should send my proposal to Steve Garber to see if my ideas matched what the band was looking for. First, I took it to my college advisor, Julia, for feedback. When I walked into her office, she asked me how studying for midterms was coming along.

"What midterm?" I asked. "This is my real exam."

Whatever Julia thought of my bullish optimism, she helped me revise the document just as she had helped me so many times over the past two years. I read it several times more and became increasingly insecure about it. I felt foolish and audacious, thinking I could send a proposal to a rock band, but I had to trust that Julia's excitement and input meant it was good enough.

One of the advantages of being so young was that I was used to not knowing. I was used to having advisors, mentors, and parents who cared about teaching me. Even today, my talents are not in being the most capable person in the room but in knowing when I need others and remaining teachable. Sometimes I fear being thought of as naive or ignorant, especially when others hold me up as a leader, but as I've discovered in my more painful moments, overconfidence can hurt the people I am trying to serve. Listening to people who know more than I do, being vulnerable enough to admit when I'm out of my league—these are keys to leadership, too.

And so, armed with Julia's enthusiasm, I hit send on my email to Steve and hoped that even if my ideas weren't welcomed, at least I wouldn't be mocked.

I refreshed my inbox repeatedly for several days, but I never heard back from Steve. I went back to studying for my midterms and researching post-graduation internships in D.C.

Then Dan Haseltine's name popped up on my email feed. The band liked what I had sent, and they wanted to talk. They emailed back the document with answers to questions I had posed. They included questions for me.

I read the email over and over. I grabbed my roommates and had them read it. The five of us jumped up and down and squealed like we were all thirteen and at an Ace of Base concert.

Dan jokes today about the stunned reaction the band had when Steve forwarded my proposal to them. It was the first time the band had encountered someone who took their vision as seriously as they did—maybe even more.

. . .

As soon as midterms were over, I flew home to Colorado for Thanksgiving break. I showed my parents what I had written and how the band had responded. In between eating turkey and visiting with family, I holed up in my dad's basement office, reworking and further developing my ideas. I skimmed through Dad's business books on strategic planning, dissected the band's answers to my questions, and crystallized my own thoughts into a more thorough document.

The first proposal I'd sent Steve was a few pages long. This one was twenty-five pages—what Dan now refers to as "the manifesto." I look at those pages today, and I'm embarrassed at how my inexperience and ignorance shine through them. But like so many things that don't end up working as planned—choosing to be a nursing major when you faint at the sight of blood, for instance—it got something good started.

In February 2004, the band members asked me to move to Nashville as soon as I graduated and help them start Blood:Water. I said yes without hesitating, even though I knew the band had only about a thousand dollars in donations to start the organization with, and it was unclear whether or not they would be paying me to take on this new responsibility. Perhaps I should have been more cautious, but naïveté was my guardian angel in those early years. Looking back, "no" would have been a safer answer—and the loss of a greater story.

During that final semester of college, Dan and I spoke regularly about how to launch the organization. We asked ourselves a lot of questions, but really, what complications could a rock band and a college student foresee when neither had ever started a nonprofit organization before? Those lessons would come in the days and years ahead, through both struggle and grace. In the meantime, my classes felt laborious in the wake of the work that the band and I were doing on the side.

One day that spring, my phone rang multiple times in class. The phone vibrated in my backpack, and each time I pulled it out, it was Dan. After the third call, I rushed out to the hallway with my phone.

"Hey," I whispered. "I'm in class. What's up?"

"I got it!" he said.

"Got what?"

"Our first campaign. I've got it."

"Yeah?" I asked, walking outside to stop the whispering.

"People in the U.S. are scared to talk about AIDS. We know that; the statistics confirm that. So our attempts to raise money for AIDS are going to be really challenging because people feel hesitant about it."

"Yeah, totally," I agreed.

"Okay, but we're Blood:Water. We're HIV and water. We know that safe water is essential for people with HIV."

"Yeah," I said. "Okay." This was not news to me, and I was getting anxious about the length of my bathroom break from class.

"The 1000 Wells Project," he proclaimed. "Let's provide a thousand communities in Africa, especially the ones affected by HIV, with clean water."

"Wow," I said. "I love it!"

I did love it. But I also was thinking about all we had yet to do, such as file as a nonprofit, find capital to fund the start-up, and, well, graduate from college.

"A thousand seems a bit ambitious," I admitted. "Do you think we should start with the Hundred Wells Project, or the Ten Wells Project? I'm a little uncomfortable with a thousand."

"Jena," Dan responded. "A thousand is a number that we shouldn't be comfortable with. If we get there, we know it wasn't because of us. It's audacious; it's not possible. But it has to be done."

"Okay," I said. "I need to run back to class, but let me figure out how we can do this."

I spent the following nights and weekends reaching out to anybody in my small network who could help us think strategically about Dan's vision for the 1000 Wells Project. HIV/AIDS was my passion, and that was where I had spent my time and studies for the last couple of years. Despite our hours of idealistic phone calls, I had very little knowledge about how to get water to sub-Saharan Africa. But I also knew Dan was on to something about how the message of clean water might overcome the barriers Americans had to caring about AIDS.

As I met with people, the reaction was always the same: excitement and a desire to help. Friends, professors, and colleagues from my volunteer work were eager to participate in something extraordinary.

This was my first experience seeing the power of a specific vision to fuel change. Dan's vision *was* ambitious, but we, as human beings, love to have something to chase after. Our best selves want our actions to benefit others, even people we haven't met.

"African communities without water?" people responded. "What can I do? How can we start?"

So with my manifesto tucked in my duffel, I flew out to meet the band in Nashville, skipping classes once again. I drifted among the homes of the band members for a few days, getting to know their families. We looked for office space for Blood:Water, set up a post office box, and met with some Nashville music contacts.

On the plane ride home I realized that I'd forgotten (again) to ask if my "job" would pay anything. My idealism would be a gift and a struggle—a severe mercy—in the years to come.

⋅ ⋅ ⋅

My last few months of school, I floated around Whitworth's campus elated about the dream job I had just landed—with or without a salary. Most of my peers called me lucky, and I was. In a larger narrative, I had been preparing for this moment ever since I had encountered the homeless man. I had been practicing activism for most of my life. But I had learned that the alignment of passion, skill set, and opportunity—those three pulses at the heart of vocation—is hard to find.

Though I believe that alignment of vocation awaits every one of us, I realize that trying to determine a personal vocation sometimes feels like searching for your own constellation amid a trillion stars. I had been looking at the night sky through my youthful eyes for years. I was giddy to see lights shape themselves into something I could recognize.

The band didn't truly know me, but they believed in me, and though I didn't truly know them, I believed in what they envisioned. I had an insatiable desire to make my life matter, to find how I could use my whole self to change the world. That was all I needed to risk saying yes—which was good, because at the time a shared passion was all that we had. Oh, and one thousand dollars in the bank account.

But the stars were bright.

9

Something Better

I never really went on spring break, at least not the MTV-type with kegs and dancing. Looking back, maybe I should have had a little more fun. But in keeping with my earnest demeanor and my desire to serve, I volunteered each spring in college to travel to Tijuana, Mexico, with fifty high school students from a local Presbyterian church. We built houses and played with children at an orphanage and tried to get our minds around the reality of poverty just over the border from San Diego.

My senior year in college, during those months I was moving toward graduation more slowly than I wanted to, I met a quiet, confident volunteer living in the Tijuana orphanage. His name was Joel.

Joel had grown up in Spokane, near my college, but we had never met before. He had taken these same spring break trips to Tijuana with his youth group for several years as a high school student and now was living there for a year. Although he attended a Christian church back home, his mom was Jewish—which of course I loved.

Joel's interest was global health for the poor, and he planned to attend medical school at the University of California in San Francisco. How could a young AIDS activist not notice a passionate young man who loved God and who had dedicated a whole year to living and serving in an orphanage in Mexico before becoming a doctor for the poor? His desire to care for Jesus by caring for the least of these was similar to mine. I was smitten.

We talked together every night after the high school kids went to bed. Joel told me stories about water projects in Nicaragua he had volunteered on during a study-abroad trip while he was at Dartmouth.

"You know about water?" I asked. "I have been looking for someone who knows about water!"

At that point, my encouraging conversations about the 1000 Wells Project hadn't led to any definite plan. I was growing anxious about delivering concrete ideas to the band. I may have been overly eager to talk with someone else who cared, but Joel pretended not to mind.

Throughout the week in Mexico, Joel and I frequently stole away from the group and talked about the things that I loved to talk about: God and poverty and how to figure out the right ways to make a difference in the world. I asked him questions about what he knew about getting clean water to the developing world. I furiously took notes.

But I liked more about Joel than just his knowledge of digging wells. He had an adventure-ready appeal and a dark, scruffy face. He carried himself with ease. His Spanish was beautiful, his approach with people was gentle, and his certainty about how the world ought to be was inspiring. I ached to have that same kind of confidence—to be comfortable in a place as jarring and unpredictable as Tijuana, to be unwavering in my convictions about the future, and to hold fast to the belief that I could do what I set out to do.

Not much had changed for me since my junior high days of avoiding boys to hide my insecurities. My bra size was the same, and so was my relational inexperience. I had had countless crushes along the way, but I rarely acted on them. In a span of ten years, I dated twice—once in high school and once the summer before my freshman year of college, when a cute guy said that God told him we were supposed to be together. Despite the divine forecasting, that relationship did not end well, and at the age of nineteen I had settled back into a defensive position with guys.

But meeting Joel made me rethink my hesitations. He took interest in my endeavors—and in me. Here was a peer who was genuinely interested in what I believed.

. . .

After I returned to Spokane that spring, I had my first opportunity to appear in public as a Blood:Water representative—despite the fact that Blood:Water was only a dream and a P.O. box at that point.

Jars of Clay had received an invitation to attend a White House event on faith-based organizations addressing issues such as AIDS. It would be at the Washington, D.C., Hilton, and President George W. Bush would be speaking. But the band was booked for shows during that time and asked that I go in their stead. I didn't need long to think about it.

The band didn't have a budget to cover my travel expenses, so my college advisor Julia found a way to get the political studies department to pay for a plane ticket and a room at the Red Roof Inn in Chinatown. I was thrilled. I had been to D.C. only once before, on a study tour of the civil rights movement my junior year of college. We had arrived by Amtrak and stayed in hostels. So this would be a new experience in several ways.

After checking in to the hotel and getting dressed, I fumbled my way through the metro system and eventually arrived at Dupont Circle. The thick humidity and the cacophony of the seventeen-year cicadas made Spokane feel far away. I wiped the sweat from my face as I entered the grand hotel and its air-conditioned climate. The lobby—or should I say, lobbies—were packed with important-looking people. I found the registration table.

With my name tag on, I looked around, hoping to find someone to talk to. I felt confident and happy to be there. Then I realized that the whole room was wearing grown-up attire: men in suits and women in pantsuits. Here I was, a twenty-two-year-old college advocate, wearing the nicest outfit I had, which happened to be a hot pink floral skirt, a V-neck t-shirt, and black flip-flops. I looked like a girl who'd gotten lost on the way to a church picnic. I was Walmart on an Ann Taylor and Brooks Brothers stage. I wanted to hide in the bathroom.

At dinner, I sat at my assigned table feeling like a kid who'd been invited to the grown-ups' table at Thanksgiving. I used my napkin to cover my skirt and prayed that no one would notice me. But I was sure it was obvious to everyone, including the president, that I was out of my league.

Now that I've lived east of the Mississippi for more than a decade, I realize that my young adult fashion sense was mostly cultural. If I had been at an event in California or Colorado, I would have seen others in floral skirts and flip-flops, maybe even with a CamelBak water bottle poking out from their messenger bag. I also realize that whenever I'm called to Washington, D.C., I should leave the flip-flops at home.

• • •

Back in Spokane, I spent several days with Joel after his return from Tijuana.

"So, tell me again how you are going to drill a thousand wells in Africa?" he asked as we walked through the manicured park near his parents' home.

"I have no idea. I was hoping you could help me figure that out?" I said, half-flirting, half-serious.

Apparently my ability to flirt was still questionable, because he responded, "What are the band's parameters? What do they want?"

"They're trusting me to come up with the plan."

"No one wants to hear it, but do you guys know how often good intentions are the most harmful for poor communities? Everyone thinks they want to do the right thing until they realize that the right thing isn't always the easiest approach. In fact, it hardly ever is. You know that, right?"

I smiled like I understood, but I had no idea what he was talking about.

As we walked on, Joel listed examples of what he meant. Aid agencies had tried to bring clean water to communities in Bangladesh. They drilled millions of tube wells across the country. But one in five of those wells were contaminated with arsenic higher than the government standard. As a result, as many as 35 million people were at risk of detrimental health effects due to arsenic poisoning—an unintended consequence of good intentions.[4] He added that there had been a movement in the eighties to provide clean water across the African continent. Outsiders had come in to drill wells for communities, but most of them ended up in disrepair.[5]

"That's hundreds of millions of dollars that didn't make a lasting change."

"How did that happen?" I asked him.

"Imagine a bunch of Russians showed up on your block and started building something without consulting you, maybe something you didn't even want."

"That's a far-fetched example . . ." I started to defend.

"Well, that's how crazy it is see a bunch of Americans coming into a rural African village. The Americans don't know these communities, but they have the audacity to believe that they know what's best for them. They don't even consult the people living there."

Joel's words did not fit with my assurance that I was going to make a difference—for good—or even with Dan's impressions upon returning from Africa.

I pushed back on some of the things he was saying, calling them issues of semantics. He pushed back harder with examples of how words and images can be tools for oppression.

"Take a look at how the poor are portrayed in the media," he challenged me as we were hiking one day. "And then imagine your worst day. You're home with the flu. You look awful. You feel miserable."

"Okay."

"How would you feel if a photojournalist who was doing a piece on influenza took a photo of you on that worst day and then published it for the world to see? Then his company put your photo on a billboard to raise money for influenza research. They don't know who you are; they didn't ask you, but they took something from you." I thought about photos of children with distended bellies and flies on their faces.

"Wow," I said.

"The band wants to do what's right?" he continued. "It will be the hardest thing to do. Jena, not enough people take the time to put themselves in the shoes of the poor, to have actual relationships with them." I thought about how Joel had spent the last year living in the orphanage. He had earned the right to speak this way.

"So many times, outsiders strip dignity from the poor in their attempts to help. We could do something different. We could be an example of something better." My lofty thoughts toward Africa turned into a warm excitement that he was using the word "we."

After Joel left Spokane to begin a joint medical and public health degree in San Francisco, I immersed myself in the writings of his author heroes. I could see immediately how these leaders had shaped Joel's worldview. I was finally reading what would really matter in my mission, books like *A Theology of Liberation: History, Politics and Salvation* by Gustavo Gutierrez and *Infections and Inequalities: The Modern Plagues* by Paul Farmer.

Gutierrez is a Peruvian priest who coined the term "liberation theology," a way of viewing the Christian faith through the lens of the poor's suffering. It focuses on the hope of Jesus as liberator from oppression and poverty. As part of liberation theology, the concept of preferential option for the poor demands that the moral test of any society should be based on how it treats its most vulnerable members.

Farmer's work echoes Gutierrez's preferential option for the poor by asserting that the needs of the poor should take priority over the desires of the rich. Farmer put these ideas into action by delivering high-quality health care to millions of poor people around the world.

Both Gutierrez and Farmer are quick to call out a structural injustice in which we all participate: we in developed countries are implicated in the lives of people we don't even know. These activists suggest that the powerlessness of the poor affects the whole community and that there is great benefit for all if the poor are able to become active participants in society and contribute to the common good. The call is to ensure that any attempt to help the poor focuses on empowerment and participation.

I had never heard these ideas articulated so clearly before. All I had known was that I wanted to work on behalf of the poor—or as Joel would often correct me, to work alongside the poor. But the more I read, the more I realized that this philosophy resonated with what I knew to be true from my own experiences at the homeless shelter: relationships and participation mattered as much as direct service. I couldn't do one without the other.

"The first thing we have to remember," I told Dan after my time with Joel, "is that water doesn't change a community—people do." I felt a rush of clarity in speaking it out loud. "The level of local involvement and ownership will directly affect the impact of the 1000 Wells Project. We can't just drill wells. We have to work at the grassroots level to make sure there is ownership. If we want to facilitate lasting, honest change, we have to do things that other charities don't bother to invest in. And we have to care more about the people than the numbers. That gives people dignity. Charity makes people feel needy." I had no clue what this would mean in practice, but I finally had helpful words to say. Maybe they would lead to ideas. Maybe the ideas would lead to actions.

I thought of the Code of Living my fellow campers and I developed on our first weekend together at Cheley. We named the values that we were committed to, the ideologies that bound us to one another. Joel and I ensured that a Code of Living was set for Blood:Water before the mission ever began. In those early conversations, he required me to ask the most difficult questions first. I've tried to keep that mind-set ever since. And so our fledgling organization became tied to values of community, dignity, teachability, integrity, and responsibility—and to relationship above all.

10

Sailboat, Sailboat, Sailboat

My dad and I arrived in Nashville, Tennessee, on July 12, 2004, after a 2,200-mile journey from Colorado in my Honda CRV. It was still unclear where I would actually live and how I would be paid, so Dan and his wife and two boys offered me their spare bedroom until we figured out the plan. Dad and I dropped my duffel bags in a dark corner of the windowless room in the basement across from their laundry room.

Dan had also found a church basement for me to work from. He took us there to see it. The room was about the size of a walk-in closet, with a narrow window on one side that allowed in light from the garden walkway above. A rusty table, like the ones from the junior high cafeteria, and a metal folding chair completed the look. I put my clunky college laptop down on the table.

I smiled, thrilled that we had finally arrived at this moment. This was our beginning. This was our chance. A lowly basement room would soon become the hub for a dream in action, with papers shuffling and phones ringing.

Dad looked nervous.

That afternoon, I dropped Dad off at the Nashville airport for his return flight home. He told me how proud of me he was. But he knew better than I did that I had picked a difficult path.

With his hands on my shoulders, he said, "Jena Roo, you know that there's a place for you in Colorado if this doesn't pan out."

"Dad, this is going to work!" I said with confidence.

He hugged me and then walked through the sliding glass doors of the airport.

.   .   .

Steve Garber had connected me to the band, but he didn't stop there. He flipped through his mind's Rolodex in search of other people who could lend expertise and support to Blood:Water. He then invited them to our first "board meeting" in the living room of record producer Charlie Peacock.

Steve had recruited people with significant résumés like Clydette Powell, a medical doctor from the United States Agency for International Development with a focus on global HIV/AIDS and tuberculosis. Joel came out from medical school in California to introduce Jars and the rest of the board to the idea of a preferential option for the poor. The band members and their spouses were there. Steve had also invited Roger Parrott, the president of Belhaven University, who was representing a foundation in Kansas City that had shown interest in funding our work.

I couldn't believe so many incredible people from across the country had come to hash out the founding vision for the organization. As Steve would say, our time together was less of a board meeting and more of a "conversation with consequences."

Steve and Roger asked the most questions, getting to the heart of what Blood:Water ought to be about, and Dan formed most of the answers. Dan spoke about how he wanted Blood:Water to challenge the evangelical church that was afraid to talk about AIDS. He called out Hollywood celebrities who knew Africa only as a cause. He wanted Blood:Water to be different than aid agencies that tended toward transactional interactions—instituting a program rather than getting to know a community. Dan spoke with the voice of an artist determined to do what was right, even if it was more difficult or less popular than other options.

Africa had become a trendy topic. Hollywood celebrities had adopted the ONE Campaign. The most popular musicians in the world had participated in Live 8 benefit concerts preceding the G8 summit, on a mission to "Make Poverty History." The media had begun to cover more stories on AIDS, famine, war, and poverty.

As Dan noted, it was getting easier to consider Africans a cause to be advertised on a wristband or a t-shirt or a guitar case instead of a people who reflect God's image just as we do. I was aware of the media attention Africa was receiving—I had a collection of articles in my journals and taped on my walls in college—but I hadn't considered the dangers of that. It was counterintuitive, but so were Joel's explanations of how good intentions could create detrimental results.

"As we try to advocate for Africa, it's hard to reach beyond simple awareness," Dan admitted. "Although awareness is a vital first breath in the conversation about injustice, we are called to something more transformational. We're called not just to knowledge but to the intentional decision to be present in someone else's suffering."

"But what would this look like?" Roger pressed in.

"Most of the international development models we have seen are focused on how aid agencies are saving Africans from poverty," Dan said. "This existing narrative is more about Americans as heroes and Africans as beneficiaries. I just don't see it that way." Dan was speaking the truths we had learned through Joel: many aid models ignored the capabilities of the poor while highlighting the altruism of the rich.

Roger continued to ask questions to which we had no answers—questions about what strategy we had for turning Dan's convictions into an operational reality.

"I don't know," Dan said finally. "But somehow we need to be about identifying *Africa's* hidden heroes and to partner with *them* in their vision for change. Whatever it is, whatever it becomes, I have no desire for us to gallivant across Africa with our own personal agendas."

I looked over at Joel. He was beaming. In fact, everyone was. The intimate collection of artists and doctors and consultants and medical students and mothers and fathers and recent college graduates in that room agreed with Dan. Blood:Water would be more about Africa and less about us.

Roger spoke up with his observations as a consultant. He responded with admiration for Dan's convictions, noting that the band was far from reducing their advocacy to a cause on a t-shirt. Their sense of moral responsibility was palpable. Their integrity was sincere.

I loved Roger's observations because I believed them to be true. I felt privileged to be in the company of the band and our new friends and advisors.

Roger took another deep breath.

"I'm not sure, however, that you understand the commitment a vision like this requires of you." He looked at the band. "And I worry that you will quickly run out of steam."

I felt a tug of fear at Roger's words. I wondered what the band and their spouses were thinking.

"To partner with Africans in the way that you have described is the nobler approach to development," Roger went on. "It will also be the more difficult model not only to create, but also to sustain."

Then Roger gave us an image that has become critical to the entire philosophy of Blood:Water.

"My challenge to you is to ask yourselves whether you want Blood: Water to be a motorboat or a sailboat. Think of it this way: A motorboat will get you to your destination quickly. It's fancy and efficient. It runs on fuel and doesn't require much skill. One person can drive it. You'll make waves along the way, and that wake may cause problems for others on the water. A sailboat, on the other hand, is a lot less predictable. It requires a team of people with various skill sets. It will take longer to get somewhere. It requires leadership and teamwork. It puts its sail up and is at the mercy of the wind, or perhaps God, to set the pace. Sometimes the boat doesn't move at all, regardless of how much you will it to do so. And sometimes you have to be willing to change direction or make other adjustments to find the wind. But that means that the journey in the water matters as much, if not more than, the destination itself."[6]

Roger paused and looked around the room.

Sailboat, sailboat, sailboat, I thought.

Out of the silence, Dan spoke for all of us: "Well, let's set sail."

.   .   .

Time after time in those early years we talked about the image of the sailboat. We did encounter days of steady sailing, when the wind was at our backs and we believed clean water in Africa would be as plentiful as our proverbial ocean. Other days the boat did not move, no matter how high or strong our sail was perched. Some days the boat took us backward, because we naively placed the rudder in the wrong direction. We watched other organizations pass us by like motorboats on waves of success and grandeur. But we moved slowly, if we moved at all, enabling one community at a time to join us. The relationships we forged with African communities and with the Americans who funded the work were what made the journey worth anything—and what made arriving at the destination so sweet.

Had we been in a room with executives that day, we probably would have walked out with a business strategy, annual benchmarks, and a five-year plan. Those meetings would happen for Blood:Water eventually. But first we heard from the artists. After all, blood and water do not come from a think tank. Blood and water are carnal, spiritual. Prophetic and poetic.

They are theology in action, an invitation to stand in solidarity with the poor, to see one another as image bearers of a just and loving God.

This was the start-up season for us, a period of grace and chaos when anything was possible. Before water flowed or clinics opened, the logistics of running a multimillion-dollar operation were merely hypothetical. A band of artists was still dreaming, looking toward a boundless horizon.

11

"There's a *Girl* on the Bus?"

That evening after the meeting wrapped up, it was time to hit the road. Jars of Clay toured around the country almost every week of the year. They would board a tour bus around midnight on Wednesday, perform in various cities on Thursday, Friday, Saturday, and Sunday nights, and then return home to Nashville on Monday afternoon.

They had only Monday afternoon through Wednesday evening to be with their wives and young children, so it made sense for the work of Blood:Water to happen while the band was on the road and not during those home days. My charge to start Blood:Water meant that I needed to go wherever the band's bus took them. That's when I realized that although my college degree had equipped me for the basics of international relations—the culture of places like Mexico or Kenya—nothing had prepared me for the culture of a tour bus.

At about nine that night after the board meeting, I climbed the stairs of the forty-foot bus with a small duffel bag over my shoulder, and I entered the private world of the band. The front room of the rented bus had booth seating, a couple TVs, and a small kitchenette. It was better than what I had imagined for a rock star bus. I couldn't believe I was invited to live here for a while.

"Ah, man, there's a *girl* on the bus?" complained Bobby, the XXL road manager.

"Girls have *cooties*," yelled Jay, the fridge-size sound guy. I smiled in the hope that their juvenile distaste was a joke.

Bobby and Jay were both guys whose personalities were as big as their bodies. In their black Harley-Davidson shirts, they were loud and opinionated and in charge.

Bobby was a proud Texan who kept the time, managed the band, and oversaw the entire production of a show. The band did what Bobby told them to do. He had served as their road manager since 1996, so he was naturally protective. He was like the band's personal bouncer.

My bus mates consisted of the four permanent band members of Jars of Clay, Jay and Bobby, three other supporting musicians (all men), and the driver hired for that run. I felt rather unwelcome, completely out of place, and a lot like a groupie.

As the bus began rolling, Charlie, the keyboardist, kindly gave me an orientation to the bus, his three-year-old son Micah in tow. (Micah was a last-minute addition.)

One look inside the fridge and cabinets signaled the end of my low-carb diet. Both were stocked with every chip and cookie and ice cream imaginable.

Charlie opened the door next to the kitchen to show me the one toilet on the bus.

"This is just for number one. No number two allowed on the bus. Just ask the driver to pull over at a station if you need to go."

Yeah right, I thought. *Like I'm going to let these guys know when I need to poop.*

We walked into the bunk room, where two sets of bunks stacked three beds high lined both walls. The middle and bottom bunks were already claimed. The ones remaining were the top bunks: six feet off the ground. They were the designated "junk bunks," extra storage space for equipment and bags—things the band termed "shenanigans." Not only was I a girl, I was a shenanigan in a junk bunk.

I threw my duffel bag on the top bunk and looked into the back room, where a few of the guys were engrossed in a game of Madden NFL. I meandered out to the front room, where I watched a movie with everyone before making my way to bed.

Getting into the top bunk while the bus was moving was more awkward than I'd anticipated. On my first try, I heaved myself up but slipped and thwacked my knee on the ledge. After ensuring no one was watching, I maneuvered my way into the bunk and closed the privacy curtain. I tried to journal, but it was hard to process the excitement and surrealism of my new situation. Soon the highway lulled me to sleep.

.   .   .

I spent the next several months touring with the band and learning a thing or two about the rhythm of road life. The Jars of Clay guys woke up with cereal and coffee on the bus. Depending on the season, they might go for a run before they showered at the venue. They called their wives and spoke to their children. Then they began their workday in the afternoon with a sound check. They made final decisions on the set list and worked out any kinks. After a bit of downtime, they had a catered dinner at the venue, and then the evening began.

It started with a formal meet and greet with VIP fans during the opening band's set. The four guys signed autographs, had their pictures taken, and listened to fans' testimonies of how Jars of Clay's music had affected their lives or which shows they'd seen, each fan believing that their fandom couldn't be rivaled.

After the opening band finished, Jars showed up to rock it out brilliantly on stage with incredible passion and craft. The cheers called them back up for an encore, and then they retreated back to the green room or bus at the end of the evening. They occasionally invited friends or family who were at the show to come and visit until the crew had packed up the equipment, finished the paperwork with the promoter, closed out the merchandise sales, and ensured that the bus driver who was sleeping at a nearby hotel was picked up and ready to drive through the night to the next city. It usually took a couple hours to come down from the adrenaline rush of the performance, which they tempered with microwave popcorn, beer, and SportsCenter. By one or two in the morning, everyone retreated to their individual bunks and then woke up in a new city, be it Chicago or Tucson, and repeated the routine.

Despite the packed bus, we had ample space and opportunity to bring Blood:Water on the road. No matter what city we were in, we filled our pockets of downtime with purpose.

We knew that we were not experts and that the only way we could succeed in Africa would be to recruit as much support as we could find. So whether we were in California or Minnesota, we worked to find like-minded friends and fans who would sit down with us and discuss Blood:Water. I studied the list of contacts from the band, Steve Garber, and my own college Rolodex and planned meetings prior to our arrival in each city. In between sound checks and other meetings, we grabbed coffee and lunches with professors, lawyers, development workers, businessmen, pastors, parents, and college students. We passed out AIDS ribbons and business cards to anyone we could find. Dan used every media interview as an opportunity to bring awareness to the AIDS and water crises in Africa. He spoke eloquently about Blood:Water, painting a vision of who we strived to be, even though we were just a touring band with a girl in the junk bunk with big dreams.

Bobby, the road manager, became my ally in securing meeting times with the band when their schedule was open. Aaron, the bassist, became my administrative partner in the meetings. We tackled issues such as crafting a mission statement, pursuing potential board members, creating a logo, and planning the launch of the 1000 Wells Project.

Dan and I talked for hours about Africa. We dreamed together about fixing broken things, about restorative justice, about real redemption. We discussed Joel's ideas and committed ourselves to doing the right thing, even if it was harder. I emailed Joel at the end of each day to update him on my conversations with the band. I took comfort in knowing that Joel cared about the details of my days and that he was proud of my commitment to our shared ideals.

As it turns out, traveling on a bus across the country with ten guys was a great way for me to transition from college life. I enjoyed getting to know these new colleagues who were the primary caretakers of Blood:Water in its infancy and, in a weird way, of me. I learned to love the adventure of new cities and new people and the opportunities to fill in wherever the band or crew needed me.

I often stood with the band during their meetings with fans in autograph lines and supplied them with Sharpies or took the fans' photos for them, allowing Bobby and Jay to work on other duties at the venue. I let people know when time was almost up and made sure the band had what they needed before and after the shows. Sometimes I tried too hard to fit in with the guys, accompanying them to see *Anchorman* when I would rather have read a book, or pretending to laugh along with their avid *Arrested Development* viewing even though I didn't understand the humor.

But I was thankful for the haven that the bus provided. I spent hours staring out the window with the landscape blurring by and thinking, *How did I get so lucky? How am I able to do this?* Those months on the road with the band still hold some of the most treasured experiences of my life.

. . .

When I first talked with Dan after his presentation at Whitworth, I heard him allude to the band's frustration with being labeled "Christian." At the time, I considered it nitpicky to hear a band say that they didn't consider themselves a Christian band but rather a band made up of Christians. After all, in high school and college, I was part of the market that wanted to consider them a Christian band.

Once I started touring with Jars, it didn't take me long to figure out what they meant—and to rethink my commitment to the labels of Christian culture.

Jars of Clay had entered the music scene when evangelical culture was asserting itself as separate from mainstream culture. "Christian" became an adjective, a stamp of approval in certain circles, like "organic" on a milk carton. It gave evangelicals confidence that their purchase was in keeping with their worldview.

Though Jars of Clay's song "Flood" soared the Billboard charts in the mid-nineties as a mainstream success, it was the Christian music labels, radio stations, and loyal fans that kept the band from becoming a one-hit wonder. Jars became the darling of the Christian music industry, putting out ten successful albums in less than twenty years. But with that, they had to accept being labeled as a *Christian* band, which was a seal of approval in the faith community and a kiss of death in the mainstream market.

The problem with "Christian" goods was that they could be seen as knockoffs, just as those signs in Station 316 boldly admitted. The Christian industry sometimes placed greater value on a product's Christian appearance than its quality. It meant that music was sold not because the sound was unique, but because the lyrics made direct references to Jesus or were simple and repetitive enough to be used in a church worship service.

Not only did this business model conflict with the band's aesthetic, it also made a theological statement that the world fell into categories of secular and sacred. Those of us who grew up within the influence of evangelical Christianity were encouraged to protect ourselves from the secular by buying into the Christian subculture. It was an outward act of faithfulness to consume differently than the rest of the world, even at the expense of authenticity.

This dichotomy was a chronic conflict for the members of Jars of Clay, who believe that art and faith transcend constructed divisions. Once they became known as a Christian band, they had to follow "Christian" expectations that they felt limited them as performing artists. If they wanted radio play or a large platform at a summer festival, their songs needed to be explicitly Christian by the industry's standard. ("Jesus per minute," or JPM, is an actual measure that some radio stations use. If you don't say "Jesus" enough in your songs, you can't get radio play on those stations.)

Dan once said in an interview, "Our songs . . . are not really there to explain our faith," rather, they are written about lives that are shaped by faith. He believes that art can "make people feel what's true rather than telling them."[7] This paradox did not fit well in the Christian industry's paradigm.

The band was also expected to be as spiritually competent as a pastor of a church and act accordingly. Many festival hosts asked the band to do an altar call at the end of their set, which the guys respectfully but uncomfortably declined. Most nights, vulnerable fans asked specific members of the band to pray for them. Other fans had "a word from God," a divine message they believed they were supposed to share with the band.

I watched in awe, night after night, as each band member graciously listened and responded with compassion to the fans, despite being grossly misunderstood. I soon became uncomfortable with the "Christian" labeling of products and ideas as I saw its implications. Those touring days set me on a path toward realizing that I can be a serious follower of Jesus even if I don't have his name on my t-shirt.

At first I wavered between guilt over betraying evangelical Christianity's unwritten rules and cynicism about that subculture. God had used my youth group, my Christian music store, and even my Christian t-shirts to shape my faith as a teenager. I wanted to recognize the value in that rather than become bitter about it. But I also wanted to be more authentic to the faith I'd had at the shelter: I can love Jesus through loving others.

Jars of Clay faced a catch-22 I would soon come to know well. They wanted to create something true that was inspired and informed by a Christian faith—but the mainstream music industry marked the band as "too Christian." They also wanted to write lyrics that moved beyond traditional religious language, words that wouldn't alienate those seeking God—and the Christian music industry marked them "not Christian enough."

As I observed this happening, I began to ask questions that continue to shape me, and Blood:Water, today: *How can we place anything—commerce, opinion, semantics—before caring for those in need? How can we paint "secular" and "sacred" labels while missing the vision that all things God touches are sacred, even if they are broken?* And most of all: *When do we overlook opportunities to love others because we're so concerned with keeping ourselves safe?*

Touring with the band, I was also let in on one of their greatest stress relievers: karaoke. One night after an outdoor festival show for more than ten thousand fans in Chicago, the bus driver took us across town and dropped us off at a karaoke joint. Actually, he dropped us off four blocks from a karaoke joint, so we could remain undercover. When we got to the bar at the end of a dark street, the bouncer carded me while the rest of the group grabbed tables and began flipping through the sticky sleeves of the song list binders.

When I finally joined them, a guy about the same age as the band was showboating his best high school musical voice through the microphone.

He was serious about his karaoke. He was also a sucker for any audience on a random Thursday night.

After about thirty minutes of letting this local Karaoke King have his way with the place, Jars of Clay's guitarist Steve Mason slyly made his way to the microphone. As the intro to a piano ballad filled the room, the unsuspecting audience continued to drink their beers and smoke their cigarettes and flirt with their dates. The karaoke "piano" finished its descending *dum, dum, dum, dum, dum*, and Steve crept into the first two lines of Elton John's "Don't Let the Sun Go Down on Me."

As the song continued, Steve leaned into the chorus. He hit a high note, and the middle-aged couple at the table next to us glanced in his direction. The Karaoke King looked up.

Then, as soon as the chorus ended, Steve pointed his arm in the direction of our table and proclaimed, "Ladies and gentlemen, Sir Elton John!"

Jay the sound guy rose from our table, adjusted his shirt down over his belly, and picked up the second microphone just in time to begin the second verse. He belted out the ballad.

The Karaoke King looked dumbfounded. I couldn't believe it either. Jay had the finest Elton John voice in all of central Illinois.

Steve and Jay crooned through the chorus in harmony while spectators threw expletives to their friends. The local King stood, awed. He was in the presence of karaoke greatness, and all he could do at that point was worship. The duo held the high note in the chorus, and whistles and cheers filled the small room.

As the recording ended, the locals stood up with cheers and applause. Jay and Steve walked nonchalantly back to the table, sat down, and finished their beers.

Before people could catch their breath from the disbelief, Dan approached the stage. Brilliantly imitating Neil Diamond's raspy voice in "America," Dan gave the table away for the karaoke sharks they were.

The Karaoke King approached the band at the table after Dan sat down amid many cheers. "Who *are* you?" the King asked. "You *have* to join our team for Wednesday night's sing-off!" His feet shuffled as he spoke, "You *have* to be there. That was *sick*!"

And so the tour went: the karaoke sharks of the Grammy Award–winning Jars of Clay moved stealthily through each unsuspecting city and town. Different cities, different venues. Same entrance, same act, same audience response. They were a tiny flash mob, before such a thing was popular.

In these strange little bars across the country, the band found an escape from the monotony of road life. They found respite from the holy Christian expectations of their day jobs. And karaoke sharking helped us all remember, in the midst of starting a nonprofit organization to change the world, that some moments need not be taken so seriously.

·   ·   ·

When the band had first told me we had one thousand dollars to start the organization, I didn't see it for the warning that it was. For a twenty-two-year-old, a thousand dollars is an enormous amount of cash. A thousand dollars means gas money for a year or one hundred movie tickets or a four-year college supply of Domino's pizza. But when I received the bill for the legal fees to file as a nonprofit, I realized that a thousand dollars to start an organization means you might as well not start.

When our account quickly hit zero, I was surprised that the band did not refill it.

"Jena, there are some things that I think you need to know," said Matt's wife, Kristen, over lunch one day. "You know we're facing a lot of challenges right now, right?"

I thought I knew. "You mean with too many tour dates and not enough time home with family? I definitely get that and can feel it everywhere."

"Yes, but there's more," she said as she fiddled her fork into her salad. "It's a classic story. We were young and naive in the music business. We thought we would be making more money but it's not that simple." Kristen had just turned thirty. They had all been my age when the band hit the Billboard charts.

"I thought you all were rich," I admitted. I felt like Dorothy discovering that the great wizard was just a man behind a curtain: the celebrities of my adolescence were just musicians trying to make a living.

Kristen smiled painfully and shrugged her shoulders.

I hadn't yet cost the organization any money. On the road, I ate the catered meals backstage and had a bunk bed on the bus at night. On the two nights each week that we were back in Nashville, I didn't have a home. I had stayed for a while in Dan and Katie's basement, and other members of the band had offered to host me in their guest rooms, but I was growing keenly aware of how precious their family time was. Travel and young children strained their marriages, and I did not want to get in the way.

So I became a nonprofit vagabond, staying in guest rooms of complete strangers and in empty dorm rooms on Belmont University's campus. I cat-sat and dog-sat for more friends of the band than I can remember, despite being allergic to animals. In moments of utter crudeness, I pocketed the junk food from the bus, poached wireless internet from motel parking lots, and babysat for families so I could eat from their cupboards.

But Blood:Water certainly wasn't making any money either. We needed a more immediate plan.

We learned from a well-established water organization that one dollar could provide a year of clean drinking water for one person living in Africa. In our value for the individual story, perhaps we could fundraise one person at a time? The band had as many as three thousand fans per show, with four shows a week. If we asked for one dollar from each person, we could come away with as much as twelve thousand dollars in any given week, covering the cost for up to four wells. We had to move beyond our late-night planning discussions and start making this pitch.

At a show in Indiana, Dan planned to talk about Africa when the band returned on stage for the encore. He would invite people to give dollar bills on their way out of the venue. With Bobby's help, I found volunteers and organized them to stand at the doors to collect donations. As the band came back onto the stage in response to the standing ovation, Dan approached the microphone and spoke eloquently but generally about Africa and justice. It was personal and compelling, but at the moment when he was supposed to invite people to give a dollar to the cause, he simply introduced the next song and the band began to play.

I stood in the back of the concert hall with the confused volunteers at the doors. I couldn't believe it—Dan hadn't made the ask. I collected the buckets from the volunteers, apologized for the mixup, and walked back onto the empty bus, where I slumped on the couch until the band finished.

"I couldn't do it," Dan apologized later. "It just didn't feel right. We have already asked our fans to pay to come and hear us play, and we ask them to buy our stuff. It doesn't seem right to ask them for more money in addition to that."

"But this wasn't for you, Dan," I said self-righteously.

"I know. I just couldn't do it."

I curled myself into my top bunk with hot tears. It was just one concert . . . but it had held such potential. If Dan wasn't willing to pose a simple question at the end of a concert, was our dream going to languish in a pile of Post-it Notes?

.   .   .

Dan, the band, and I knew where we wanted to go. We hadn't realized what it would cost to get there. When Dan balked at taking the next step for Blood:Water, or when I groaned about traipsing across Nashville from one house to another, we were forgetting that getting to the glory of our goal meant a lot of altitude adjustment—and we had not trained to climb this mountain.

My way of dealing with that was to push harder, scheduling almost every minute of the band's free time and frustrating the rhythm that Bobby, as their road manager, had known for ten years.

Then one night, I pushed too hard. The band had a run of shows on the east coast, and I had booked meetings for them throughout the weekend. Bobby had to do a lot of extra planning to adjust the guys' schedules for yet more Blood:Water meetings. In the green room of a venue in Annapolis, Maryland, he announced with irritation and sarcasm that he needed to meet with the band to discuss the fall touring schedule.

"I don't know if it's possible with all this Blood:Water crap that has trumped our meetings, but I hope two minutes of your time won't be too much," he said. "Will that work?"

The guys looked at me.

"Yeah," I said to Bobby. "We're free during lunch tomorrow."

Bobby whirled around to face me and yelled: "*You are not invited!*" He then unleashed the frustrations that had been building in him for months as he worked hard to manage four young men who were now activists as well as artists. I tried hard not to cry.

It wasn't Bobby's words that wounded me. I understood that the crew had not signed up to be a part of Blood:Water and had to adjust frequently to accommodate the band's new pet project. What upset me was that the Jars guys didn't say a word. Not one of them defended me or told Bobby to shut up. They all just stood in awkward silence.

I tried to shake off the experience, but I couldn't. After that night, I decided to take a break from the tour and spend a few weeks at home in Nashville. I used the fact that I would soon be flying to Kenya to investigate partners for Blood:Water as an excuse.

Weeks before I left, I sent the band a thorough email to update them on all the activities of the mission. I heard nothing back. I assumed they had not taken the time to read it. *Typical,* I thought.

Whether they knew it or not, the band and I were on a break. Everything associated with Jars of Clay put me in a bad mood. If a Jars song came on the radio, I turned it off. Aaron called me three times, and I didn't answer. The background picture on my computer was of Dan and me, and I changed it. I was mad at them and there was nothing they could do about it—especially because they didn't even know we were fighting.

What I had trouble remembering at the time was that Blood:Water held no professional or monetary benefit for the band. It made no sense for them to add a twenty-two-year-old and a nonprofit organization to their burdens. In the years to come, the energies they could have put into making money they instead invested into their vision for serving communities in Africa. They gave up concert revenue to play benefits. They stayed out extra days on the road to meet with board members and advisors. Their families had many dinners without them because of these sacrifices. We didn't know then that Blood:Water's revenue would one day exceed that of Jars of Clay—all because four guys chose to put others' needs before their own.

In our individual ways, each of us was just beginning to learn that making an impact with your life is risky. Missional vocation will break you, taunt you, do whatever it can to test whether you mean it when you say you want to serve the poor or provide clean water in Africa or conquer a mountain.

We would need grace to carry us through.

12

Promising Not to Promise

Given my hostility toward the majority of the people I worked most closely with, it was a great time to leave the country. Joel, serving as a Blood:Water volunteer, and I would be traveling across Kenya to visit water organizations that a reputable nonprofit in the United States suggested we observe. The band had asked us to help them shape the strategy for the 1000 Wells Project. Since the project was only a name and a logo at that point, friends and family helped finance our trip, with the remaining balance charged to our personal credit cards.

Instead of looking forward to the adventure, I was overcome with fears of malaria, kidnapping, and food poisoning. I feared aggressive street vendors, unruly roads, and the confusion of currency conversion. Most of all, I feared standing out. I feared being in an environment and culture that were totally unfamiliar. My inner Archery Girl had resurfaced.

A week before we left, I wrote a will. I wanted my beloved 1997 Honda CRV to go to a family that needed it. I gave instructions for songs to play at my funeral, including a note to my parents asking them to embrace forgiveness if my death were a result of malice. I made my final phone calls from the pay phone in the Nashville airport. Dad wished me traveling mercies and proclaimed, "You're on a mission from God, Jena." That's when I was sure that I was coming home in a body bag.

After the twenty-four-hour journey from one continent to another, I walked out of the Nairobi airport with a racing heart and a disoriented sense of self. I had finally arrived at the place I'd dreamed of, with my newspaper clippings and journaled hopes. My expectations were grand, though my fear of the unknown was palpable.

Joel had flown in from San Francisco the night before, so I was on my own at first. I timidly accepted the offer of an assertive cabdriver, rolled up the back window of the beaten Toyota Corolla, locked the door, and held my backpack close to me as we drove into the unmoving traffic. Street hawkers wove their way through the lanes selling canvas shoes, soccer balls, sunglasses, and other items one might find at the dollar store. Vehicles puked black fumes. Pedestrians scrambled along nonexistent shoulders of the highway, chaotically dodging motorbikes, oncoming traffic, and one another.

Amid the stops and starts of the cab, I was sure we would strike a child on the way to school or a mother on the way to the market. Instead of stoplights, cops in blue-collared shirts under worn-out navy blue sweaters attempted to guide traffic while clutching walkie-talkies. The roundabouts were islands of acacia trees. Luxury Land Rovers paraded past barefoot peddlers.

As a student, I had traveled internationally. I had also studied race relations on a train tour across America, and I had spent hundreds of hours with homeless vets. But arriving in Kenya on that first official Blood:Water trip was different. The stakes were higher. Traveling as a young, single white female did not help. I was keenly aware of my youth and my otherness.

My anxiety calmed as I reunited with Joel. Upon seeing him again, I momentarily forgot about my impending illness/injury/death. We smiled at each other. I had dreamed of finding a partner with whom I could travel and serve, and here I was in Kenya with Joel. These were the adventures for which I had been waiting.

We went over our plans for the month, pulling up notes that outlined the questions we wanted to answer. We were on a mission to learn how to apply our values to actual projects in Africa. We believed the best way to learn would be to see what other organizations were already doing and ask them questions: *What is working? Where are the gaps? What would you change if you were to start over today?* We still had to raise the money for the wells, but we wanted to lay the groundwork for the 1000 Wells Project in the expectation that it would take off at some point. Unlike many large organizations that could work only with well-established African partners, Blood:Water could reach the smaller, fledgling organizations and help them soar.

The next day, we visited a highly recommended local organization that was bringing water to communities in western Kenya. To get there, we took a small plane from Nairobi to Kisumu, the third largest city in Kenya. The forty-five-minute flight kept us low to the earth, allowing us to see a land of greens and browns through the patches of clouds. We were south of the Kinshasa Highway, the dense vector of human and animal traffic along which, near the time I was born, HIV had begun its march against humanity.

As I looked out the window at a panorama I had seen only in movies, I realized my desire for adventure was still alive in me. Flying over rural Kenya elicits romantic images of vast landscapes, exotic animals, and village living. I wanted to experience those places almost as much as I wanted to help the people living there. I had flown thousands of miles closer to this place named Calling, and I realized again the joy that comes, even at the intersection of need and pain, when we are where God wants us to be.

What I would come to understand is that although working in the developing world is often lauded as self-sacrificial, if you have an ounce of wanderlust in you, the work is never purely altruistic. Many humanitarians find a curious tension in enjoying the expedition of a place as much as the service itself. The thrill of new landscapes, extraordinary culture, peculiar transportation, unfamiliar flavors, and diverse relationships all feed the soul of the globe-trotter. The journey can be therapeutic, cathartic even.

We landed on a quaint runway next to Lake Victoria, its waters covered in green hyacinth. Joel and I walked down the steps of the plane and picked up our suitcases from a cart. The airport was small, like a Jiffy Lube. Only two planes flew in and out each day.

A leader of the local water organization, a man named Moses, was supposed to pick us up. We knew it would be easy for him to find us because Joel and I were the only white people at the airport.

Several cabdrivers approached us. Eager for a fare, they called me "sister" and tugged at my suitcase. I gripped my bag tightly, while Joel told them to leave us alone. He and I walked to a shaded area of the building and waited to be found. After an hour of sitting and letting my mind wander into worst-case scenarios, a man and woman cautiously approached and asked our names. When we answered, the man smiled with relief.

"I'm Moses," he said as he shook my hand. He was a sturdy man with a small gut, round face, and wide nose. His mustache disappeared against his dark skin. He exuded confidence and warmth. "This is my wife, Irene." He put his arm on her small shoulder. Irene was as thin as Moses was round, and she was stunning.

"*Karibu* Kenya," she said as she shook our hands and took my suitcase.

"I was told we were picking up a lady director, but we did not think it was you," Moses explained. "Forgive me, but I expected you would be older."

We laughed together as Moses loaded our luggage into the back of a baby blue pickup. I couldn't blame Moses for missing me at first glance. I did look about fifteen. (Even today, I still find leaders ignoring me while they scan the crowd for someone more important-looking. Visitors to Blood:Water offices sometimes ask me if I'm an intern. I continue to be carded at my own fundraising events. I have guest lectured at universities where I've been mistaken for a student. The misunderstanding hurts my feelings, but it keeps my ego in check. I've also found that low expectations from strangers can be a gift—you can surprise your skeptics, and later, yourself.)

Moses's organization, Water for Women's Groups (WWG), was only a few years old, but it was providing water and health support to several rural villages on the outskirts of Kisumu. He had a small team of health care trainers, well drillers, and community organizers. The organization partnered with the poorest villages to support them in the provision of water, sanitation, and hygiene.

WWG caught our eye as a potential partner because it mobilized women's groups from each village and trained them to manage their own projects. Joel and I appreciated WWG's approach in doing the work *with* the poor community, which fit our philosophy for locally led development. We'd read reports from people in the women's groups telling about their achievements, not WWG's, in bringing in a well or latrine.

We met the WWG team in their small office in Kisumu and took tea together. Among them was John Gideon the head driller, Elizabeth the hygiene trainer, and Lillian the community health promoter.

Even though English is a national language in Kenya, there are forty-two local dialects which affect the way English is spoken. And English is typically the third language of a Kenyan (first, the local language and second, Swahili). I quickly realized that Kenyan English rolls off the tongue quite differently than American English. I became terribly timid because I could understand only about one sentence in every three. The soft *i* in American English is pronounced as *ee* in Kenyan English. This really confused me when I thought I heard Moses say, "We do not *geev-a-sheet.*" *What? I couldn't have heard that right.* He was explaining how WWG does not do handouts but rather partners with existing leadership in the community. He was actually saying, "We do not initiate." Ah, that made more sense.

Perhaps Moses sensed my confusion, because after a while he said, "We can make you full with words, but you will learn the most by hearing from the communities."

We loaded into the pickup again, this time with John Gideon, Elizabeth, and Lillian piled in the bed of the truck. The main highway of Kisumu was a circus of buses, small public vans called *matatus*, men on rusty bicycles with bags of grain strapped on the backs, women carrying yellow plastic jerricans full of river water, motorcycle rickshaws called *tuk tuks*, and lopsided buses loaded with supplies and bags of food. Phone credit kiosks lined the roads, and secondhand clothing hung on a wire like laundry drying in the baking sun. Buildings were painted colorfully with advertisements for Rhino Cement, DuraCoat Paint, and Coca-Cola products. Men stood under trees with their motor taxis, waiting to be hired. Goats roamed the Kenol gas station. Dilapidated buildings were marked with large *X*'s, indicating the government's intention to remove the buildings for highway expansion.

Forty minutes into our drive, we turned off the main highway and bounced our way through interior villages. The sky was big against the green, low mountains. Chickens and cows roamed around the dirt paths. Each of the scattered mud homes had a thatched roof and a plot of farming land.

We drove as far as the truck could go, and then we walked another twenty minutes along smaller paths to the village Moses wanted us to see. John Gideon translated for us since many of the villagers spoke only their mother tongue of Dholuo and a little bit of Swahili.

In a tucked-away community called Karao I met Joseph Otieno. He was fourteen years old, quiet and unsure. His tie-dyed red shirt was ripped in various places, his dry skin peeking through the holes. I learned that he had been eight when his parents had died from AIDS, though the look on his face made it seem as though they had died yesterday. Joseph and his little brother lived with their eighty-year-old grandfather.

Joseph was responsible for collecting water twice in the morning before school and twice in the evening after school. He cooked and did the domestic work to assist his ailing grandfather, who wove baskets and sold them to support his grandchildren. If Joseph's grandfather was lucky, he would make seventy shillings a day—less than one U.S. dollar.

Joseph had white scabs all over his arms and legs.

"The scabs come and go," he told us. "These are about three weeks old."

I imagined that the filthy water he drank was making him sick. I also wondered if he was HIV positive.

Joseph said he was quiet because he was always thinking about his parents, wondering what it would be like if they were still alive.

"What makes you smile?" I asked through the help of John Gideon. Joseph said he couldn't really think of anything and that he didn't like jokes. Older kids often beat him and punched him.

"What do you hope for?" I asked, unaware how naive my questions were.

"To go to the hospital." He looked down at his oversize and ragged shirt and added quietly, "And a shirt and some food." Joseph wanted to be a doctor. He was a smart and hardworking student, but he would never be able to afford secondary school.

We followed Joseph and his grandfather to their home. The hut was made from a mixture of mud and cow dung. The floor was dirt. The two eldest children slept on a single bed, and Joseph's two cousins slept on the ground. The grandfather stayed in a separate shelter under worse conditions. I was horrified.

We walked with the women, Joseph, and the other children to a small stagnant pond filled with mud, feces, and algae. A herd of cows stood in the water, one of them defecating into it. Meanwhile, we filled our buckets from the same water source. I watched the children put their buckets on their heads, and I did my best to do the same. Two women helped lift the weight upon my head. I held the sloshing container of disease-ridden fluid and walked with the others back to the village. My neck ached, and my arms lost all their strength. Step by step, I remembered that Joseph and the rest of this community did this four times a day. Even worse, they consumed what they carried.

We then met a woman in a green dress with silver buttons down the front. Her name was Pamela, and she wore a Catholic Jesus charm around her neck. A white wrap covered her shaved head.

As a widow who was HIV positive, Pamela feared she would die and no one would be left to care for her three children. You know something is deeply wrong with the world when you meet a mother who prays that her babies will die before her. Despite the battle for her family's survival, Pamela joined the women's group that was working with Moses and WWG in hopes of bringing clean water to their community. Perhaps if she and her children did live, they could have a better life.

Coming from a culture in which even one coffee drink comes with an infinite number of varieties, I assumed that *choice* was a universal experience. That day I saw differently. Joseph and his community could drink the filthy, bacteria-ridden pond water or drink nothing. They could walk an hour to get contaminated water or another hour to get more contaminated water. Pamela could go to bed with the fishermen who would give food in return or let her children go to bed hungry. In other words, these men and women and children had no choices at all.

After a long, hot morning walking through other villages where WWG worked, we gathered under a towering tree to meet with WWG committee members. A set of chairs was arranged under the shade for the other guests and me. In front of us to the left were about ten men, also in chairs. To our right were about twenty women seated in the dirt. It felt uncomfortably imbalanced as I, because of the color of my skin, was given the status of a man. Lillian sat on the ground with the other women. A small girl with splints on both her legs sat in her lap.

"That's Zinnat," John Gideon said about the small girl. "She was orphaned by AIDS but has also not walked because of clubfeet." He paused, watching her. "Sometimes we must answer God's call to go above and beyond our means."

I learned later that the entire WWG staff were contributing their own money to pay for an upcoming surgery for Zinnat. As a clinical officer (the equivalent of a physician's assistant), Lillian had taken it upon herself to bring Zinnat to her appointments and volunteered to monitor her recovery. I wondered what it would feel like to be so generous when your own finances were so limited.

Moses introduced Joel and me to the gathering, explaining that we were there to listen and learn. The cultural exchange required a formality of speeches, songs, dancing, and testimonies. Over the years, this community ritual would become one of my most familiar experiences.

Several committee members stood up to speak, sharing with us about the water crisis in their community and the work they were doing in partnership with WWG to improve the conditions. They spoke of what they had already done: Elizabeth had trained them in WASH (water, sanitation, and hygiene) practices, money had been raised to pay for sand and cement to build the base of a well, and a number of the committee members were qualified to maintain the hand-pump well, should they ever receive one. The chairlady of the women's group explained to us that a different organization had started putting in a well. WWG had then done their portion of the work to bring clean water to their village, but the former donor had pulled out of the project. The women's group and WWG were one thousand five hundred dollars short of being able to drill the two wells for which they had worked. They asked if we could help.

Under the shade of the tree, the crowd waited expectantly for speeches from us, the visitors. I nervously asked Joel to speak on our behalf, but when he finished, they pointed in my direction, asking to hear from the "lady director." I had spoken at my college graduation, and the experience had been slightly anxiety producing. But standing in front of this village of strangers was one of the most terrifying experiences of my life.

I remembered Joel's words about the good but harmful intentions of Westerners, especially in the form of broken promises.

"Westerners come to a place like Kenya or Tijuana," Joel had said to me on one of our walks together. "Their hearts bleed from what they see; they hear need; they know they have resources back home. They make promises to the poor. Then they get home and realize that getting the resources was harder than they had thought. Or they get caught up in the bustle of their normal life and forget that they made any promise at all."

"That's a harsh assumption," I defended.

"No, hear me out," Joel urged. "Meanwhile, the woman at the river goes about her days with the expectation that the promise will be fulfilled. She waits and wonders. She waits some more. She worries that something horrible has happened to the friend who made the promise. She wonders if she did anything wrong to cause the stranger to break the promise. She eventually accepts that it will not be fulfilled. Then another visitor comes with another promise that sounds similar to the previous one. And then another, to the point that promises become tools for oppression—words the oppressor uses to relieve his or her own sense of guilt in the moment, received by the oppressed as yet another empty gesture."

"Okay, Joel," I said. "I get it. No promises."

"Do you promise to not promise?"

"I promise."

Standing in the shade that day, I had a million and a half promises ready to give, even though I possessed no answers to the unfathomable stories in front of me. Despite all our late-night conversations, and despite having a project with a name, I felt as if we had nothing to offer in real life, especially because I had made The Promise Not to Promise. I understood the urge to tell the community that we would do something. How could I not? I stood up and fumbled through my words. The work of translation required that I speak one sentence at a time, which gave me extra time to make sure I didn't say anything too stupid.

"I want to, um, thank you for taking the time to be with us today." I paused for the translation. "It means so much to hear your stories. It is amazing to consider all the ways you have addressed the challenges in your community." The crowd clapped and whistled in response.

"I am so sorry to hear about your orphan problem and how AIDS has taken your loved ones. We sympathize with you on the challenge of the water crisis and the incomplete water project." The women sitting on the ground nodded their heads and looked at me with expectation. I wanted to help them. I wanted to tell them we would fix the problem. But I knew I couldn't.

"Regarding these challenges, I can't make any promises to you today. Well, actually, I do have one promise to make." I looked back at Joel's nervous eyes. "I promise to take your stories and, well, I promise to share them with our friends in the United States." Joel gave me a look of approval. As I sat down, I saw several of the women smile.

13

Secrets of Change

That afternoon, our Kenyan hosts invited us to lunch in a village home. It was the first of many meals I would share with African friends. It is always humbling to receive tea and food from those who live in extreme poverty.

That first day, about twenty of us crammed into a rectangular hut. It would become a familiar scene to me: eating around a low table in a dark room that had a couple of windows, several wooden chairs with laced cushions, education certificates, and images of Jesus Christ and President Kibaki facing off on the walls.

The owner of this home, Andrew, was a tall, wrinkled man with big teeth and slouched shoulders. As we sat down, he lined three women in front of us for introductions and proudly presented them as his wives. *He has three wives?* I wondered incredulously. Each wife had her own hut in a circle of huts.

I had thought, naively, that polygamy was a thing of the past. Moses leaned over and whispered, "I will tell you later why this is a problem."

The women brought out various dishes, crowding the coffee table between us. Chicken, collard greens, rice, and *ugali* (a doughlike substance that looks like a slice of white clay). They loaded our plates with the food and handed them to Joel and me. No utensils, all hands.

I watched Joel eat and drink all that he was served. I felt expectant eyes on me. I picked up the chicken and struggled to bite the meat from the bone. It felt like rubber, and I wasn't quite sure how to politely consume this bird. When the hosts looked away, I shoved the remaining chicken onto Joel's plate and popped a Pepto-Bismol. In retrospect, I shouldn't have feared a dish that was more local and free-range than anything available to me in my urban American life, but it took time and experience for my ignorant fears to ease.

.   .   .

Moses's team helped me understand that drilling a well was only one part of reducing waterborne diseases.

"What good is it to have clean water flowing from a well when it is stored in a dirty bucket?" Moses explained. "And if you wash your potatoes with clean water, but your hands are still dirty from responding to the call of nature, the people eating your potatoes will still have stomachaches."

"That is why we ensure that all the community members where WWG works learn proper care for water, sanitation, and hygiene. We call it 'WASH.'"

"But what about the communities that don't have clean water?" I asked. "Isn't washing with dirty water just as bad as not washing at all?"

"You do not give a man a truck before he knows how to change the oil," Moses explained. "You do not provide clean water for a community before they know how to care for it and make the most of it."

I learned that the WASH trainings are designed to equip community members with basic information that helps them adopt health-seeking behaviors like hand-washing and clean water storage. Even in places where they don't yet have access to clean water, they can learn healthier practices and creative ways to filter and treat the water they do have.

Moses invited Joel and me to come and see.

With only a stack of butcher paper and markers, a mud-walled church, and a remarkable teacher, my friends in Kenya gave me a new paradigm for lasting change on my first visit there. They sat facing one another on backless benches that wobbled on the uneven dirt of the dimly lit room. The building, offered by the congregation for this gathering, was no bigger than an American living room. Its walls were smoothed with mud and manure. Uneven wood beams from endangered local trees stretched from one wall to the other, holding up the corrugated tin roof that provided shelter from the unforgiving equatorial sun and unpredictable downpours. Brilliant sunlight found its way only through the open door and through scattered holes across the tin.

A roll of masking tape and a red marker made its way from one person to another. Mothers, fathers, teachers, sons, daughters. The women's heads, with closely shaven hair, were wrapped with bright fabrics. Their plastic flip-flops and canvas shoes were crusted with earth. They had been pulling weeds and cutting sugarcane before the sun rose. Colorfully patterned skirts hid the dark leathery skin, while worn-in t-shirts revealed the shapes and sizes of breasts not constrained by Western undergarments. Some women were holding babies, like accessories.

The men looked distinguished, with collared shirts tucked nicely into their slacks. Their shoes were "smart," in their words, the kind of shoes an American businessman would drop off at Goodwill after too many days at the office.

Each participant carefully wrote his or her name on the curved surface of the tape. Maurice. Naomi. Irene. Dennis. Rebecca. Jared. Benta. Each person with hopes, expectations, motivations. Some wanted to be seen as leaders in their community. Some were tired of watching their babies die and had heard that the information in this class could prevent more deaths. Others wanted the certificate that came at the end of the course—they had not had the opportunity to complete anything worthy of acknowledgment, not even primary school.

Elizabeth walked around the circle with her dark skin, perfect smile, and carefully cornrowed braids hanging just above her strong shoulders. She was wearing wire-framed glasses that darken in sunlight. She wore a solid black skirt that ended near her rough ankles and canvas shoes. I learned that if it were up to Elizabeth, she would have been wearing pants, but the church had complained the last time she arrived in what they considered to be men's attire. If the skirt misrepresented her, the words on her neon yellow shirt reflected her greatest passion: SAFE WATER: CONSERVE IT. SHARE IT. ALL PEOPLE NEED IT.

"*Oyawore*," Elizabeth said to the class as she took an open seat on one of the benches in the circle. She invited us to share our expectations of the training. It was quiet at first, awkward. But like the good teacher that she was, she waited in silence.

Maurice cut the silence with the obvious right answer: "*To gain knowledge about WASH.*"

Elizabeth wrote Maurice's response on the butcher paper that was taped to the wall.

"What is another expectation?"

"*To know how to build a latrine,*" said another. It went up on the paper.

"*To improve my family's health,*" said Naomi, a mother of six who also cared for her paralyzed husband.

"*For certificate,*" answered another. Many agreed and nodded their heads.

Others chimed in that they were there for the t-shirt. In a community where people live on less than one dollar a day, a powerful local currency is the neon green t-shirt reserved for those who have completed the training and demonstrated the changes in their home.

According to Elizabeth, the most important outcome was to increase the number of trained community members. The information she would provide in the following five days could very well save their lives.

On another piece of butcher paper, we created our own set of rules for class: *arrive on time, group prayer before class, raise your hand if you have an answer, respect one another,* and *put cell phones on silent.*

Here lay a great irony: this group of people in a mud-walled, dirt-floored room did not yet know basic germ theory, but each of them owned a cell phone that would interrupt the class like any modern meeting if it were not silenced. This community had cell phones but no toilets. I still marvel at that juxtaposition every time I see it.

Now that the Code of Living was established, the class was ready to begin. It was Camp Cheley for sanitation.

Over the next five days—a total of thirty-five hours—Elizabeth guided us through lifesaving information that most of the developed world takes for granted. First, she laid several laminated pictures along the floor of the circle: cartoon drawings of a pile of feces, a fly, a person's hands, a person's mouth, a plate of food. She put them in a particular order: the feces first, then the fly, then the food, the hands, and the mouth. Did the students see the connection? Initially, no. But Elizabeth took a string and connected one to the other. Heads nodded in agreement and understanding. Yes, a fly lands on the poop and then flies onto the food. We then take the food in our hands and put it in our mouth. That is one way that we are getting sick.

Let's try another: pictures of a river, animals bathing in the river, a pile of vegetables, a mouth. The water is contaminated by its proximity to animals. When we wash our vegetables with the river water, the contamination enters our bodies. This is another way that we are getting sick.

Yet another: open feces, a chicken, dishes on the ground, food, hands, mouth. The chicken steps in the poop and then steps on the clean dishes, which then contaminate the food. Of course we get sick.

With those disease pathways in line, Elizabeth revealed a new set of drawings that she introduced as blockages. A latrine, covered food, water-treatment activities, a hand-washing station. She handed a blockage drawing to each participant. They were then responsible for placing their blocking activity between the pictures. Dennis placed his drawing of fenced-in chickens between the chicken and the dishes. Norma's picture of a latrine went between the poop and the chicken. Rebecca laid the hand-washing station between the hands and the mouth.

These patterns seem obvious to Western eyes, but they presented a new way of living for my bright and eager classmates. Seeing the connection between actions and consequences also reinforced the idea that change was within their power.

Every day of class we learned from one another as Elizabeth facilitated lessons through reading stories, writing songs and poems, performing skits (or as they call them, "dramas"), taking notes, sharing ideas, and reinforcing key messages.

Today, my classmates walk around their communities in the neon green t-shirts they earned through their commitment to change. They will proudly show you their hand-dug latrine and adjacent hand-washing station, their drying rack for dishes, their healthy children. And a corner of darkness tears itself away in a place that was considered a lost cause.

Every day I spent in Kenya, I learned more of the complexity of African life: resilient communities caring for one another and trying to make life better despite extreme poverty and disease. I began to realize that the secrets of change are not found in places of power or advantage. They are hidden in the experience and knowledge of the poor.

Elizabeth became a hero to me as she faithfully worked in partnership with community groups to train villagers in healthy practices. Hers was a story I wanted to tell.

•

The following days in Kenya were filled with visits to several more local WWG groups across Kano Plains. WWG showed us how effective it was to work through community groups. Even though Joel and I had yet to decide how Blood:Water would intersect with organizations like WWG, each meeting taught me something more about AIDS and water and poverty and the complexity of it all.

The community visit format would shape the way I and others from Blood:Water would enter communities for years to come. They came with stories to share. We came with a blank notebook in hand. We visited homes and heard testimonies. We answered their questions about Americans, about our families, and about which God we prayed to. True to my original promise, we brought their stories back with us.

The community members emphasized time and time again how much it meant to them that we would come to sit with them, eat with them, dance with them, pray with them, dream with them.

"Most Americans come and tell us what to do," the chairlady of Okana village shared with me. "They make promises to come back, but they never do. They steal our picture and leave."

I had read a lot about how to work with the poor, but in rural Kenya, I first saw the creeds of Gustavo Gutierrez lived out. I saw how Africans like Elizabeth, along with Pamela and Joseph and other community participants, would be the ones to solve the problems of their continent. They were motivated to lead because the challenges of HIV and water were personal for them, and their own Christian faith called them to be agents of love. They had lost family members and neighbors to diseases that were preventable and treatable, and they wanted to stop the losses.

After Joel and I said our goodbyes to the WWG team, we visited other organizations and parts of Kenya. We quickly came to realize that what we encountered with Moses was different than most approaches to water and development. We discovered that many communities had wells, but the wells were in disrepair. Joel asked community members why they were broken and what they were planning to do to repair them. We learned that Outsiders had come in to drill the well. The Outsiders didn't engage the community, and therefore the community did not see it as their project. When the well broke down, the people waited for the Outsiders to come back and fix it.

"Empty promise, empty plate," Jars of Clay wrote upon hearing stories of an American pastor gallivanting through an African village offering large checks and larger moral promises. His actions would not make a lasting difference in Africa because he didn't engage the communities. By contrast, when the people are involved, local leaders show pride in their care for the wells and the health that accompanies access to clean water. This was the type of insight we'd been hoping to receive on this trip.

At the end of our visit, we found the local bus station to return to Nairobi. A fifteen-passenger minibus, the matatu, is the most common form of public transportation in Kenya. The conductor of the matatu recruits passengers, takes payments, and stops the driver when a passenger is ready to get off. The general rule is that a matatu will not leave the station until all the seats are filled with paying passengers.

Joel and I learned the hard way that it requires a bit of cultural savvy to get out of the station. A conductor came up to us to show us that there were just two seats left in his matatu, meaning that as soon as we boarded, the matatu would head out. We paid our fee, got into the vehicle, and all of a sudden five people exited the matatu. Seat fillers. So we sat in the station for another hour and forty-five minutes before we had fifteen real paying passengers. As we drove along, the conductor frequently stopped the vehicle, and more people piled into the hot space. At one point, more than twenty people crammed into the fifteen-passenger vehicle.

For hours, Joel and I sat in the back among Kenyan men, women, children, and an occasional chicken. Smells blended together, a mixture of exhaust, body odor, roasted corn bought through the window, and bad breath. Many Kenyans define personal space differently than Americans, oftentimes meaning there is no such thing. My left foot fell asleep, and my forehead dripped with sweat.

Along the stop-and-go journey, Joel and I spoke quietly about what we had seen and experienced over the last few weeks. He took my brown journal, opened it to a blank page, and wrote, "What will Blood:Water be about?"

We talked back and forth. It was a continuation of our conversations in Tijuana and Spokane, but this time it wasn't distant or hypothetical. It was present and real.

"What if we discovered African-led organizations across Africa that are already doing great work in the areas of water and HIV/AIDS? Could we provide small grants to these organizations and support their growth? That way we can make sure that *Africans* are solving the challenges on their continent."

I still have the notebook in which I wrote what is now such an integral part of Blood:Water that it seems obvious. But in the back of that tightly packed vehicle, it was the first moment that the strategy for our dreaming became clear: if we ever had resources or influence to be a part of this HIV/AIDS and water fight, we would partner with the communities and their existing leaders. We would champion them, listen to them, humanize the experience, and try our best never to strip dignity from another. Our business model would recognize that emerging heroes in Africa know their communities better than we ever could.

Among the sweat and the smell and the growing discomfort of my tingling left foot, I realized that God had just delivered an actionable vision. God had breathed into us his hope for Blood:Water. We had found our foundation and our future.

The matatu continued to jostle us against each other as we let our epiphanies settle in our minds. And even in the grandness of the moment for Blood:Water, I couldn't help but wonder, *Could Joel and I have a future, too?*

⋯

My eyes fought to stay open as I walked off the airplane, jet-lagged and glad that my legs still worked after the twenty-hour flight. I had my passport and forms in hand to present to the customs official who wanted proof that I was bringing no guns, fruit, or terrorists with me from Africa.

"What were you doing in Kenya?" he asked me. When I told him, his response was "I need your shoes."

"I'm sorry?" I asked, convinced that my exhaustion had impaired my hearing.

"Ma'am, your shoes have been to some uncommon places. We need to disinfect them."

I unbuckled my worn-out red Keens that had walked me miles across a land so different than the one I had returned to. The man sprayed my shoes and returned them to me. Too tired to put them back on, I walked barefoot through the Detroit airport to my connecting flight. I stared at my shoes and thought about where they had been. I thought about Atticus Finch's wise words to his daughter, Scout, in *To Kill a Mockingbird:* "You never really know a man until you stand in his shoes and walk around in them."

I thought about Joseph and the journey we took to gather water. I tried to feel what it meant to multiply his story by 14 million—the number of orphans in Africa.

Just briefly, I had worn the shoes of others. Seeing their courage and their offer of friendship humbled me. Recognizing that I could always put my own shoes back on, return home, and order takeout brought me to silence. I also remembered Jesus, the greatest example of what it means to walk in another's shoes. God himself, taking on flesh and walking in the shoes of humanity. To be present with our brothers and sisters in Africa, to understand their suffering, we would need to risk being fully human with one another. I took courage in knowing Jesus could relate to each person's burdens and hopes, even if I could not.

What I could do was tell their stories.

14

The Six Flags Miracle

My routine in Nashville included at least one, if not two or three, visits to our post office box every day. The mail was distributed throughout the day, and I didn't want to miss any deliveries. Since very few people sent checks to support Blood:Water, the visit was usually disappointing. Sometimes I found advertisements and junk mail. Every now and then, I picked up a letter with a check inside from a friend or family member. Their belief in this pursuit carried me through the moments when I doubted the most. Because most days, despite my faithful visits, the box was empty.

The one letter in the box when I returned from Kenya was the one I didn't want. Roger, the consultant from the foundation in Kansas City who had come to our first board meeting, had sent his report to the foundation's program directors in response to our request for one hundred thousand dollars in start-up funding. Roger's conclusion was that we were too risky. His letter read, "Blood:Water has the opportunity to become one of the greatest social justice movements for young people in the church or to die under its own weight." The rejection confirmed that the foundation believed we just didn't have what it would take.

I drove myself to my next house-sitting assignment, found the hidden key in the drainpipe, dragged my Africa suitcase into the living room, and collapsed onto the dog-haired couch. I began to feel sorry for myself. I had come back from Africa with momentum, only to be reminded of how impossible this task was. I still hadn't heard back from the guys in the band in response to the email I'd sent before going to Kenya. I could hear my dad's words at the airport reminding me that I had a home in Colorado should the dream fail.

I thought about Joseph and Pamela and the Kenyan community that had worked so hard to usher health and water through new wells—only to have their partner donor pull out. *Sometimes even hard work doesn't pay off,* I thought miserably. *So many people and forces outside of yourself have to cooperate in order for a vision to become real.*

I was pouring my life into this idea and this dream, but it was impossible for me to do it alone. I felt as if I were on a matatu thinking we were about to take off when I discovered half the people around me were just seat fillers. I opened my journal and tried to pen a prayer to God, but I began to doubt if God was even in support of this crazy path I had taken.

.   .   .

Two weeks after returning home from Kenya, I did the only thing I knew to do next: I got back on the bus with the band. Jars, the crew, and even Bobby welcomed me warmly without acknowledging that we had been on a break. I was still frustrated with them. But America felt different to me after having spent so many days in rural Africa, and boarding a bus in Nashville at midnight granted me familiar comfort. I tossed my duffel to the top bunk. The bus carried us to the northeast while we slept.

I had seen the band perform in clubs, theaters, churches, outdoor festivals, and college campuses. But this time they were slated to perform at Six Flags Great Adventure Park in Jackson, New Jersey. The bus wound around the back gates of the park and pulled up behind a large grandstand where the band would perform in the evening.

Joel arrived around midday to help me report back to the band about Kenya. I probably could have done it on my own, but I continued to seek excuses to see him. I hoped he wanted to see me, too—and I knew he welcomed any break from the research library. I also wanted the support that I wasn't sure would come from Jars.

The band gathered on the beaten couches of the backstage trailer while Joel and I presented our findings. The guys were already on board with the idea of local empowerment. So when we proposed that the 1000 Wells Project should be accomplished through partnerships with local organizations such as WWG, they were sold.

I passed around photos of the WWG team, the Karao village, and Joseph and Pamela. I told them about the fifteen hundred dollars needed to drill two wells in the community. Joel explained the hard work that the village leaders had already done. We shared their stories.

A shot of hope ran through me as I watched the band reconnect with their dream. They led chaotic, ever-demanding lives as husbands, dads, and touring musicians. But I saw them take the time to look at our photographs from Kenya and remember what they had started. Seeing the faces of these new African friends reminded them that the need was urgent.

Dan looked up. "Let's raise the money for the two wells."

"Tonight?" I asked, remembering the grand disappointment from the Indiana show.

"We need to do this. How could we not?"

Joel and I looked at each other like two siblings whose parents just gave them permission to extend their curfew. We needed to come up with a quick plan because the showtime was in an hour.

"Let's just do what we tried to do before, but this time I have a story to tell." Dan's band mates nodded in agreement.

"Are we even allowed to raise money inside a theme park?" Matt, the always-practical one, asked. He tasked Bobby to find out.

About thirty minutes before the show, Bobby came back, holding stacked theme park popcorn buckets in both hands.

"All right, here's the deal, kids," he began. "There is a policy against fundraising here that is not park-sponsored. It gets complicated the minute we try to sell or raise money inside the park."

It didn't surprise me. Empty mailboxes, rejection letters, a disconnected band—and right when the guys were ready to try again, theme park rules stopped us in our tracks. We hadn't raised so much as a thousand dollars in the past six months, so why would we succeed tonight?

"But," Bobby smirked, "I say we do it anyway. If it causes a stir, I'll take the heat."

He turned to me. "We don't have a lot to work with. This is the best I could find." He handed me the popcorn buckets and then gave me a friendly jab in the arm. "Go get 'em, Nonprofit Girl!"

Joel and I split the buckets and ran out to the grassy field where the audience was gathering. I had college friends meeting me at the park for the show, and I recruited them to collect money. We found other fans in the audience who volunteered to help.

That night, Jars of Clay played for seven hundred theme park enthusiasts seated on the grassy spread between two towering roller coasters. For most in the crowd, it had been a long day of lines and screams and cotton candy. Parents and children sipped from Styrofoam cups and snacked from popcorn buckets that looked remarkably similar to money collection devices. The crowd moved along to the band's songs as the roller coasters roared loudly from above. The fall evening was still muggy.

As the band finished, the whole crowd stood, half-cheering, half-shuffling around to gather their items and quickly leave the park to beat the traffic. Then Dan boldly came back to the microphone and asked for a few minutes of their attention.

"Our lives have been turned upside down since the concept of 'neighbor' has expanded itself to Africa," he began. He talked about the numbing nature of statistics—the same words he spoke when he presented at my college. He spouted the numbers off and asked, "What do those numbers mean to us? They hardly mean anything, because they are grand abstractions. But I'm not here to tell you about those statistics. I want to tell you about one person, and her name is Pamela . . ."

And there, in the midst of the Six Flags Great Adventure Park of Jackson, New Jersey, Dan fulfilled the one promise we had made to our friends in Kenya. He did not tell a sob story to induce a guilt trip. He told a story of compassion, hard work, and resilience in the midst of dirty water, orphans, and AIDS—all the while offering dignity and grace to Pamela and her community. I think they would have been so proud, so honored had they been there that night.

Dan continued, "We're not about the abstractions or the hundreds of millions. We are about the one. Tonight, you have the opportunity to make a difference in Africa, to wrap yourselves around these communities, and to show that you care because we are called to love well. We learned recently that one dollar can provide a year of water for one person in Africa. What's amazing about that is that anyone can come up with a dollar. You don't have to be a billionaire or a rock star to affect the life of another. I'd love for you to just take one dollar and think about one person."

My hands were shaking from the excitement and Dan's inspired words.

"If each person here tonight gave a dollar, we would be close to being able to call our friends in Kenya tomorrow and tell them to start digging. You'll find volunteers around holding popcorn buckets. Place your dollar there and think of one person."

The crowd applauded and the band closed with a final song. And hundreds of theme park vacationers-turned-momentary-philanthropists dug into their pockets for dollar bills. Parents handed dollar bills to children, who walked up to us and placed them in the bucket. Someone put a ten into the bucket. Another person, a twenty.

This accidental community did something extraordinary that night as they opened their hearts to the story of another—trusting the invitation from a band they loved—and responded with joyful giving. My small popcorn bucket was filled with crumpled dollar bills, the greatest manifestation of encouragement that I had received so far.

Late that evening, Steve, Dan, Charlie, Matt, Aaron, Joel, and I piled into the back room of the bus with ten popcorn buckets that were overflowing with dollar bills. As the bus rolled home, we unfolded the crinkled offerings and made piles of bills and then stacked them to a hundred and bound the hundreds in rubber bands. Aaron kept the tally as we continued to unfold. Dan was quiet, shaking his head as he laid one dollar on top of another. I wondered what he thought of this direct result of his advocacy. No one else could do it for him.

We waited for Aaron to finalize the count, wondering how close to our fifteen hundred–dollar goal we had come.

With a full grin, he answered, "Six Flags New Jersey has just raised us one thousand five hundred thirty-nine dollars!"

We couldn't believe it.

We gave it a second look, and it was indeed the exact amount of money that we needed, including the wiring fee from our account to Kenya. We would call Moses in the morning with the good news. Over the poor phone connection, he responded with gratitude and noted the privilege of drilling our first well. We no longer lived in the hypothetical. Our words had become water.

The truth was that we had no money, no experience, and no backing to address something as enormous as HIV/AIDS and water in Africa. We were much more likely to live out the latter prediction of the foundation's consultant: we would be a group that died under our own weight. But that night at Six Flags changed all of us—the band, the crew, the volunteers, the audience. It was bigger than us. It had little to do with *us* at all.

On a personal level, since the moment I'd signed on with Blood:Water, I had waited to hear a resounding word from God that would confirm my choice or direct me elsewhere. I never heard a peep, at least not one that I recognized. I often remembered the uncomfortable feeling I'd had in high school when my youth group leader asked what I was hearing from God and I had no answer to give.

And yet, on that crowded bus departing Six Flags Great Adventure, in the company of this unlikely band of brothers, holding $1,539, I heard a voice in the depths of me. It wasn't much, but it was enough. It was a faint whisper that said, *Keep going.*

Part Two

Coming Together

"If you are coming to help me, you are wasting your time. But if you have come because your liberation is bound up with mine, then let us work together."

—Aboriginal activist group, Queensland, 1970s

15

Fundraising by *Harambee*

The money we raised at Six Flags infused the band with a renewed sense of purpose. Though we were still afraid to publicly proclaim our 1000 Wells goal, Dan was making a pitch from the stage each night based on the promise that one dollar provides a year of clean water for a single person in Africa.

I stood anxiously in the back of each venue, hoping he would nail all the talking points on the role we each could play in addressing injustice. Sometimes he crisply made these points in a few minutes. Sometimes he meandered for more than fifteen minutes while the rest of the band fidgeted, ready to get the music going again. But the ask was always the same: one person, one dollar. It was a wonderfully unassuming request, and we were blessed with generous crowds. We began to believe that one thousand wells was a realistic goal and planned for the day we would take the 1000 Wells Project on a national scale.

Every time I returned from a tour, I went straight to our post office box to see if anyone was sending in support. Often the box was empty, but sometimes I found letters with checks inside. I opened the envelopes in my car like Charlie Bucket unwrapping his chocolate bars hoping to find the golden ticket. Inevitably, one of the envelopes held one or two dollars and a note from a child who wanted his or her allowance to help a child in Africa get water. I folded up those sweet letters to take to the children I hoped to see in Africa again one day.

In the meantime, I attended every course I could at the Center for Nonprofit Management in Nashville. I met regularly with my first contact with Jars: Steve Garber. I also sought mentorship from Gary Haugen, the president of the International Justice Mission. I read and read about missions organizations, nonprofits, and people management. I was insatiably curious about how to do the things I didn't know how to do yet—and there were a lot of them. When I reached my limit on what I could do or learn myself, I found people who could help me.

That meant solidifying a board of directors for Blood:Water. Dan, Steve, and I called on the people who had first gathered in Charlie Peacock's living room the year before. We asked if they would commit to meeting quarterly to discuss the national launch of the 1000 Wells Project. We called in others who could help fill the gaps in our knowledge—those from the business world, the medical world, the nonprofit world, and the complex world of politics. We found a seasoned executive named Rich Hoops who had a passion for helping boards. I had been feeling overwhelmed trying to lead a board. In fact, I was so nervous at our first regular board gathering that I made Joel facilitate the meeting. Now with Rich, I had a coach to help me grow into my title as executive director of Blood:Water.

In one of our first meetings as a formed board, Dan shared his desire to cultivate the fundraising efforts of kids, teenagers, college students, and families. We not only wanted to bring water to one thousand communities, we wanted to do it in a way that would be mutually transformative—valuable for our friends in Africa but also for our friends in America, many of whom had never seen themselves as implicated in the lives of people on another continent.

We had an idea for a fundraising model: in villages all over Africa, community groups chip in to help someone in need. Perhaps someone is facing a poor harvest, has a sickness in the family, or has a child entering high school. The group members each contribute a small amount.

In Swahili this is called *harambee,* a time when everyone in a community comes together—those with status, those without status, those with much, those with little—to contribute whatever they can to a collective cause. It is as much about participating in the communal act of giving as it is about the amount that any one person gives. The point is that "we all give together" because we all share our burdens together. I have seen elderly widows bring two ears of corn to a church harambee, and the corn was auctioned off for a few coins toward the collection basket.

As we started Blood:Water, we wanted our method for giving to be just as inspired as the water projects. We believed that through the act of giving itself, a community can be transformed.

Despite some hesitations about whether it would yield results, the board signed off on this grassroots fundraising strategy. Then, as if led by the spirit of communal giving themselves, the members threw a sort of harambee to cover basic costs and provide me with a living stipend so I could move into an apartment. Each board member and band member committed to bringing in one thousand dollars within thirty days, whether from their own pockets or through friends, family, and other connections. And that's how Blood:Water's first donors came to include my parents, Joel's grandmother, Matt's parents and mother-in-law, the band's studio producer, and my college professors.

Over time, this dollar-by-dollar approach became infectious. Social media did not exist then, so we had to rely on word of mouth. At four or five concerts a week, Dan told stories about Africa. Fans graciously responded every time and told others. Jars of Clay became known for advocacy as well as music.

Even people who weren't at concerts started helping. A woman gave up plans of improving her home sprinkler system and instead donated money for a well. Ten-year-olds sent in wads of dollar bills and coins from their neighborhood lemonade stand. Nashville-based musicians took the message on the road and passed buckets at their own shows, bringing in thousands more dollars. People of means contributed what they could, and checks for one thousand dollars and five thousand dollars joined the collection. A group of twentysomethings rode their bikes across the country and raised money in every city they stopped in. The band's recording label donated its staff and supplies to create promotional materials for the launch of 1000 Wells. We were living out harambee.

As a result of this web of generosity, my life in Nashville began to expand. On days when my basement office got lonely, I stopped by the headquarters of the band's label and worked alongside the creative team on our printing projects, making friends along the way. The band began to do more acoustic tours to save money. This freed up Aaron, the bass player, to cut his time on the road in half so he could provide back-end support in the office (as he does to this day, full-time and full-heartedly). A longtime fan of Jars of Clay took a four-month sabbatical from her job in New Jersey to work at our office daily, assisting in any way possible. Dan's wife, Katie, took care of all the organizational correspondence. Collin, a local lawyer who worked for Bono's advocacy organization, provided all of our legal needs for free.

In an act of true sacrifice, two of my childhood friends, Amy and Rachel, moved from Colorado to Nashville to be my social support. We rented an apartment together with my new friend, Autumn, and they cooked me meals and hosted events for Blood:Water. This coming together around the cause gave me the first sense of belonging I'd had since college, other than the tour bus.

Joel continued to squeeze in medical school while spending hours on the phone with me late at night as we evaluated our programmatic plans for Africa. I stopped by the Haseltines' several evenings a week, where Katie fed me, their boys entertained me, and Dan and I caught up on the work we needed to do together. A collective missional spirit guided each of us.

A film company made an unexpected contribution. A couple guys in the band introduced me to Ken Carpenter, the president of Franklin Films, who happened to go to their church. One afternoon I met with him to talk about a video we wanted to make to help launch 1000 Wells. He showed me other promotional videos they had done for other artists' causes. We brainstormed for a couple hours on what a video for Blood:Water would look like. Eventually, Ken realized we were getting ahead ourselves. "I should have asked this earlier, but what is your budget for this, Jena?"

I knew little about negotiating, but I was pretty sure that my first answer should never be my actual answer. I had a total of fifteen hundred dollars.

"We have about a thousand dollars for this," I answered professionally.

Ken put his pen and notebook down. Clearly, it was game over.

"Well, actually, we could spend fourteen hundred dollars." As if I could use one hundred dollars for leverage later.

Ken leaned toward me across the table, looking at me more as a loving parent than as a business associate.

"Jena, do you have a sense of how much money it costs to do the films like the ones I just showed you?"

My face got hot.

"Five thousand?" I said sheepishly.

"Times ten," Ken said, assuming incorrectly that I was good at mental math.

"Seriously?" I asked, acting surprised because I was. "I'm so sorry. I am very new at this." My naïveté was wasting this man's time and diminishing whatever credibility had got me the meeting.

I closed my notebook and shuffled my things into my backpack.

"You know what, Jena?" Ken added. "I love the Jars of Clay guys, and I really respect them."

"Me, too," I said, standing up.

"More than that, I believe in the power of their message and what you guys are trying to do in Africa. My family went to Africa last year, and we have never been the same."

"Thanks, Ken." He was so kind in the midst of an embarrassing scenario.

He continued, "I am convinced that we can make you a powerful video that will represent Blood:Water as you want it. I also believe that the message is so powerful that you will inevitably raise money for the cause."

"I am seriously not holding out on you, Ken," I assured him, wondering if this was part of a sales pitch. "I don't have any more than fourteen hundred. Well, I have fifteen hundred, but I don't think that makes a difference."

"My point is this," Ken continued. "Let's make a deal: we make the video for you, and then you pay us back when you have the money."

Harambee! Generosity is a powerful force in the world, maybe because it is always a risk. It is also invigorating, even exciting. As people who enjoy giving away their resources have discovered, it's one of the best rushes you can experience.

Within two months, we had assembled a nationwide team of more than a hundred people—people like Ken who believed along with us that this mission would take off.

•　　　•　　　•

During this time, the band and I traveled to San Luis Obispo to attend a water conference hosted by one of our new partners, Lifewater International. Joel drove down from San Francisco to meet us there, and I joined him on his way back to the Bay Area. We planned to spend a few days in between Joel's classes to finalize more partnership agreements with Africa-based organizations such as WWG. I was excited to have more time with Joel and wondered if we might be more honest with each other about our feelings.

On the four-hour drive back, we debriefed the conference and talked about what we wanted to tackle that week, but our conversation faded with unusual speed. We listened to the radio and looked anywhere but at each other as we drove along the 101.

"So, I wanted to talk to you about something," Joel finally said, still keeping his eyes on the road.

Thank goodness, I thought.

"I've really enjoyed the way our friendship has developed over the last year."

"Me, too," I said, maybe too quickly. I could feel my heart pounding.

"I want to be sensitive to your feelings. I don't take them lightly. I worry that they might confuse our friendship and our partnership."

Huh?

"I've started to feel some pressure," he continued. "You are a wonderful friend, and that's how I see you. As a friend." He glanced at me, waiting for a response.

You bring this up with three hours left in a car ride together?

My head throbbed. I felt claustrophobic—not just in the moment, but in anticipation of the next several days we had planned together. *Could I please jump out of the car and walk back to Nashville now?*

"I *do* like you," I confessed. "But I haven't known if it was mutual." I couldn't believe we were having this conversation. "Which obviously it's not," I added.

"Oh, man," Joel said nervously. "We should have prayed together before talking about this." He went on to say a bunch of nothing to fill the space, to soften the blow. "All reason points to you," he said in conclusion, offering me a phrase I would analyze for months.

Ultimately, I told myself, *reason means nothing if feelings are not there.*

I can't remember how we got through the next three hours. I was trying hard not to let on that I was crushed. Somehow we found our way out of our forest of feelings (or lack thereof) and made our way to other topics. But in the back of my mind, I continued to process our conversation. I felt so alone. That night when we arrived in Berkeley, I sneaked out and called my dad and my best friend, Amy.

"Joel has a plan for his life," Dad explained, as if he'd been anticipating my call. "You complicate that plan."

"I know it hurts, dear," Amy said. "I'm proud of you for telling him you like him."

I decided to make the most of Joel's answer and continue to enjoy our friendship—at least until I could cry freely back home. He and I went to coffee shops and studied and read and worked on Blood:Water plans. We climbed a mountain with his friends. We ate Thai food at midnight and laughed a lot. We continued the long conversation about community development. We went to see Bob Dylan perform. (I had gone to Best Buy three weeks earlier and bought *The Best of Bob Dylan* to be sure I knew a song or two.) We had extravagant dinners with his roommates from Chile and Spain. I bonded with his neighbor, Cora, who was studying Buddhism and loved talking about religion.

One evening, Cora asked me if it was hard to have a long-distance relationship.

"Uh, we're not dating," I responded. She was shocked. *Thank you, Cora.*

And we prayed together—and included the request that God would guard our friendship.

When I returned to Nashville, I hung a quote up on my bedroom wall:

I get up.
I walk.
I fall down.
Meanwhile, I keep dancing.

—Hillel

Blood:Water was taking off. I had a job, friends, and a lot of work to do. I chose to let my feet keep bouncing.

.   .   .

We officially launched the 1000 Wells Project in February 2005, coinciding with the band's twenty-city spring tour across the country. It had been nearly eighteen months since the band and I had first met. Our vision was always clear, but our pathway was not. We'd known tears and doubts and the sheer effort of trying to be taken seriously. But then, slowly, something eased. Whether by sweat equity or grace or a little bit of both, the world around us began to soften on our behalf.

We worked on the 1000 Wells launch materials up to the last minute before the tour. By the time we hit the road, we had customized an experience for each show that included videos, stories, and opportunities to give. We had defined our values, assembled a body of volunteers, and committed to our mission statement. We had built relationships with Africa-based organizations like Moses's Women's Water Group. We had developed detailed plans about providing grants to these organizations to drill wells and train communities in WASH. But we needed the resources to do it. We were all eager to have enough money to turn our focus away from marketing and toward the water projects themselves.

At the end of each show, Dan made his ask, and then the volunteers and I circulated with buckets. Afterward we piled into the bus and poured the wads of cash on the back table. Each night, in each city, we opened dollar bills that translated into water for thousands of Africans. Whether they were crisp, sticky, or torn, we unfolded each one as if it were a love letter.

We believed that we were receiving dollars that would probably have been spent on things like coffee or a great new ringtone—at least, that's what we would have spent them on. Just as our African brothers and sisters needed relief from the AIDS and water crises, our American brothers and sisters needed reprieve from trivial wants and worries.

The woman who had given up her sprinkler system wrote a letter thanking us for reminding her about what truly matters in the world. A touring musician who had raised thousands of dollars for Blood:Water explained how exhausting it had been to self-promote every night. He found delight and freedom by sharing the stories of communities in Africa and inviting his fans to dig into the story with him. Through giving, people were seeing themselves differently, seeing their lives differently. Generosity has a redemptive nature. It is a dual rescue.

I became a familiar face in our local bank, approaching the counter with a smile and a backpack full of cash. The tellers initially avoided eye contact with me, hoping to be spared the laborious task of running the bills through the counting machine. But after several visits, the people behind the counter showed interest in counting our cash and finding out details about the show and our updates from Africa.

Within the first three months of launching the 1000 Wells Project, we had raised twenty thousand dollars. And then our harambee took on a national scale.

I received a call from a Christian radio station based in northern California. K-LOVE Radio had five million listeners across the country, and they wanted to help. They hosted annual telethons on behalf of designated charities, bringing in as much as fifty thousand dollars in one day through many small donations. I couldn't imagine what it would mean for us to raise that amount.

The band, Joel, and I arrived at the Sacramento station at 4:30 in the morning. With coffees in their hands and stories on their hearts, Dan, Matt, Charlie, and Steve faced one another in the station's recording booth to tell K-LOVE's east coast commuters about the clean water crisis. The DJs urged their listeners to call in and contribute. Within a few hours, we received reports that more than fifty thousand dollars had been raised. That was as much as we'd hoped to raise the whole day. At that point, we realized that we were in for something bigger than any of us could have imagined.

We had eighteen hours left to go in this twenty-one-hour telethon, so the band decided to take shifts, and they asked Joel and me to help them out. I had never spoken on live radio before, and it was hard to imagine hundreds of thousands of listeners behind the microphone, but I took cues from the band, and they coached me along the way.

We had a tally sheet of donations as they came in through the call center. Staff at the station brought in rounds of coffee and food throughout the day. Artist friends like Third Day, Derek Webb, and Sara Groves heard about what Jars was doing and called in on the air to encourage giving. My mom and dad sat by their living room radio all day, listening to their daughter on the air and calling their friends to tune in and give.

The energy at the station was palpable. None of us could believe the response. In one day, we had brought in two hundred fifty thousand dollars for the 1000 Wells Project.

I flew back to Nashville a couple days later on an evening flight, overwhelmed and exhausted. At midnight, I pulled into the post office parking lot and walked into the well-lit hallway. I turned the key to our box, as I did every day I was in town, but the lock resisted. I jiggled it a bit and yanked the metal door open. Piles of envelopes fell to my feet. I broke into tears.

The once-barren mailbox was overflowing with letters from people across the country who had heard us on the radio. I slid down against the wall and sat on the floor of the vacant hallway, opening one envelope after another. Checks for twenty dollars. Checks for a thousand dollars.

Fifty thousand additional dollars for Africa lay at my feet.

I read with gratitude the names and addresses of the supporters nationwide who had just given us the opportunity to partner with Africa to end the HIV/AIDS and water crises. Our grassroots approach was working. Like our friends in Africa, we were aggregating small donations to address the needs of our neighbors. We were giving together.

And so the world bent. I leaned into it with joy.

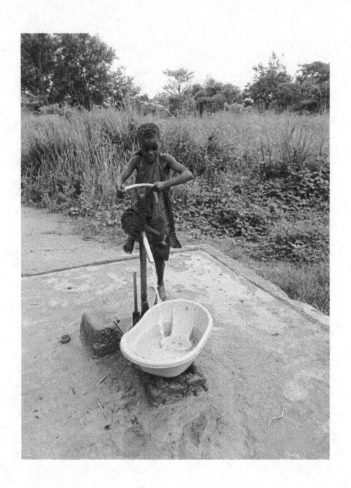

Project: No. 127

Location: Sangala, Central African Republic

Partner: Water for Good

Currently the only operating water organization in Central African Republic, Water for Good's team maintains a network of wells around the country like this one in the Sangala community, which serves a village of 337 people and is still operating today in spite of the civil conflicts that continue to destabilize the nation.

Photo Credit: Jon Allen, Water for Good.

16

A Bridge of Water

Less than a year after Joel and I had traveled to Africa with only a notebook of questions and possibilities, we were on our way back with the means to begin the work of 1000 Wells. We set out for five weeks to visit the East African partnerships that our initial fundraising efforts had supported. Joel planned to travel from East Africa to Uganda for a brief consulting job with another nonprofit. He found any excuse to get out of the classroom and into the communities, like I had in college.

This time, Moses picked us up with ease from the Kisumu airport. Elizabeth, Lillian, and John Gideon were with him. We embraced with a sense of homecoming and drove straight to greet the communities across the Kano Plains. As our bodies ricocheted inside the vehicle on the cratered road, we told the team about launching 1000 Wells, the radio campaign, the concerts, and the generous response from Americans.

Moses's delight was palpable. "Just wait until you see the work that the communities here have done," he responded with his big smile.

We returned to Karao village where we had met Joseph, the orphan with the skin infections. As we drove in I could see about twenty-five men and women seated under the shade of a large tree. They rose with enthusiasm and began to sing in their local language, what I would later know well as Dholuo. With hands in the air and hips shaking side to side, a small group of women approached the truck. I jumped out and greeted them with hugs and handshakes and then joined their line to dance.

And as I danced, I saw it. Just beyond the dirt path was a well. *Our* well. *Their* well. While the band and I were mobilizing money and volunteers across the United States, the Women's Water Group team came alongside this Kenyan village to donate materials, help them organize, elect a committee, and complete their training in water, sanitation, and hygiene. Finally, John Gideon and his team came to drill. Now five hundred people were benefiting from this source of water—something they could not have afforded without the funds from Blood:Water or cared for without the support of WWG.

To show off the new well, a child was pumping water into a bucket. The community continued to sing. The women grabbed my arms and pulled me closer. I cupped my hands to the water and felt joy running through my fingers. I put my hands to my mouth and tasted this outpouring of love.

News reporters who portray Africa as a lost cause would be gratified to stand among a community of dreamers and doers in Karao village singing and dancing around a fountain of clean water.

I spotted Joseph in the crowd, wearing the same torn red t-shirt he'd had on a year ago. Our young acquaintance showed us where the scabs on his arms had disappeared. He told us how his stomachaches had vanished.

"We are implicated in the lives of others, even those we have never met," Steve Garber had often reminded me. Here in Karao village, I knew he was right. In a globalized world, our actions affect people oceans away. Eight thousand miles from home, I began to understand.

In the midst of a village in Kenya, I had neighbors whose lives were better because of the tour-bus dreams of four guys in a rock band. Water had become a bridge.

With John Gideon serving as our translator, Joel and I told the community that thousands of Americans supported them in their building of the well. "Thousands of Americans participated in a big harambee," we said. "And this time, it was for you."

That day alone we visited four more villages to celebrate more new wells, water committees, and health clubs in primary schools. Elizabeth had been training hundreds of community members in the same class-room style that Joel and I had witnessed on our first visit with WWG. She proudly introduced us to the graduates of each community. They would be the ones to ensure that the wells remained functional, that their neighbors practiced health-seeking behaviors like hand-washing, and that the water was properly stored. I remained convinced that the true transformation was happening within those training sessions. The wells were a catalyst for the community to work together to accomplish something. The biggest reward was the way they learned to work together.

We prayed with our new neighbors, giving thanks for the changes, and we ate together in communion. By day's end, my small stomach was bursting from five separate celebrations—a sensation I have known many times since. Joel and I retired to Moses's home, where his wife Irene insisted that the two of us stay with them and their children.

Moses's home village of Okana is about fifteen miles south of Kisumu city off a small dirt road. The homes of Okana are primarily huts, each about 300 square feet, but Moses's residence was a gated property with a solid-structure home of about 1500 square feet. His small living area included the typical Kenyan wood-framed couches with square foam cushions covered in faded bed sheets. Lace coverings adorned the furniture.

"You may feel the call of nature in the evening when you are sleeping, but you are safe to respond here in the night." Moses pointed at the stick-walled latrine at the end of the property. "We have a Maasai who has killed a lion with his bare hands and a spear. They are the most reliable security in all of Kenya. That guy is here every night to ensure you are safe."

"You have lions here?" I asked.

Moses laughed at my misunderstanding. "No, you will not find a lion here. But we have thieves, and thieves are worse than lions."

We walked to the metal hand-pump well in the front of his home. This was where we would gather water for a bucket shower, brush our teeth, fill our water bottles for the day, help with the dishes, and wash our clothes. It was a luxury to have a private well, and Moses knew firsthand the gift of clean water. He was on a mission to ensure other communities in his area would have the same gift.

Even though we were in the business of providing safe water for communities through the provision of hand-pump wells, I was skeptical about drinking from one myself. I had heard horror stories about Westerners whose immune systems couldn't handle what Africa had to offer.

Joel was a shining example of an American who refused to let any place or circumstance make him uncomfortable. He did as the Kenyans did, and I would do my best to follow suit in the days ahead, though I would still sneak in a Pepto-Bismol or two.

Moses grabbed our bags and placed them in a bedroom that had one full-size bed under a mosquito net. He proudly told us that the wood-framed bed had a brand-new mattress that he had just purchased from Nakumatt, the Kenyan equivalent of Target. The bed had a dust ruffle on top of the mattress, serving as the bottom sheet, with a floral sheet folded at the foot of the bed.

Joel and I looked at each other with confusion. *Did Moses think we were a couple? Or was this the only bed they had? Would he be offended if we spoke up?* I was too shy to ask.

My Christian college had rules against cohabitation. My parents had even stricter rules. Here I was in the middle of an African village trying to live out my commitment to God, being asked to go against another commitment from my upbringing.

Joel seemed to get over the situation quickly, and he was soon asleep on his side of the hard mattress. I, on the other hand, sat on the edge thinking, *There's a boy in my bed.*

A year before, I would have been glad to be put in the same room as Joel. It certainly would have fulfilled my daydreams of falling in love with a boy in the middle of Africa. But the truth was, my relationship with Joel had changed since our first visit to Kenya when I was hopeful for something more between us. Our friendship ran deep, but the question of romance had faded since our California car conversation. I also had a growing network of support in Nashville and beyond, so I was less dependent on Joel for conversation, support, or professional guidance. In the meantime, Joel had settled into medical school and had rekindled a friendship with a girl he knew from college. We both needed less of each other.

I kept my headlamp on and tried to read myself to sleep, but I was too uncomfortable with my rule-breaking circumstance. Eventually, I moved my folded sweatshirt pillow to the foot of the bed and slept on top of the sheet that covered Joel, thinking about how ironic it was that by the time we'd found nearness in Moses's guest bedroom, we had already separated.

.　　.　　.

The days were full. We visited about three villages each day, spending several hours in each place for conversation, dancing, learning, and—without fail—eating. Everywhere we went, the women had prepared meals the size of a Thanksgiving dinner and insisted that we partake.

"You have given us a gift of water," they would say, "so we must give you the gift we can offer." They joyfully presented their dishes of chicken, goat, ugali, rice, collard greens, and *githeri* (roasted corn and beans). I came to think of this as "missionary eating" and willingly gained ten pounds that summer from the marathon meals the generous families across the Kano Plains prepared. I later learned that many rural families ate chicken only a few times a year, at weddings or funerals. This was the greatest gift they could give.

Moses, Joel, and I had spent late nights in Moses's living room with mugs of African tea and shortbread biscuits ("bis-*quit*," Moses would say, just like he would say "mos-*kweee*-toe), discussing the issues of the day. Joel and I were full of questions, observations, and ideas about how our partnership could revolutionize the concept of aid and charity in Africa. We dreamed about empowering each woman in a village with education about water, sanitation, and hygiene. She could sell clean water at a market, and then use income from the water to start poultry projects or a sewing business. We would be the advocates for grassroots development work, and these communities would be the ones to prove its power.

Those nights in Moses's living room invigorated my soul. No longer pretending to be something, Blood:Water had reached the beginning of real partnership, real relationship, real projects, and real funds. Joel was the conscience of the organization, ensuring that we wouldn't lose sight of the equalizing, humanizing approaches to the work. Moses was the practitioner, giving us the ability to put our shared ideas into action. And I was the engine, doing all that I could to keep this start-up dream moving forward.

Along the way, we learned more about Moses's story.

"Irene is not my first wife," he told us. I assumed he was speaking of polygamy, something that I was now aware of. "My first wife—we were young," he began. "I was in the U.S. for schooling in engineering. We had a child together, a happy marriage. And the dangerous roads took her life." It took me a while to understand that she'd died in a car accident.

Moses spoke with an air of dismissal—a cover of protection, I imagined. "But with Irene, I am pleased. She is my joy," he said, looking her way toward the cooking room of the home. "I have found happiness as the director of WWG and the husband of Irene."

More recently, Moses's twin brother died. "It was too late when he found out he was positive," Moses reflected. "His body was already dying when they told him it was AIDS. I could not even grieve his passing."

Moses's culture discouraged the presence of a twin at a funeral. It reminds the grieving too much of the one they have just lost; they believe that if a twin is at the funeral he will also die soon.

One night as Joel and I sat with Moses in his living room, the lightbulb hanging from the ceiling went out. The sound of the rented generator went silent, and the house went dark. I fished around for my headlamp while Irene lit the oil lamp. It was not uncommon for the generator to run out of gas, and we knew we were getting the royal treatment to have any semblance of electricity in a place like Okana.

We finished our conversation by the light of the oil lamp, and Joel and I found our way back to the close quarters of our room. By the light of the headlamp, I noticed movement in the suitcase on the floor. Driver ants had found a half-eaten Luna Bar and flooded my pile of clothes. I squirmed as I imagined insects crawling on my skin. I could do little at that moment but set the Luna Bar in the corner of the room and hope that the colony would move with it.

As I was inspecting the ant damage in my suitcase the next morning, Moses knocked on our door. With a look of anguish, he reported, "It wasn't out of fuel. They stole it."

"The generator?" we asked. "Who stole it?"

"I don't know," he lamented. "But there are thieves out there. They must know that foreigners are in our home."

We were collectively defying common practice, both for Moses to host Americans in his village and for Americans to forego the Kisumu city guesthouses for a village residence. Despite Joel's hopes of living in solidarity together and Moses's desire to show us African hospitality, we had caused a village stir and had inadvertently brought trouble to Moses.

"Irene has booked you rooms at a guesthouse in town," he apologized. "We are not wanting to take any more risks on your safety." I wondered how much our visit had truly cost Moses and his family. We were embarrassed about the fuss they made on our behalf; they were embarrassed for disappointing us with African realities. I was secretly glad to have a room of my own without the inconvenience of a boy or biting ants.

As I rolled my suitcase to the corner of the small Kisumu guesthouse room, I wondered about this notion of equality that Joel continued to champion. Were we simply pretending to be on equal footing when, in reality, we were so far from one another's experiences? Moses's greatest efforts to make his home comfortable for us would never equal the homes in which Joel and I had grown up. It still felt like roughing it to bathe from a bucket and squat in an outdoor latrine lined with sticks. And yet, the rest of Moses's community didn't even have the luxury of mattresses, linoleum floors, and Maasai guards.

So many times I have tried to enter a world I did not come from, whether in the homeless shelter in Colorado Springs or the orphanage in Tijuana or a village in Kenya, but I cannot wash the white from my skin or leave behind the culture I represent. In those early days I believed, somehow, that I could eventually blend in. I have yet to achieve that.

.   .   .

As Joel and I traveled, our education soared. Our biggest lesson was that we should not simply drill a thousand holes in the ground and bring water up out of the earth. That had been our original, vague idea, but in our travels we saw so many broken, unrepaired wells that we knew simply digging wells alone would not be the answer.

We realized our true goal was for one thousand communities in Africa to have access to clean drinking water. Each place we visited needed a different route to water access. In arid communities, borehole wells would be ineffective. Other villages had broken wells, so repair would be most appropriate. Rainy areas needed catchment tanks to harvest roof runoff. Some communities had rivers and ponds but no way to treat this water, so filtration methods would be most helpful. Bringing clean water to one thousand communities required a patchwork of methods based on individual needs. It required us to be connected to local knowledge of landscape, culture, and environment. It would take more time and care, but it was the only way to make a lasting change.

We saw in person what we had begun to articulate on the matatu on our first trip to Kenya: as a young American organization, we did not know best what African villages needed. Africans did. As we'd seen with Moses and WWG, local partner organizations had the better view. They, not us, had the personal knowledge to implement our one thousand water projects. We would provide funding and guidance, but they would decide the best technologies and water methods for their communities.

We also learned that addressing water alone was simplistic. Water is one leg of a three-legged stool if you're trying to achieve real changes in health. The other two legs are hygiene and sanitation. More people in Africa lack access to toilets than water. As Elizabeth knew when leading WASH programs, open defecation and poor hand-washing can cancel the benefits of clean water. Holistic health transformation for each community we served would mean improvements not only to water access but also to sanitation and hygiene practices.

We knew all of this would be less satisfying to our donor audience. A well sounds much more romantic than a water filter or hygiene training. Focusing on a variety of methods to get water, educating people about how to use that water, and using the power and insight of local organizations would be more difficult from a logistical standpoint as well, but it would have more impact. It would also be more expensive at the beginning but more sustainable at the end.

With these lessons in hand, Blood:Water started giving small grants to Africa-based organizations focused on water, sanitation, and hygiene. We were different than other organizations in that we made sure our support covered not just the water technology, but also the community mobilizing efforts of WASH, drilling rigs, transportation vehicles, staff salaries, and financial systems improvements. For example, an organization we worked with called MOUCECORE would reach communities in the hills of Cyanika, Rwanda, to construct rain tanks as an act of post-genocide reconciliation. Another organization called Divine Waters would reach refugee camps in Lira, Uganda, amid the country's chronic civil war. Seeds of Hope International Partnerships in Zambia converted slum-dwelling river water into clean water through the construction of cement-based biosand filters. Water for Good in Central African Republic would drill wells for a marginalized pygmy population. Water for Women's Groups in Kenya would partner with village committees in water provision across multiple communities.

Blood:Water was feeling more and more like a reflection of my own dreams, rather than just a response to Dan's vision. And each visit with our African partners confirmed my conviction that true change comes only when Africans are free to be the heroes of their own stories.

Project: No. 172
Location: Kanyonyera, Rwanda
Partner: ARAMET

Safe water often comes from far away, using earth's gravity to pipe water from sources higher up. The 140 families in Kanyonyera community were collecting water from Lake Cyohoha and using it without any kind of treatment. Now this gravity-fed system pipes safe water directly into their village, and a water committee made of community members manages it in collaboration with local government. *Photo Credit: Barak Bruerd, Blood:Water.*

17

Image Bearers

Joel and I were in an internet café in Kisumu when he received an email from his college friend Milton. As we ate lunch, Joel told me Milton's remarkable story.

Milton is a Kenyan from a rural village called Lwala that is tucked away on a dirt path seven miles from a main road. His parents were schoolteachers and strong leaders in their community. Despite their humble origins, Milton and his younger brother, Fred, were exceptional students who were admitted to the most prestigious boarding school in the country. Following graduation from secondary school, Milton was awarded a scholarship to attend Dartmouth College in New Hampshire. He didn't, however, have the means to get to the United States. The people of Lwala lived on less than one dollar a day—a nine hundred–dollar plane ticket was impossible.

But in Africa, you don't belong just to your parents, you belong to everyone. The village organized a harambee, selling their chickens, cows, and sugarcane crops to send their son to the United States. *Now, when you go there,* the community told young Milton as they invested their hard-earned bills and coins into his future, *don't you forget about us.*

Milton's younger brother, Fred, also earned a scholarship to Dartmouth. While the brothers were in college, their mother Margaret died of AIDS. It was devastating, and many people on campus were aware of the brothers' loss, including Joel, who had met Milton on a spring break service project in Nicaragua.

Now, eighteen months later in 2005, their father, Erastus, had also died. Seven thousand miles from Lwala, the two brothers had become orphaned in a land that was not their home.

Milton and Fred emailed Joel to say they were on their way back to Kenya for the funeral. Knowing that Joel was already there, they invited him to visit them in Lwala. Despite my resistance to changing our prearranged travel schedule, Joel and I shoved ourselves and our suitcases into a public matatu for the eighty-five-mile stop-and-go journey of people and luggage and chickens on our way to a place that couldn't be found on a map. We had written the name Rongo, a nearby town, on a piece of paper, and at each stop we showed it to the conductor. He shook his head and waved us off. We weren't there yet. I shifted my weight from one hip to the other and prayed we weren't making a foolish decision.

We arrived at a curve in the highway where twenty other matatus were loading and unloading from the shoulder. The conductor snapped his extended hand in our direction and gave Joel a nod.

"This is Rongo?" Joel asked, and the conductor affirmed with, "Ehh."

We walked down the side of the highway, rolling our suitcases toward the small town. In front of the local bank, Milton, Fred, and an American classmate of theirs named Caitlin were waiting for us. Milton's eyes were wide and his smile was bright with the excitement of seeing Joel. Fred was tall, with a thin face, and he was shier than his brother. They were both chuckling at seeing two Americans come out of a matatu.

"Man, you are like real Kenyans!" Milton laughed with congratulations. I received his comment like a badge of honor.

The six of us piled into the back of a low-riding pickup truck and drove a short distance on the highway before turning onto an unmarked dirt crossway. The path looked more like a hiking trail than a road for vehicles.

We bounced and jerked, like kernels popping in hot oil. I gripped the edge of the truck and tried to keep my suitcase from falling out.

Milton slammed his hand against the truck door, "*Omera, pole pole!*" he yelled in a mix of Swahili and Dholuo. The driver slowed down.

As we drove, we saw villagers on foot and a few on rusty bikes with metal seats. Like the places Moses took us, the villages were scattered with mud huts that had thatched or tin roofs. Children walked barefoot while men and women wore their finest collared shirts. Goats tangled in their own ropes grazed on bushes, and boys with sticks herded bulls with lethal horns. Children in Goodwill clothing chewed on stalks of sugarcane and ran alongside the truck yelling *"Mzungu, mzungu!"* (White person, white person!)

In contrast to the Kano Plains, however, these villages sat among the lush greens of banana trees, grass, and bushes, like the rolling hills of Tuscany. The air was cool, and the landscape of fields, hills, and greenery was idyllic. *It looks like Eden,* I thought. This place was something special. I could feel it. I didn't know it then, but the bed of that truck included the community of my future. The road we were taking, I would take a hundred times again. I was coming home.

Milton greeted people as we jostled by. *That's Mr. Abuya. This is my aunt Grace. Pastor Samson, Oimore!* Small kiosks made of crooked wood and rusted tin sold Coca-Cola and Safaricom phone credit. We passed a brick building with open-air windows and children inside.

"This is where I attended school," Fred said. "Our mom used to be a teacher here."

Used to be a teacher, I thought. *Used to be.* Not because she is retired. I thought of my own mom and couldn't imagine speaking about her in the past tense.

The curves of the road became windier until we arrived on a small compound where four huts circled a grassy area.

"*Karibu* Lwala," Milton said. Welcome to Lwala.

Five women emerged from their respective huts and greeted us with full-bodied hugs and high-pitched calls of joyous noise. They began to sing, *Wail-come the vee-zee-tors, wail-come. Wail-come the vee-zee-tors, Wail-come, Lwala village!* I loved it already.

Milton and Fred's parents' home was nicer than the surrounding huts. Made of cement, the building had glass windows, a spacious main room, and cushioned furniture. There were two bedrooms off the main room, and Joel and I were each given our own room with a bed and a mosquito net.

I met Milton and Fred's older brother, Omondi, and their younger sisters, Grace and Flo. Their grandmother, Dani Sarah, and their aunts Yuka, Grace, Flora, and Baba joined us for a banquet of ugali, chicken, rice, and chapati. The gathering was rambunctious and joyful. Joel and I were welcomed as if we were joining the family. I felt the same comfort I had found in the homeless shelter. *This is my place.*

Amid the fellowship, it occurred to me that no one mentioned their parents; no one seemed to be grieving. I whispered to Joel about it, wondering if he noticed the same thing.

"The funeral was last week, and that was the place for mourning," he whispered back. I later learned that traditional mourning used to last several months, accompanied with various rituals. But once HIV increased the incidences of death, communities abandoned tradition and only mourn on the day of burial. People then try not to show their grief after their loved one is buried.

Today, after I've lost many African friends to death, this attitude makes more sense to me. Lwala may appear to be a rural paradise, but its physical beauty masks underlying social ills.

Kenya has an HIV prevalence rate of 6 percent, but in the region where Lwala is, the prevalence rate is 16 to 20 percent, which means that almost one in five adults is infected with HIV. Two of them were Milton and Fred's parents. So my handshake out of every five touches the hand of someone harboring a silent killer. Children in this part of Kenya are almost twenty times as likely to die before the age of five than children in the United States. The leading causes of death for children are malaria, HIV, dehydration caused by diarrhea, measles, and malnutrition. All this leads to an average life expectancy of about forty-six years for this county. (Kenya's national life expectancy is sixty-one years.) By virtue of where you are born, your life span is cut in half. In Lwala, death is so common that bodies are brought home from mortuaries each Friday afternoon. It would be difficult for a community with those circumstances to thrive if they gave grief more attention. *And yet,* I wondered that evening and many evenings since then, *does ignoring grief cause different kinds of pain?*

I knew that many factors in rural Africa escalate the spread of HIV/AIDS. Polygamy, wife inheritance, gender violence, and girls' inability to attend school are among them. Also, circumcised men are much less likely to contract HIV, but many cultures, such as the Luo culture in Lwala, do not practice circumcision. But the greatest challenge I saw in Lwala was the stigma associated with HIV, just as Dan had told us at Whitworth. I remembered Bill, the HIV-positive man in Spokane, who'd said his community ostracized him when they knew his status. As in Moses's village and all over Africa, HIV is seen as a curse. No one must know.

In the following days of that first visit to Lwala, Joel and I met a woman named Leah who appeared to be in her late thirties but was actually ten years younger. She had a bright smile with failing teeth, a long handsome face, and deep-set eyes. Leah's appearance was so frail that it was easy to wonder if she was HIV positive.

Leah wore a brightly colored wrap around her head. Her smile was as labored as her breathing, but her welcome was profound. She invited us into her home, a typical hut with dirt floors, mud walls, and a corrugated tin roof and door. It was dark inside as we sat across from one another in the small room. She told us that her husband, Oyugis, had died suddenly after showing signs of sickness for about two years.

"We loved each other," Leah said. "He was a handsome man. Hard-working. A loving husband. Also a loving parent to his children." She said that she didn't know the cause of his death. She has simply been left as a widow with her three children.

It did not look as if Leah was strong enough to take care of herself, let alone her kids. She moved slowly through her home as she poured us tea and laid out a plate of tea biscuits. It was hard to imagine that Leah was just a few years older than me.

In our time together, Leah never said the words "HIV" or "AIDS," but she did acknowledge that she was sick with symptoms that were similar to what her husband had suffered. She had not admitted her sickness to any-one in the community. Most people probably suspected something, but no one spoke of it. If Leah wanted medical assistance, she would have to travel far from Lwala, which she couldn't afford to do.

I don't know what it was about Leah that captivated me, but she made a deep impression. Her story mattered. I wished I could do more for her.

. . .

Caitlin, the other American woman who was there volunteering for the summer, and I were some of the first white women to visit Lwala. We im-mediately attracted attention from the other women, who stayed with us in the living room after dinner one evening. The ladies wanted to touch my straight black hair and Caitlin's red curls and fair skin. They sat close to us on the couches, their colorful sarongs wrapped high on their waists, their t-shirts decorated with logos of American baseball teams and church events from the nineties.

Joel went to bed, but Milton stayed with us around the oil lamp in the living room, serving as our translator of both language and culture.

The conversation moved its way to questions about being a woman in America.

"What is the name of your husband?" they asked me.

"My husband?" I laughed. "I'm not married. I'm only twenty-three years old."

"But you should be married by now," they responded. "You should be bearing children." It became real to me that women in rural places around the world live in circumstances different than my own. The average age in the room that night was twenty-two, and most of the women were mothers of at least three children. In the United States we assume that marriage usually comes after education, and we consider teenage mothers young.

I remembered a conversation that Lillian, the health promoter, and I had had as we visited the WWG communities. She had spoken about the cultural pressure for girls to marry, even before completing their education. Lillian expressed to me the loneliness she encountered because she wanted to stay single in her twenties so she could pursue her studies as a nurse practitioner. She told me this with embarrassment, as if she had confessed a desire to join a traveling circus. As an ambitious young woman, I was sensitive to the equality battles that women in the United States fight. But I could see that our complaints paled in comparison to the cultural obstacles that equally ambitious young women like Lillian faced.

Those of us sitting around the living room were curious about one another's differences, so the conversation continued. "Do the women in America share a husband like we do?"

"No, we are a monogamous culture. A man takes only one wife."

"How does the man choose the woman?"

"We call it 'dating.' A man and a woman who have mutual interest in each other spend time together and are romantic with each other. If it goes well, it leads to marriage. If it doesn't, they each move on and try again with someone else." Here I was, the girl who hardly dated, posing as the resident expert on American romance.

"Ehh," they half-gasped, half-laughed. "You *are* polygamous! You just practice it like it is like serial polygamy."

They were on to something. It turns out that most Americans do have more sexual partners in their lifetime than their African peers. Even though I wasn't one of those Americans, I thought about Joel asleep in the other room and wondered who my someone else might be.

Caitlin and I asked them about AIDS. Did they know how it was contracted? The women were hesitant to answer, but Milton rephrased the question and encouraged them to guess. Some of them answered that it was from sex. A couple of them said it was from someone else cursing you.

"How is Lwala being affected by AIDS?"

"People keep dying and no one is talking about it," they said as we sat in the home of someone with two family members who had died of AIDS.

"Have any of you been tested for HIV?"

They shook their heads.

"Do you have access to condoms? Do you know that they can help prevent the spread of HIV?"

The women looked confused and continued to dialogue with Milton as Caitlin and I watched with curiosity. Milton finally turned from the fast-paced Dholuo conversation to us. "They said they have heard of condoms but have never seen them. They said that if they had access to condoms the men would never use them. The men would probably beat them for suggesting something like that."

Caitlin and I exchanged glances of horror.

"Do your husbands beat you?"

They laughed, slapping their hands upon their thighs. "Ehh."

"All of you have a husband that beats you?" Caitlin asked again in disbelief. They all nodded their heads.

"What are the reasons they beat you?"

Milton relayed their answers: refusing sex, or disobedience, or when their husbands were drunk. Caitlin and I told them that in America, it is against the law for a man to beat his wife.

To this, they responded, "American women are more civilized than us. We African women are too unruly." They laughed and believed what they said. Milton's eyes got big as he looked at us. It seemed that most of the information he was hearing from his own community was as surprising to him as it was to us.

The three of us tried to explain that geography and culture should not determine whether or not a person is valuable. Milton spent time in a long dialogue with the women, his eyes continuing to bulge. He laughed in his own discomfort.

"Okay," he told us, shaking his head. "They are saying that there is a story in the Bible where Noah has three sons—one black, one white, one brown—and the black one is cursed. Then God curses Africans and their descendants to slavery, and as a result they are less civilized and less blessed than white people." Milton paused. "That's their justification for being beaten by their husbands. They believe they are supposed to accept the curse of God."

There is no such story in the Bible. This legend loosely refers to an Old Testament account of Noah's son Ham, who is cursed for a transgression. It is a story, however, that some have used to justify the oppression of those with black skin. Most of the women in the room were illiterate, so their knowledge of the story had to have come from someone telling them. They were churchgoing women who spent the Sabbath in the pews of the church with songs and prayers and attentiveness to whatever the village preacher spoke. Knowing that most Africans came to Christian faith by way of colonialism, I feared that, in an act of oppression, the story of Ham had come from outsiders who had been there decades ago. Lies handed down through generations still shaped the thoughts these women had about their own value.

I asked the women what they would change if they could change one thing in their lives. About half of them said they would go back to being young girls so they could be educated and not get married. The other half said that they wished they were men. They wanted their husbands to know what it felt like to be beaten, overworked, and abandoned.

It's easy for outsiders to simplify the problems of Africa to issues of laziness or corruption or drunkenness. As Caitlin and I sat there with these women, I realized how little I understood. While Burlingame, California, had handed me a world of opportunities, Lwala had handed these women tremendous limitations.

Each of the women showed tremendous strength, beauty, and resolve. And yet they accepted the abuses. I thought of the residents of the homeless shelter in Colorado Springs who had believed the messages delivered to them: they weren't good enough; they were failures; they deserved to be on the streets. The same sentiments seemed to exist in these women. They believed they deserved to be treated like property—they couldn't imagine anything different.

That evening marked the beginning of a new set of questions for me: *What part of someone else's culture am I supposed to respect, and what part am I supposed to disrupt? How do I know the line between my truth and someone else's truth?* I continue to struggle with the answers.

It was 2:00 a.m., and the women would have talked through the night, but Caitlin and I were exhausted.

"They are saying that they have never had a place to talk about such things," Milton relayed back to us. "They are grateful."

But I felt that Caitlin and I were as grateful as they were. As I went to bed that night, I realized how much I still didn't know.

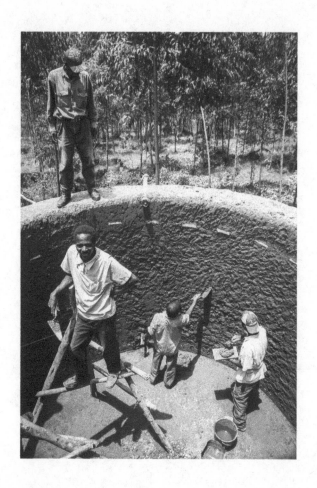

Project: No. 251

Location: Runaba Secondary School, Rwanda

Partner: ARASI

It is estimated that 443 million school days are lost each year globally due to water-related diseases. Blood:Water partnered with local organization ARASI to construct water systems like this one, which benefitted more than 1,800 children in two schools, many of whom spent two hours before school fetching water. *Photo Credit: Barak Bruerd, Blood:Water.*

18

Daughter of Lwala

In the living room of his parents' home the next day, Milton pulled out a set of blueprints for Joel and me to see. "This was my father's dream."

The plans he showed us included a long building with five rooms. Each room was labeled with a word: EXAMINATION, CONSULTATION, LABORATORY, ADMINISTRATION, KITCHEN. They were drawings for a clinic, right there in Lwala.

"We have pushed sick people in wheelbarrows for hours to the nearest facility," Milton reflected. "If this clinic existed, my parents would have had access to care that would have saved their lives."

We folded up the blueprints and followed Milton out of his parents' home, up a small trail, and through two more homesteads before reaching an open plot of land that looked as though the crops had been harvested and the land tilled.

"Well, here it is." Milton smiled proudly as we looked over the stretch of dirt.

Perhaps if I'd been ten years older, I would have seen that plot for the challenge that it was: the dying wish of an HIV-positive schoolteacher in an extremely poor and overlooked community. This area didn't have running water or electricity or paved roads. It was central to nothing but sugarcane fields and peasant farmers. Realists would have thought about what a clinic, located down a dirt path in a last-mile community, would cost to run over time.

But I was twenty-three. And I lived in a world in which dreamers, artists, and believers were the ones who made the greatest contributions to humanity. The foolish ones.

As Milton, Joel, and I stood upon the expanse of the barren land, we could see it. We could see the clinic that would bring hope to a community wrought with loss. A place that would save lives and equip men, women, and children with knowledge, health care, and medicine. We could see it because the community, right before our eyes, was beginning to build it. A group of young men stood in a line, passing large stones from one person to another. Others pushed wheelbarrows of sand from the distant river up the hill. This small community was responding to their beloved friend's dream, in his memory. They labored with hope that their futures could be different.

Joel and I looked at each other with excitement as we saw yet another example of a community taking ownership of their future. I felt alive with possibility.

.   .   .

Focused so intently on the 1000 Wells Project, Blood:Water had yet to determine how it would respond directly to HIV/AIDS. Lwala came to us like a gift.

"Milton, do you still live in New Hampshire?" I asked one day, realizing I was learning a lot about Lwala but knew very little about him.

"Oh, no," he responded. "I graduated two years ago. I'm in medical school at Vanderbilt."

"In Nashville?"

He nodded.

We laughed, realizing that we lived a few blocks from each other. Yes, this partnership with Lwala could continue. Another bridge handed to us with generous providence.

Just before Joel and I left, Leah walked through the cornfields to pray with us. She held my hands. "If we do not live to greet one another again," she stated with the seriousness that one knows only when looking death in the face, "we know we will be together in heaven."

But I want to see you again on earth, I thought. *I want to return here again and again.*

As I got on the pickup truck again, I spoke in basic Dholuo to wish the women well.

"*Nyasaye ogwedhu,*" *God bless you,* I told them. "*Abogombou ahinya.*" *I will miss you very much.*

They cheered and called back to me, "*Oriti NyaLwala.*"

"What did they say?" I asked Milton.

"They have given you a name," he said, laughing. "They are calling you *NyaLwala.* Daughter of Lwala."

.   .   .

The final leg of our trip took us to a world of even greater brokenness, and greater fear, across the Nile.

When Joel and I had planned to visit our new projects in Uganda, I didn't realize that we were heading up to northern Uganda, a place where the Lord's Resistance Army had waged guerrilla warfare for almost twenty years in villages all across the region. In the capital of Kampala we met up with Edward and Vincent, representatives of our local partnership, and drove five hours north to a place called Lira, just on the outskirts of the violence.

There we stood in a displacement camp that held 1,300 people who had limited food, unreliable water, and fading hope.

"All the people in the camp rely on this water source," Vincent said as he showed us the community well. "But the pump broke, and it sits here, useless. In a place like this, they can't raise the money for a repair.

Even if they could accumulate what they need, no one trusts anyone to keep it."

"How much would it cost to fix this pump?" I asked.

Vincent spoke to the camp leader and the crowd standing around us. After much debate, he had an answer. "They think it would cost ninety thousand Ugandan shillings," he said. "About sixty U.S. dollars."

That night, Joel and I shared a meal with Edward, Vincent, and their colleague Tonny to debrief the day. Our lodging was a small guesthouse two blocks down from the camp. I was full of questions. I had spent so much time focused on war against HIV/AIDS and the water crisis that I hadn't considered what it's like to know physical war, too. If you're living with the sheer terror of abduction and rape and child soldiers, you're not going to take time to learn about how to wash your hands properly. I lay awake that night, realizing that my worldview had been shaken yet again.

Why is it that I have every physical need met? I asked myself. *Why is it that I get to leave this camp and fly home to a place of freedom and abundance? How is it ever possible to apply ideals to reality?* These were hardworking, loving people who faced disease and discomfort every day, who had no home because rebels had driven them away, who cared, empty-handed, for starving children. They didn't complain. They just tried every day to survive.

The next day, I made sure that Blood:Water would cover the cost of the well repair. It ended up being 140,000 Ugandan shillings—just about one hundred dollars. I knew it wasn't going to be the fix we all wanted it to be. It also went against our ideals of long-term development. But sometimes best practices are less important than mercy.

．．．

Joel and I had been in East Africa for more than a month. I had seen, touched, smelled, and encountered the reality of extreme poverty. I was closer to grasping that more than a billion people live on a dollar a day, that poor countries are unable to address their own development because they are funneling all their funds toward debt repayment to rich and unforgiving countries, that preventable diseases continue to steal lives by the millions, that human beings still terrorize one another.

I had walked with women who carry filthy water on their heads for miles every day. I sat with people living with AIDS who knew they would not survive because they could not access medical care. I saw mothers whose babies died of malaria because they could not afford a mosquito net. I met orphans who could not pay the pennies needed to go to school.

Each day on that trip and every trip since then, I saw people whom I would never see again because they would not survive. I carried more and more heavily the burden of knowing how easy it would be for those with resources to give to those with little—and how that assistance would dramatically change this continent. The actions of these communities and local organizations were humbling and extraordinary. But they could not do the work without help from nations and individuals who hold resources in abundance.

I returned home with more stories to tell.

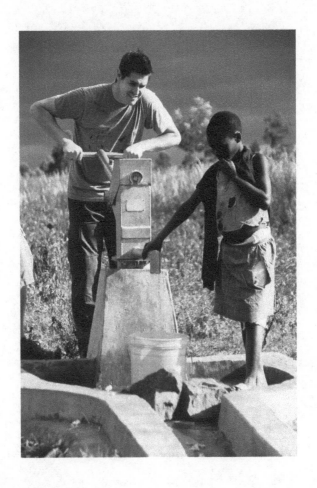

Project: No. 285
Location: Lwala, Kenya
Partner: Lwala Community Alliance
Blood:Water cofounder Dan Haseltine pumps water from the first safe water source in Lwala, Kenya. This pump sits outside the Lwala hospital, funded by Blood:Water in 2007. *Photo Credit: Barak Bruerd, Blood:Water.*

19

The View from the Clouds

In November 2006, I found out that my dad was going to be in Washington, D.C., on business during one of my upcoming visits to meet with board members. We met for burgers at Union Station's Thunder Grill, just off the main hall of the Mass Ave. entrance of the airy station. We talked football and books and shared stories of our recent travels. As we were finishing up, Dad asked me if I remembered our daddy/daughter dates on Saturday mornings in California.

"Of course," I said. "Those hash browns at Carl's Jr. were the only fried food we could sneak by Mom."

"And to think now we're dining together in Union Station." Dad wiped his face with the cloth napkin. "There's something I've been wanting to talk to you about. But I don't want you to take it the wrong way."

"Okay," I said, shifting in my seat.

"Mom and I couldn't be more proud of who you are and how you are serving the Lord with your whole heart. Just look at what you have been able to achieve at such a young age. And here you are, jet-setting around the world."

I had no idea where Dad was going with this.

"We've been behind you since the day you wrote the proposal to the band. And we're still cheering you on, of course."

Now I was nervous.

"But," he sighed. "I'm worried that Blood:Water has become your whole life, that there is nothing left for you beyond it."

Not what I expected him to say.

"It *is* my whole life, Dad," I defended. "It's my calling."

"I believe that there is more to your calling than Blood:Water."

"Okay," I said cautiously.

"You know that the army was my Blood:Water. It aligned with my values and the vision I had for my life. It gave me the ability to serve my country, see the world, rise beyond the conditions of my childhood. It was all-consuming, and I loved it."

"I know, Dad."

"But everything that the army gave me paled in comparison to what my life became when I met your mom and had Jessica and you and Eric."

"So, you want me to get married?" Now I was getting annoyed.

"Not today, but someday. I can't tell if that's something that you want in your life. It just doesn't seem like you're interested in dating."

"I'm not interested in dating," I confessed. "I'm interested in Blood:Water."

"I know, Jena Roo. And I'm not here to give you dating advice. But I have a small challenge for you: keep doing what you're doing right now, but maybe a year from now, consider keeping your heart open for someone else. I'll let you off the hook for another twelve months, but after that, I may bug you a bit more about it."

"Okay, Dad," I said politely. We gathered our things and browsed through the Hudson News bookstore together before we said our good-byes. I took the escalators down to the metro, thinking about my dad's challenge.

The truth was, though I had a lot of community in Kenya and a lot of Blood:Water connections, I did long to be in partnership with one other person. Though I felt peaceful about the end of my nonexistent romance with Joel, I was missing the dream of that possibility.

Then my junior high insecurities surfaced. *Wasn't the disconnect between Joel and me a reminder me that compatibility is hard to find? Was I really cut out for romance in the first place? For one thing, how would I find the time?* Despite all my questions, I realized that Dad was right: I did hope for more beyond Blood:Water, I was just too afraid to pursue it. I was afraid it wouldn't come true.

.   .   .

Back in Nashville, our mailbox remained full. Aaron and I moved the Blood:Water offices out of the church basement to a larger donated office space. We hired a small staff and began to build the infrastructure required for growth. Our partnership with WWG and Moses continued to thrive while we forged new partnerships in Kenya, Uganda, Zambia, and Central African Republic, each new connection teaching us more than the one before.

In the midst of the rush we felt at Blood:Water's momentum, Lwala became an integral part of who we were. Joel and I had sensed the region's significance when we'd first arrived by pickup truck. Our love for the place and the people had only grown. Joel's ambivalence about medical school only increased as his desire to be in Lwala became clearer. He decided to take a year off from school to partner with Lwala in its vision for establishing health care in the village.

Lwala captivated the band, too. Within months of their first visit, they were back on the road raising money for a village that their audience would not be able to find on a map. Soon after, in the fall of 2006, Blood:Water provided sixty thousand dollars for start-up funding for the clinic in Lwala. All our stories began to weave into one another.

In January 2007, I took Steve Garber and his son Elliott; Charlie from Jars of Clay and his wife, Sonja; and two other artist advocates to see the efforts that Joel and the Lwala community were making toward building the clinic. Though it takes more than twenty-four hours to get to Kenya, the flights from Nashville to Nairobi became as unremarkable to me as any commuter's drive to work.

I had discovered that a routine allowed me to feel at home even with the disorienting experience of international travel. So on this trip, as on any other trip to Kenya, I arrived at the Nashville airport two hours before my flight. I spent my time at the gate finishing up last-minute emails, calling my bank, and calling my nervous but encouraging parents. In Detroit, I ate at the sushi restaurant in Terminal A and then walked back and forth along the terminal before the eight-hour flight to Amsterdam. I watched one movie on the way across the ocean and then took a Benadryl and slept for the rest of the flight.

Sleepy-eyed and groggy after we landed, I continued on with my usual Amsterdam routine: brush my teeth, wash my face, buy bottled water at an absurdly high price. Then I stood in line with the Blood:Water group to board the KLM 565 flight to Nairobi, which was another eight hours.

"Jena?" said someone in the line ahead of us. A handsome young man with dark hair, a perfect smile, and brilliant blue eyes behind his designer-framed glasses waved at me with enthusiasm.

"Hey!" I answered, waving back.

"Who is *that*?" Charlie asked me, elbowing me teasingly.

"I have no idea," I whispered with a smile. Perhaps the Benadryl from my previous flight was still hanging on. He looked familiar, but I couldn't place him. He stood on the other side of the security check and waited for me to come through. Charlie agreed to help me out.

"Hey, I'm Charlie," he said, extending his hand to the mystery guy.

"I'm James," he replied, shaking Charlie's hand. "I met Jena in New York in November."

Yes, of course. I remembered. Two months before, I had been in New York for a global water event at the United Nations. I invited my friend

Scott Harrison to join me. Scott was on a similar mission to provide water for the world's poorest through his new organization called charity: water. We had spent a couple days together in New York, and as I was leaving his office, I needed directions to the airport. James, who was volunteering for them, had just walked into the office. He was headed to Uganda the next day to film projects for Scott's upcoming fundraising gala. James's jacket was soaked from the pouring rain outside, and he advised me to take the subway instead of trying to hail a cab. He even kindly wrote down the trains I needed to take to get to JFK.

The Amsterdam–Nairobi flight was uncharacteristically empty, and passengers spread out to enjoy full rows of the baby blue seats. About an hour into the flight, I walked around the plane to check on my traveling team. I walked past James, who had a book in his hand and a row to himself, and he invited me to join him. He shifted to the window seat, and I took the aisle. As I sat down, I asked him about the book he was reading.

"Oh, man," James said, as he handed me the small paperback *Beasts of No Nation* by Uzodinma Iweala. He leaned his head back in exhaustion.

"It's so intense, so well written. It's from the perspective of a child soldier, but I have to keep putting it down. It's so painful." He looked over and smiled at me. "I'm grateful for an excuse to take a break from it."

I handed the book back to him, and we began with the obvious why-are-you-flying-to-Kenya introductions. I learned that James was a twenty-nine-year-old classically trained actor working in film, television, and theater in New York City. I wasn't surprised—he was as good-looking as the guys from *Dawson's Creek* that my girlfriends and I had had crushes on as teenagers. Not the kind of guy you would expect to see on a plane to Africa.

James told me that spending his college summers in Central Asia and Latin America had given him a passion for communities in the developing world. When he moved to New York seven years ago, he supplemented his acting career by running a private tutoring business for some of the city's wealthiest families and decided to donate a portion of his profits to education initiatives in Africa. He believed that education was one of the greatest launching points for rising above extreme poverty—especially for girls.

"I'm a bit of a Robin Hood."

"Except for the stealing part, right?"

"Yeah," he laughed. "Okay, more like if Robin Hood were a social entrepreneur."

After his recent travels to Uganda, James was considering a career shift from acting to international development. This trip to Kenya would help him determine that; he was on his way to volunteer in a school in a Maasai community for three months.

We talked more about Uganda and realized that the refugee camps he visited in the northern part of the country were the same ones I had been to a year before.

"I came to realize that no matter what direction you take in your life— be it acting, business, or any job you may love—you still have to take into account the fact that places like northern Uganda exist," he said.

James picked up the small novel on the seat between us. For a moment, he looked down and fanned through the pages of the book with his thumb. "Or that stories like this are not just well-written fiction, but that they represent real accounts of injustice in the world." He put the book down and rested his head back against the seat.

"I guess I continue to live with that tension," he said.

I know exactly what you mean, I thought.

James looked out the window. "Hey, now, I've talked the whole time we've been flying over southern Europe," he said. "It's your turn."

I wasn't ready to share. James's stories intrigued me and I wanted to hear more. I tried to stall, but it didn't work.

"You have to talk until we get past Libya," he said, "or at least until we're over the Mediterranean."

I shared briefly about founding Blood:Water with Jars. I told him about sending the band my proposal from my college duplex, the invitation they gave in response, and my move to Nashville.

"Wait," James interrupted, "you were *twenty-one* when you started this?" He made me feel like the most interesting person on the plane. "What made you do it?"

I was suddenly grateful that Libya was still hundreds of miles away.

I shared about the homeless man in San Francisco, my failed efforts as a nursing student, my college activism, and how my faith convictions led me to this particular vocational path. James continued to smile as I spoke. He chimed in with comments and observations that made me feel unusually understood.

"There's this quote that guides me," I explained. "It says that the place God calls you to is the place where your deep gladness and the world's deep hunger meet."

"Frederick Buechner," James answered. "I have a shelf full of Buechner." We both smiled.

As our view out the window of the Boeing 777 gave us glimpses of the Mediterranean Sea, the edges of Libya, and then the vast deserts of Egypt and Sudan, we discovered shared dreams, values, and interests that wove our unique narratives into mutual worldviews. We shared about our families and our upbringing, our college experiences and our social justice heroes. We found commonality in our respect for Paul Farmer's work and our convictions about the preferential option for the poor. We both found our way in the Presbyterian church and loved the writing of Anne Lamott. Our conversation rode into the night until we crossed Ethiopia.

And just like that, six hours passed.

As we parted in the Nairobi airport, I handed James the book I was reading, with a note inside. To my surprise, James handed me a note in return.

For the next week, we sent text messages to each other on our cheap Kenyan Nokia phones—a recent luxury for international travel. When James's vehicle broke down, leaving him and his driver on the side of the road through the night, he texted: "Only by being stranded on the side of a dirt road in the middle of the Kenyan night can you truly appreciate the stars." I looked up from my hut in Lwala village and texted him in agreement. Twice, we tried to talk by phone, but our calls crossed when I was in a village gathering and when James was in a school meeting. We sent one more friendly text exchange before I returned to the United States.

Despite the obvious connection James and I discovered, I was certain that my life would not be compatible with that of an actor from New York City. Once I returned to Nashville, we stopped communicating. I didn't expect I would ever see him again.

·   ·   ·

Dad's challenge clock didn't start for another nine months, but as an overachiever, I went ahead and took it up anyway. Two guys asked me out within a week of each other. Jonathan was a personal trainer at my gym, and we would chat together on occasion during workouts. Rodrigo was from Mexico and was part of my neighborhood running club. I didn't know either of them very well, but I was open to getting to know them better.

In the strangest of coincidences, both guys asked me out to Predators hockey games. The dates were friendly—and boring.

"Have you been a longtime Predators fan?" I asked Jonathan as I grabbed a handful of popcorn from the bag we shared. The Predators were hosting the San Jose Sharks for the first play-off game. I like sports, so I was looking forward to the game.

"Hockey's not really my gig," he answered, with a sip of beer. "But when the tickets are free, it's easy to root for them."

We watched more of the game.

Jena from the top of South Arapaho Peak (13,397 feet).

Jena attending a Jars of Clay concert in San Francisco, 1997.

Meeting Jars of Clay at Whitworth University,
Spokane, WA.

The junk bunk.

Meeting on the bus (*left to right:* Jena, Matthew Odmark, Stephen Mason, Dan Haseltine, Charlie Lowell, and Aaron Sands).

Dan and Jena on the air for the K-LOVE radio campaign.

Jena, Joel, and a community group at the site of a well.

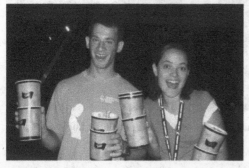

Joel and Jena holding popcorn buckets of cash at Six Flags.

Jars of Clay and Jena at the site of a well in Kenya (*left to right:* Stephen Mason, Matthew Odmark, Jena, Charlie Lowell, and Dan Haseltine).

Jena, Edward Kiwanuka, Joel, and Tonny Okullu visit an Internally Displaced Person (IDP) camp in Lira, Uganda.

Jena and a community member in Rwanda.

Jumping rope with school children.

Lillian and Zinnat after her surgery.

Well driller, John Gideon.

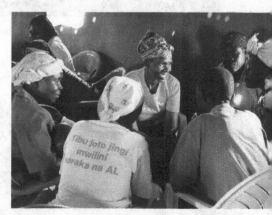

Leah facilitating a WASH training.

Elizabeth inspecting a family latrine.

Participating in a community WASH training.

Charlie Lowell, Steve Garber, and Jena celebrating at a well dedication ceremony.

Jena and her dad, Gus Lee, celebrating Veterans Day in Washington, DC.

James and Jena in Brooklyn, NY.

James and Jena received a goat from a community in Kenya as a wedding gift.

Jena and Milton Ochieng' in front of the clinic in Lwala, Kenya.

James and Jena on the Lwala Community Hospital compound.

James unloading from the plane in Amboseli National Park.

Brooke Baxter (*left*) carrying water with children in Lwala and with her colleague, Emily Anne Patt.

Standing in a dry dam during the drought in Marsabit.

Jena and a community member near a limited water source in Marsabit.

James and the Ochieng' brothers (*left:* Fred Ochieng' in dark suit, *right:* Milton Ochieng' in gray shirt and tie) celebrate with the Lwala community on the opening of a new maternity ward.

Jena's parents visit Lwala (*left to right:* Gus Lee, Diane Elliott-Lee, Jena, and James).

Jars of Clay receives the Gospel Angels Award at the DOVE Awards for their work with Blood:Water.

"What about you?"

"Um, I don't know a whole lot about the team this year. I'm originally from California, so I remember going to a Sharks game and getting to meet some of the players afterward."

"Oh, cool."

"My high school in Colorado had a really good hockey team. They won state when I was a senior."

"Nice."

I returned home, proud that I had gone out, but more certain than ever that I would never find someone interested in what I felt passionate about.

Later that night, I flipped through my journal in search of the note that James had given me when we parted in Nairobi. On it, he had written the web address of his personal blog, *Notes from Africa*. I opened my laptop and discovered James's account of his first two months in Kenya.

To my surprise, this actor from New York City was a beautiful writer. He used vivid detail to describe his experiences, taking me right back into the ideas we had shared on the plane. He told stories about the noble dreams of his students who could hardly afford their school uniforms, stories about the sounds of the birds and wildlife near his village home, stories about trying to make the plays of Shakespeare alive to the students in his classroom, stories about struggling to find the words to pray with a student who had been abused and then abandoned by his family. I read every entry, savoring his words, suddenly motivated to reconnect with him.

I looked at my calendar. *When will I be in New York again?*

I sent a quick email, our first communication since Africa, and we decided to meet up the next time I would be in the city, which was just a couple days after James's return from Kenya. I planned to visit New York for a Sunday night Jars of Clay show at Irving Plaza. I invited James to the Jars concert, and we also planned a breakfast for the following day.

That Sunday marked the most rain the city had experienced since 1882.

A rare spring northeaster brought more than six inches of water to the city. James's apartment was four blocks from Irving Plaza, and he invited me to come find shelter from the rain before the show. As soon as my five o'clock meeting finished, I called James for directions to his apartment.

"I'll come get you," he offered.

I stood like a drowned rat outside Irving Plaza as James walked quickly in my direction, well-dressed for the rain. He looked different than he had on our plane encounter; he had a trim beard and wasn't wearing his glasses. He was more handsome than I had remembered. We hugged each other and laughed about the weather and agreed to move quickly out of the rain. James insisted that he carry my heavy backpack.

"Did you bring a library with you?" he asked as he slung the brick-like bag over his shoulder.

"Sorry," I laughed, walking close to him under the umbrella.

We hurried up Irving Place toward a gated park in the middle of the drowning Manhattan neighborhood. He pointed to a stone statue of a man within the park.

"Have you ever heard of Edwin Booth?" James asked.

"Any relation to John Wilkes Booth?" I joked.

"He's his brother."

"Oh," I said. *Lucky guess.*

"Edwin Booth was a famous Shakespearean actor, and that statue in the middle of the park is him. When his brother killed Lincoln, Edwin retired from acting out of shame. But years later he came back to the theater and played Hamlet, which was his signature role. He was terrified that the audience would boo him off the stage or even riot. But when he finished the first soliloquy, the audience welcomed him back with a standing ovation. It was a sort of artistic redemption. The story is that Edwin was so overwhelmed by the audience's grace that he fell into his chair weeping. The statue tries to capture that moment. I love it. Anyway, he is overlooking Gramercy Park, which is a fancy place. You have to be a resident of Gramercy in order to have a key. You would not believe who has walked through here."

"Like who?" I asked, as James continued to guide us along the side of the gated park.

"Well, Steinbeck used to live here. And the Steinway piano family. Some famous actresses like Julia Roberts and Uma Thurman have lived here, too."

We crossed the street and ran into the lobby of a towering Episcopal church to take shelter. The bottoms of my jeans were dragging with water. James shook the umbrella by the door and then walked toward the elevator and pressed the button.

"So, this is where I live," he said with a smirk.

"Wait, what? You live in a church?" The elevator arrived, and James opened the door. We shuffled in.

"St. George's allocated an entire apartment floor for a few guys in the church to fix up so it could be a comfortable place for people associated with the church and be a part of the neighborhood."

"So, Steinbeck, Julia Roberts, and you?"

"It felt like a privilege before," he answered, "but I just lived in a Maasai village for the last three months. So now it's just ridiculous."

We walked out of the elevator and entered James's 1,500–square foot apartment, which, by New York standards, might as well have been a mansion. He gave me a tour of the apartment and introduced me to his roommates.

In our hours together before the concert, we dove into conversation as we had on the plane just a few months earlier. James shared a short film he had made of a Kenyan student named Damaris, and he told me about the other stories that affected him. Having just returned to the United States after three months in Kenya, James was wrestling with a lot of new questions and insights.

We attended St. George's evening service together, shared a sushi dinner, and headed to the Jars show. During the concert, I stole a moment backstage with Dan and Charlie to tell them about James.

"Jena, you know you're not allowed to date, right?" Dan joked. "We've kept you on task for so long. We can't lose you now!"

We all grabbed drinks together after the show, and the band generously took the time to get to know James.

The next morning James and I stretched breakfast into lunch and then coffee until James had to go to work. As he ran off to tutor, James handed me Anne Lamott's newest book, returning the gesture I had made at the end of our flight to Kenya.

As I stood by the gate of my delayed flight from LaGuardia that evening, I called my dad. "I just wanted you to know that I'm taking your challenge seriously," I reported.

He laughed. "Somehow, I figured you would."

Project: No. 318
Location: Cyanika, Rwanda
Partner: MOUCECORE

A community of 7,000 people situated on the side of a volcano; the women and children of Cyanika spent up to 8 hours a day collecting water from a lake 5 miles away. Blood:Water partnered with a local organization to help bring 100 percent water coverage to this community . . . one rain tank at a time. *Photo Credit: Barak Bruerd, Blood:Water.*

20

Learning What Love Requires

With James on my mind almost as much as Blood:Water was, I flew to Rwanda with two colleagues to visit Blood:Water partners there. We left the capital city of Kigali the morning after we arrived and headed north to the remote village of Runaba, a two and a half–hour drive. I had never seen a more spectacular landscape in Africa. It was no wonder Rwanda is called the "land of a thousand hills." Green, lush, perfect hills rose up on all sides of us, each one divided into clearly drawn boundaries of land. People were literally living on the sides of mountains. We passed rich soil and a variety of growing plants. I knew that the Rwandese are not dependent on any one crop because the land is so fertile and the rain so generous.

We were working with a local partner in Runaba to develop a piping system that would bring three springs together to provide water for the greater community, including two schools. We stopped at one of the spring sites and talked with the villagers.

I met a young girl named Utamuriza. She was in first grade and loved to study math. She and her nine brothers and sisters each came to the water point four times a day, walking one kilometer each way. Six villages (seven hundred households) used that water, some walking as much as two hours each way to get it. I spoke with a man named Rutikanga Fabian who had a family of seven but could get only two large canisters of water a day because of the time required to gather it. He said that the Runaba village was ready to do the communal work of bringing stones, materials, and sand. They asked for help with the cement.

We visited Runaba Secondary School, where there were two hundred sixty students and twelve teachers. It was the only school in the region whose students were passing their national exams. Their current water source was an unprotected spring, far enough to force students to spend much of their day fetching water. They were eager to participate in our partner's piping proposal.

We then met with our other partner in the area, MOUCECORE, and its leader, Michel. He said that he had told God that if he survived the genocide, he was going to use his organization to bring healing and reconciliation to the country—and he did. Michel helped develop a Solidarity Transformation Group model that empowers small groups of people to serve one another and their community. These volunteer members are trained in peace-building and reconciliation and are then equipped to lead their communities in social improvement projects concerning food and livestock, community health and water. Its focus on spiritual and social transformation helped Rwanda heal.

We drove to meet one of these groups in the Cyanika district, up the mountain toward a volcano. Five hundred people of all ages greeted us. The name "solidarity" was fitting, because that is what they demonstrated. Until just recently, the women and children had had to walk eleven miles down the mountainside to a lake and then eleven miles back up the mountain with water on their heads. The dirty water was causing typhoid, cholera, stomach issues, and eye infections.

But as a community, they decided to build rain tanks that could collect clean water during the rainy season. They began a campaign to provide tanks not only for their surrounding neighbors but also for the pygmy groups that the rest of society ignored. They had already constructed twenty-one water tanks and needed assistance to provide thirty more. Soon they would achieve 100 percent water coverage for the entire district—something very difficult to do anywhere in Africa, much less in a village on the side of a mountain. Children would be able to go to school and women could care for their community because they didn't have to walk for water. They could enjoy a life of health and hope.

I relished the excitement of what the communities were doing. I also realized how alive I felt among them. I had changed since my first nervous Kenyan luncheon—or maybe I'd just become more aware of who I was. I picked up language, customs, and attitudes with ease. I was no longer afraid of our differences and instead was so attune to how much we had in common.

That evening, I spoke in front of five hundred Rwandese. I wanted them to hear that we loved them and were humbled to know them. After I spoke, I had a chance to talk with several more people individually and get to know them more. The land of Rwanda was beautiful, but the people's resilience and courage were even more remarkable.

My last thought as I went to sleep that night was, *It's no wonder I can't stand the office!*

.   .   .

I left Rwanda for Kenya, eager to see the progress of the clinic in Lwala. Two of the young village leaders, Japolo and Joshua, met me in Kisumu, and we boarded the back of a full matatu toward Rongo. The rain came pouring down during our two and a half–hour drive. Everything was green and vibrant as streams of water flowed along the side of the road.

I fell asleep amid the rough rhythm of bumps and sudden stops and the occasional splash of rainwater through the cracks of the matatu window. When I woke, I discovered a few text messages from James, and my thoughts, daydreams, and prayers about him consumed the rest of the ride. Despite being on separate continents and time zones, James and I were in contact every day. On the phone across the ocean, we articulated how our feelings and interests were mutual. We made plans for him to come to Nashville soon after I returned home.

The rain continued to dump, *koth chue mang'eny.* We ran outside when the matatu came to a stop and became drenched in an instant. We found refuge in a small restaurant that was doing great business simply because it was one of the few dry options in the tiny bus stop town. As we sat for a cup of chai, the driver, Josi, complained about the muddy roads and the low pay and tried to get out of taking us to Lwala. Japolo and Josi jabbed back and forth until Josi agreed to take us partway. We walked the rest of the way through the flooded roads to my second home.

"Ah, NyaLwala!" the people of Lwala shouted with joy on their faces as I walked in. *"Ibiro! Ibiro!" You have come! You have come!* Yuka, a small but mighty woman, placed her rough hands against my shoulders and, in an embrace, placed her cheek against mine. Mr. Odwar, a kind man with an honest countenance, asked about my parents as he shook my hand and smiled with his whole self. Susan Akoth, a young girl with a playful face who dreamed of becoming a leader someday, showed surprise upon my every return.

I decided there was nothing sweeter than showing up at a place you love, embracing people you know, and witnessing genuine joy from those who know you.

After a dinner of rice and hard-boiled eggs, I retreated to Milton and Fred's parents' house, which was now an orphanage of sorts and where I would be staying. As I got settled, I heard the girls named Dada and Phemy in the room next to me, listening to the radio and finishing their studies by candlelight. A boy, Calvin, spent the evening trying to calculate how he could come up with six thousand dollars a year to attend Nairobi University when his caretaker made only two hundred fifty dollars a month.

Every visit to Lwala reminded me how difficult it is for children to get an education there. It's the pass out of poverty, and for girls, it's their power, and yet it is often only a distant dream. I tucked myself under a mosquito net and listened to the rain dance on the tin roof of the home.

The next morning, I went to see Fred and Milton's grandmother, Dani Sarah, who at ninetysomething years old was still spreading out corn kernels to dry for the preparation of *ugali*, a dough-like Kenyan staple made of maize and water. Japolo came out of his hut and insisted that we take chai before going to visit the clinic.

Together we shared chai tea and offered a prayer: "That God be with those who are hungry and have no food, and that God be with those who have food but have no hunger, and we thank God that we have both."

Afterward, we walked to the clinic to see Suzie working registration, the nurse Rose caring for patients, the pharmacist handing out prescriptions, and a line of women and children waiting to be seen. The place was functional! I thought back to my first visit in 2005, when Joel and I stood looking at a plot of land. The clinic was far from perfect, but it was taking steps forward. This time Joel was the one to show me around. Our collective fundraising efforts and initial investment in the clinic had not been in vain. And Joel continued to seem more at home in Lwala than in medical school.

As I left early in the morning a few days later, I drifted back and forth from soaking in the last scenes of Kenya to wondering about James. I was about to leave a place that held so much of my heart, and yet I had equal excitement about going home to be with someone who was about to capture it.

. . .

With a mix of jet lag and anticipation, I stood in the Nashville airport, waiting for James to get off a plane from New York. I wasn't sure if I was going to pass out or throw up. Luckily, I did neither. James arrived clean-shaven, wearing a black shirt under a burgundy jacket and blue corduroys.

We looked at each other for a moment or two, trying to make sense of the recent shift in our relationship.

We went to Jackson's Bar and Bistro for a late-night drink. I don't remember the content of our conversation. I think I just babbled. I do remember, though, how much I loved having him hold my hand as we spoke together. We stayed until 2:00 a.m., when Jackson's closed, and then sat on my living room couch for another two and a half hours. James had his hand on my feet, and I was self-conscious about the scabs and blisters from Africa. I was a bundle of nerves and proved that by going to bed at 4:30 a.m. and waking up, wide-eyed, two hours later.

Saturday was sweet. We had a leisurely morning and then went to Percy Warner Park for a hike. The weather was perfect and so was the company. I enjoyed the conversation, holding hands, the beautiful trail, and our first kiss.

Our day together was a complete paradigm shift for me. To be engaged with someone intensely, to be touched, to be sharing myself in this way—these were brand-new things for me, and I felt unprepared.

During that trip, James sat down with some faculty and administrators at Vanderbilt. He inquired about their graduate program that was focused on international development and leadership. They told him they would love to have him enter graduate school in the fall, if only he would rush his application. So he did. My New York actor had just become my Nashville international justice advocate. And I loved them both.

There's a South African word, *ubuntu,* that Desmond Tutu made popular in his writings. It reflects the philosophy that the only thing that makes us human is the interaction and relationship with other humans. No man or woman can be without relationship and still maintain the art and essence of being human. James's entrance into my life brought me more in touch with my own humanity—the capacity to feel, to be vulnerable, to love, to risk, to allow another to be intimately connected to the most secret parts of who I was. But I had been focused on Blood:Water as my calling my whole adult life. I wrestled with how James could be part of my calling as well.

"How do I let Blood:Water *and* James be my priority?" I asked Gary Haugen during one of our mentoring sessions.

"Do you think they're in competition with each other?" he asked, already knowing the answer. Over the years, Gary had been fiercely protective of his time with his wife, Jan, and their four children, despite growing a multimillion-dollar global nonprofit.

"It just seems like I can care for one or the other, but certainly not both."

"I think that God is offering you a gift in James," Gary said. "I don't think God said, 'Jena, here are your responsibilities for reaching a thousand wells, and, oops, here is James, too.'" He smiled.

As our romance grew, James and I met with other friends and family to gather their wisdom. One evening a few weeks after we'd reconnected in Nashville, we talked with Steve Garber in a Chili's at Reagan National Airport in Washington, D.C. We asked him if we were being flippant or foolish. Should we be following a better plan?

Steve put his right hand on James's shoulder, his left hand on mine. "Dear ones," he whispered to us, "You do not fall in love and then get married. You get married and learn what love requires."[8] We understood his words as the blessing they were.

Less than a year after our meet-up in the Amsterdam airport, I stood in a white dress and James in a black suit as a circle of friends and family surrounded us. We cited our marriage values and exchanged vows in front of God and our community. And I learned that sometimes the greatest gifts show up walking—or flying—right alongside you, headed toward the same destination.

James and I quickly made our way back to Africa to celebrate our marriage with our respective Kenyan families. When we boarded the eight-seat safari plane at Wilson Airport in Nairobi, the pilot brought around snacks and asked us to shift seats to balance the weight of the plane. This is never a reassuring request. But the 150-mile flight to where James had stayed in Maasailand would shorten our trip by about six hours, so James and I scooted back a row and buckled in.

Minutes after takeoff, we were already descending on Amboseli National Park, one of Kenya's smaller reserves at just under 100,000 acres. The landing strip was in the middle of a savanna, and wild herds of buffalo and wildebeests stampeded alongside the rustic runway. The whole scene was straight out of *The Lion King.* Thousands of animals were feet from our tiny plane. Out the window was the majestic view of Mount Kilimanjaro, the world's tallest freestanding mountain. It was still white-capped at the time, though now the snow is rare.

Upon landing, tour guides dressed in traditional Maasai garb greeted us. They whisked the other couple from the flight onto safari-style Land Cruisers. We, on the other hand, were being picked up by James's old colleague David, a teacher at the school, who was nowhere to be seen. As we waited an hour in the sun, the plane loaded again and took off back to Nairobi. We were there on the strip with nothing but acacia trees and each other for company. And lots and lots of animals.

Finally, we spotted a plume of dust. Moments later a beat-up Mitsubishi Pajero pulled up. David hopped out, apologized quickly, and threw our bags in the back of the 4x4. Making little of the lateness, we drove to the ranger station, where James received resident passes to the park due to his connections to the local school. We wanted to take a spin around the park before driving the thirty minutes to the town of Kimana, our final destination in the village where James had worked the year before.

None of us knew where we were going, but Amboseli Park was beautiful and romantic. The elephants were everywhere that day. We laughed to see a female and her young playing in the mud. It was the first of many safaris that James and I would be on together.

A couple hours later we left the park and followed a dirt road toward the village. Without warning, the car started to sputter. Then came a terrible and explosive blast. Before we could say anything, flames came out of the hood and black oil sprayed up on the windshield. David was yelling, panicked. The vehicle was out of control and could not turn off. We began to roll down a hill.

James and I reached for the door to try to jump out, but the handle was jammed and we couldn't escape. Without pause, James rolled the window down, reached outside, and grabbed the exterior handle. The door swung open and we threw ourselves out and rolled. David jumped from the driver's side.

We were shocked but unhurt. As we dusted ourselves off, the SUV rolled to a stop 100 yards away, where the flames died down. We called for help, but it would be hours before that help arrived. While we waited, David admitted that the reason he had been late originally was that he had accidentally filled the diesel fuel tank on the Pajero with unleaded gasoline. He had tried to siphon the gas out of the vehicle, but the remaining fuel must have caused the fire and the disturbance in the engine. What was worse was that David had borrowed the car from an acquaintance.

After dark, old friends of James appeared with a delivery truck and a towrope. After tying our vehicle to the back of the truck, we began the slow journey to Kimana. David sat in the driver's seat and put the transmission in neutral. He had to brake every time we went down a hill to keep our vehicle from rear-ending the truck. Then each time we began an incline, the towrope yanked taut and the SUV jerked like a yo-yo reaching the end of its string.

By the time we reached our friends' home in Kimana, it was after midnight. We were exhausted by the experience and exhilarated to have lived through it. The quick plane ride, which was intended to shorten our trip, had actually been the start of a wild adventure. But I could see that day that I had married the right man, someone who would think on his feet and protect me as we dove into the world together.

· · ·

After visiting James's community in Kimana, we traveled west to stay with Moses and Irene in their newly renovated home. They were expecting their fourth child. We celebrated the miraculous result of the surgery on Zinnat's feet and witnessed with joy the care Lillian gave her. We traveled south to Lwala, and I introduced James to Leah and my other friends there. We were grateful for the homecoming we had received across Kenya and hopeful that our returns would be frequent.

We returned to our new Nashville home with great expectations for our life ahead. I was in love with the world, with James, with Africa, and with Blood:Water. I had a sense of favor upon me and the work I pursued.

In the previous years, I had overcome fears of inadequacy and failure, fears of dying in Africa, fears of boys. Early on, I decided I would try to act out justice every day even when I didn't feel like it—choosing to step in when I'd prefer to step out. I didn't always succeed. But I had made that choice on enough days that it became as habitual as getting on a plane. Risky, but familiar. Somehow those choices had accumulated into a sense of peace in who I was and what God was doing. The joy of service was ineffable.

As James continued school, I returned to communities across Rwanda, Uganda, Kenya, and Zambia every three months to see the fruit of their labor and assess ways to improve. Jars of Clay continued to raise funds from the road, despite the financial constraints of working in a struggling music industry. I attended concerts when I could, still passionate about this band that inspired thousands through their music and activism.

Then one night in an unexpected moment on the side of the stage before the band was going to share about Blood:Water to a thousand fans, Dan suggested that I be the one to do it. I was terrified, but fortunately I didn't have much time to think about it.

This turned out to be the moment that moved me to the forefront of Blood:Water, not just in title and daily life, but in the minds of the public. Jars needed to be home with their families, rather than on the road at Blood:Water events. They needed to focus on sustainability as a band. To this day, Dan and the band remain Blood:Water's most loyal advocates, talking about the mission whenever they can, but we all recognized that their formal involvement in the mission wasn't as crucial as it had been in the beginning. They were passing it on to me.

I had been speaking publicly since the beginning of Blood:Water, but after that night, I went from giving fundraising talks to being asked to speak about God, compassion, and justice in churches and religious organizations across the country. As Gary Haugen said, *by some great mystery and enormous privilege, God has chosen to use his people, empowered by his Spirit, to complete the task of pursuing justice.* Few things inspired me more than being among people who feel the weight of what it means to be a responsible, loving citizen of humanity—and who choose to use their voices and their lives to speak up for someone else. I was grateful to be one of those voices.

Blood:Water continued to bring millions of dollars into the mission, born out of the grassroots efforts of individuals across the country. And I felt the joy of it all, the alignment of calling, the thrill of connecting resources with a corner of the world's need. At twenty-six years old, I had a newfound confidence in who I was and where I was going.

Part Three

Slowly by Slowly

"We are not called to change the world. We are called to love it. So we all have to keep changing to love it better."

— Reverend Becca Stevens, Episcopal priest and
founder of Thistle Farms-Magdalene

Project: No. 361
Location: Torbi, Kenya
Partner: Food for the Hungry

Torbi community was hit by a raid from a neighboring tribe, and many of the children's parents were killed. The school and community worked together to board and take care of those children so that they could continue their education at Torbi Primary. Blood:Water partnered with Food for the Hungry to make sure that access to water and sanitation wouldn't be a barrier to their education. *Photo Credit: Barak Bruerd, Blood:Water.*

21

We Cannot Bring the Rain

The first time I fell down a mountain, it was unexpected. Most falls are.

I was seventeen years old, and my friends and I were hiking in the Indian Peaks Wilderness, the same region where I'd climbed my first mountain in junior high. As we reached the 13,000-foot summit of Mt. Audubon, the wind picked up and the rain turned to a downpour, but the views were like a drug—stealing breath and thought and awareness. I felt the familiar flush of wonder as I looked across the 360-degree view.

After cozying up for a time behind the protection of a rock wall, we began our descent. We scurried down the steep slope, chatting as water beat down on our brightly colored jackets. The rocks, of course, were wet from the rain, but we were used to such conditions. Thunder, lightning, hail—it was all part of the adventure.

Suddenly, my boot slipped on the wet scree beneath me and I fell forward. My body picked up momentum, flipping several times and stopping only because I smacked into a boulder. Though my hip and shoulders throbbed and my forehead bled, what I felt most intensely was the shock of my own carelessness. I had climbed enough mountains to know the dangers of getting too comfortable. But there I was, bruised and bleeding, no longer trusting the trail beneath me.

Our work in Africa, like a mountain storm, blindsided me just when I thought I knew what I was doing. But no one tells you about the mess that comes with trying to do a good thing in the world. Or maybe they do, but you stand convinced that your story is different than theirs: The slippery rocks won't affect *your* footing. The wind won't push *you* down.

In the early years of Blood:Water, I wasn't seasoned enough to expect the fumbling and stumbling. The head-over-heels falling. The stillness after impact. Especially not after we'd made it to at least one summit and could see the beauty of more ahead. I had no idea how difficult getting back up would be.

. . .

As I traveled to Africa again and again, one of the places where the contrast of environment and culture struck me the most was in the Marsabit Desert of northern Kenya, close to the border of Ethiopia. Its landscape is difficult to explain because it is a place of such extremes. It is not just hot—it is oppressively hot. It is not just dry—it is earth-crumbling dry. It is not just poor—it is desperately poor. As you fly above the region, the land looks like the surface of the moon. You see twisters of sand, dust, and heat dancing across the barren landscape. You feel thirsty just looking at the vast desert.

The first time I visited I was with two of my Nashville-based colleagues, Barak and Pam. We landed on a dirt airstrip and a man named Yegon met us. Yegon was the leader of our new partner in the region. Like Moses, he and his team were committed to bringing health and clean water to communities that had little of either. But rather than live in villages, the inhabitants of this desert were a nomadic people who traveled for days to find remnants of vegetation for themselves and their animals. One need only be in Marsabit for a day to feel the dramatic effects of a water crisis.

"Welcome to the end of Africa," Yegon told us as we looked across the sandy plains, seeing no signs of life from the vantage point of the small airstrip. It did look as if just past the horizon would be the ledge that marked not just the end of Africa but the end of the world.

Yegon had a vision and wanted us to see it. We traveled for hours across the moon-like terrain until we found ourselves in a remote school where a hundred children gathered to learn among an expanse of twisters and dust. These students were given an opportunity that many nomadic families do not grant their children: formal education. While their parents traveled across the Chalbi Desert, these students boarded in a basic dormitory next to the school so they could maintain their studies. I covered my head and face with a light scarf to keep the pelleting sand off my skin and out of my hair. Herds of camels, donkeys, and goats roamed the area as the sun baked my skin.

Yegon introduced us to the teachers who had been working on plans for rainwater catchment tanks that would collect water from the buildings' gutters. These tanks would be the main source of safe water for everyone at the school, allowing the children to stay in class instead of spending much of their time in search of water.

Yegon guided us up a hill that overlooked a ravine about the size of an American football field. He explained how this could become an earthen dam to provide water for Marsabit's animals—like the Hoover Dam, just smaller and made of dirt instead of concrete. It would take a bulldozer and rainfall to make it effective. He showed us the sites where they wanted to drill for deep underground water. The vision was bold, but the plans were certainly possible to execute, especially if Blood:Water partnered with them financially.

I was excited for the potential in Yegon's plans. I wondered again how I, of all people, had been given access to such remote areas and people of the world. What a gift to collect the dollars of generous individuals across North America and reallocate them toward the lifesaving work of building rain catchment tanks in a place on earth that almost no one knew about.

Later that year, I returned to the desert of Marsabit and traveled for hours with Yegon to witness the craftsmanship of the schools' rain catchment tanks, the newly constructed earthen dam for the animals, and the impressive engineering of the deep well boreholes drilled successfully in one of earth's harshest environments.

The vision Yegon had laid out and that Blood:Water had funded had taken shape, but there was one problem: no water. When I turned the tap connected to the storage tanks, I felt only hot air. I walked up the hill to view the edge of the dam. What was supposed to be filled with water for animals was a cracked prune of landscape. A goat lay on its side in the dusty sand, dead from dehydration. The new borehole was nearly dry, eking out an insufficient stream of water from a well we'd designed to serve hundreds of people and their seven thousand animals. Scattered herds of camels and donkeys stood with their owners, waiting their turn to drink from the dribble of the trough.

Marsabit had been suffering a severe and unexpected drought for more than a year. The stored water had run out nearly six months earlier. Mothers, fathers, babies, camels, donkeys, and goats were trying to live without water, which really didn't leave much life at all.

As I stood under the merciless sun, it became clear to me that return on investment doesn't apply in many places around the world. The unjust forces of nature can cripple even the strongest, most capable person, community, or ideal. In this case, all the persistence, money, and work that the people of Marsabit and Blood:Water had done had come to nothing tangible. People and animals were still dying from a drought that mocked our best intentions.

Most Americans assume that if something needs to be done, there is a way to do it. But sometimes human capability meets its threshold, and we learn the truth about what we can and cannot do.

Our limitations dumbfounded me. *Was this just a waste?* I wondered. *I thought God was with us in this.* I was again the little girl standing on a San Francisco street corner looking for that homeless man and wondering how my best intentions had made no impact at all.

In Marsabit, we can partner with the best organization in the region. We can raise all the money we need, mobilize the communities with excellent methods, train in best practices of hygiene, build solid latrines, and construct foolproof rain tanks.

But we cannot bring the rain.

So what do we do if there is little promise that rain will ever come? How do we stay with our vision? How do we stand with people on the dry land that we cannot fix? The project was a failure. I felt as though we had let the communities down. I feared the reactions of the American donors who expected successful results from their generosity.

Marsabit made me question many truths I thought I understood about the world: How hard work pays off. How hope comes through in the end. How God is merciful.

My convictions began to crumble like dirt beneath my feet.

"There is life in the desert," Yegon had told me when we first met. I found myself asking if he was impossibly optimistic, because I couldn't see it. The injustice of the situation was maddening. I could not make the rain come. Soon I would realize I could not take away the HIV/AIDS crisis either.

I had promised not to promise to everyone but myself.

.   .   .

It would be a year of questions.

In our first three months of marriage, James made two grad school trips to Bangladesh, focused on working with local schools, while I made multiple trips to Africa. Each time, he was on his way there while I was on my way home and we were able to meet for a couple days in Dubai together. Those trips reflected a lot of our early marriage: working hard, meeting halfway briefly, and then passing in the night again.

Blood:Water had been my life for enough years that I had trouble making anything else—like my husband—a priority, even though I longed to do so. I delighted to embrace this new relationship even as I struggled to understand the time, energy, and heart it required.

"We're still on the same plane together," James reminded me in a letter he tucked into my suitcase on one of my trips to Africa. "Just as we were for our first conversation. We are both seeking the same true north of justice, redemption, and reconciliation. Let's keep trying to seek it with each other."

We asked questions about our future via emails, phone calls, and intimate talks in our living room: we knew that James would pursue a job in international development after grad school, but we had not really considered what changes that might bring to our life together. Would we move to Nairobi or stay in Nashville? Were there ways to work and travel together, or did we need to keep working separate hours and separate causes? Should I follow James in his career, or should he step into Blood:Water's work? Did we live on airplanes and in hotel rooms and speak from stages, or did we dig deeply into community, find a home among those we wanted to advocate for and set our eyes on a different, less public life?

Meanwhile, the Lwala clinic was struggling. From the outside, the project looked like a success: a beautiful building, women and children lined up on a bench outside the clinic awaiting their turn, nurses and clinical officers tending to patients, shelves stocked with medicines. But without a mature system to ensure consistent access to HIV medications and to equip providers with the necessary training to enroll patients in treatment, the clinic was as good as an empty rain tank in Marsabit during a yearlong drought.

As our representative on the ground in Lwala, Joel was facing the relentless challenges of cultural differences, local politics, cronyism, and a lack of a paper trail on how donor dollars were being spent. His hopes of doing good in the world were weakening under the burden of providing health care in a place where one in five adults is HIV positive.

What made this worse was that HIV rates in this western region were escalating every day, even while they were declining in other parts of the country. Teenage girls and young women were particularly vulnerable because polygamy, sexual abuse, and gender inequality were having a terrible and cumulative effect. This verdant and rolling countryside was losing a generation of women.

HIV, the silent killer, was not simply taking advantage of the body's weak immune system; it was capitalizing on the deep social ills of places like Lwala. The late-night conversation Caitlin and I had on our first visit to Lwala about husbands beating wives and about the inaccessibility of condoms reflected a true cultural distinction. Over time, we would hear the most outrageous stories: a schoolgirl was raped by a teacher and then punished by her parents for causing the man to want her; a church community ostracized a widow who had inherited the disease through an unfaithful husband. Layers and layers of complexity covered just this one village and gave insight into the forces that were fueling the rapid spread of HIV/AIDS in the entire region.

As we looked beyond Lwala, it became clear that AIDS was destroying life at an unimaginable scale in other regions of Africa as well. It had slain adults and children. It had crippled the workforce, decreased life expectancy by two decades, reduced economic growth, weakened governance, disrupted marginal infrastructures, halted productivity, undermined national security, dissolved families, invited armed conflict, and impeded the health and educational development that are necessary to help impoverished communities rise above extreme poverty.

We felt like fools trying to put out a forest fire with a dribble of water. We had proclaimed to supporters back home that we could do it. It was a wear-flip-flops-to-meet-the-president kind of scenario: I hadn't realized what I was getting into. But this time we were dealing with people's lives, not fashion statements.

It had been four years since the band and I had launched the 1000 Wells Project. We were about halfway there, but sustaining the passion was a burden—for ourselves and others. The freshness of Blood:Water had worn off for all of us. Hundreds of boutique nonprofits had emerged on the scene, making the dollars much more difficult to raise amid the other important issues like human trafficking and orphan care. Some of our earlier supporters had moved on to other causes, yet we still had projects to deliver in Africa, staff to sustain, rent to pay, policies to establish, and a board of directors to develop. It was overwhelming to realize that we needed to scale up our efforts to mobilize support.

All the demands for maturing our organizational structure took intense time and energy, and the work was neither inspiring nor energizing to me. I continued to wrestle with questions of my own identity, realizing that there was little left of me to offer James, friends, and family outside of Blood:Water. In my most honest moments, I felt my personal conviction about the work begin to deflate. I believed in the importance of Blood:Water, but I was uncertain if I should continue as its leader.

I understand now that having the original team of an organization drift away is natural and can even be a gift. Others who were not there for the romanticism of the vision enter simply for the good of the work. But at the time, as I saw that Blood:Water was not the primary focus of Joel or Jars anymore, I felt only loneliness. As hard as those first few years of Blood:Water had been, I missed all the newness and camaraderie they held.

I also discovered that I was a naive accomplice to the very brokenness I was trying to heal.

Project: No. 440
Location: Chalbi, Kenya
Partner: Food for the Hungry

In Kenya's Chalbi Desert, primary school students walk long distances for water. This rain tank allows children easy access to drinking water during school hours. During the 2013 drought that ravaged the Horn of Africa, these and other Blood:Water-funded tanks in the region served as emergency water distribution points for humanitarian efforts. *Photo Credit: Blood:Water.*

22

A Hero Can Be Hard to Find

I was back in Kisumu, staying with Moses and his family. Despite the rockiness of my visit when the generator was stolen, Moses and Irene's home had been a respite in my frequent trips to Kenya. The amenities in their home had greatly improved due to Moses's side business of growing and selling sugarcane. I no longer used the pit latrine outside but instead had a flushing toilet across the hall from the bedroom they called "Jena's room." The leaks in the roof had been fixed, so I no longer had to contort my body when it rained at night to avoid the dripping water. The bed had a pillow. The driver ants had disappeared.

Though Blood:Water had expanded to include several more partners across Africa, Moses and the Water for Women's Groups was my favorite to visit because of the relationships I had established with the team. I considered Moses, Elizabeth, Lillian, and John Gideon good friends and enjoyed seeing them get to know James as well. Each visit was an opportunity to keep learning and growing together. So it was a surprise when Moses told me that John Gideon was no longer with WWG.

"I cannot disclose the details," he said when I asked why. "Let me just say this: he was not a team player."

John Gideon had seemed, of all the team, to be the one with the greatest amount of integrity and consideration for others. I went to Elizabeth to understand what had happened. Despite her openness to me over the years, she withheld her response and asked me not to inquire again. As did Lillian.

Several weeks later when I was back home, I received a call from another agency that was financially supporting WWG. They asked if I had heard about the allegations.

"Allegations?" I asked. "Of what?"

"A WWG staff member has sent us a letter about mismanaged funds within the organization." I wondered if that was why Moses had let John Gideon go. I felt sadness, then fear about what it meant for donor dollars that we had applied to WWG's work.

The partner organization said they would forward me the letter and informed me that they were sending outside auditors to investigate the allegations. I called my board chair and informed him of the potential liability that we had just found ourselves in. I waited with uncertainty for more information.

We soon discovered that the letter wasn't about John Gideon at all. In fact, it was *from* John Gideon, about Moses. The letter stated that Moses was keeping two different financial books, that he was double counting wells (so two donor agencies were being credited for the same well even though there was funding for two), that he was using vehicles designated for fieldwork to take Irene and the kids around town, and that he was pocketing a large percentage of his staff's salaries for himself—using the money for, among other things, the upgrades on his home that I'd been enjoying.

I couldn't believe it. I didn't want to believe it. Moses was family to me. He was the one who drilled our first well, who set the path for our work. We were partners. Surely, John Gideon was mistaken. Or was I? But the evidence coming out of the investigation of Moses was too strong to deny. I felt betrayed, and I felt foolish. The earlier concerns outsiders had about my youth and inexperience had been confirmed. I replayed our years of friendship and partnership in my mind, trying to find where I had missed the cues.

I realized that I had been too trusting. Joel and I first went to Africa determined to find a model we could believe in, a hero to back, a story worth writing—and we wanted Moses to be all of that for us.

I could see the nodding heads of the naysayers who labeled Africa a place of corruption and broken systems. A lost cause. I had refused to believe their creeds. I ferociously defended our partners against such accusations. But now, with weak knees and a bankbook of broken promises, I realized I was wrong.

I soon received another devastating phone call, this time from Elizabeth: Lillian had been killed in a car accident. *How could God allow this, another senseless death in Africa?* In my grief over Lillian, I knew that dozens of people, such as Zinnat the young orphan, had lost a significant advocate and friend. I felt a visceral loss as I watched my strongest Kenyan relationships fall away in what felt like an instant. I began to feel as though my inner compass might fall, too.

I had been so convinced that love was the greatest force for change in the world that I forgot that love could hurt. But if you stay somewhere long enough to let your life become entrenched in the lives of others, you can't take the goodness of love without the pain. And I had stayed long enough. Long enough to see senseless deaths, dry land, and now a corrupt leader.

The truth was, in the case with Moses, I was not a victim of circumstances. I was a responsible participant in the mess of it all. If I had understood our world more, I would have approached things differently. I would have ensured checks and balances so one person couldn't have that much financial influence. I would have recognized that desperation and extreme poverty make even good people do horrible things. I would have respected the mountain for the treacherous slope that it was.

Joel and I arrived at the WWG office around 6:00 p.m. We were two hours late after struggling to get a timely ride on the public matatu from Lwala to Kisumu. Joel was in the process of transition, having decided to move back to the United States amid intense vocational discouragement and a need to hit the reset button.

My visit with him and the Lwala community had been disheartening: a high percentage of babies were continuing to die, HIV-positive patients were not taking their medication, and Leah, though still alive, was living on hope.

So our matatu took us from the unfinished story of Lwala to the closing chapter of Kano Plains and WWG.

Joel and I walked up the wobbly spiral staircase to Moses's office. It was different than before, devoid of the life and activity that used to occupy the small area. Moses sat behind his desk, though he stood up to greet us with kindness and hospitality as any Kenyan would.

Elizabeth was there, too. I felt the obvious absence of John Gideon and Lillian. I was nervous, uncomfortable with the distance that circumstances had imposed on these once-easy friendships. We sat facing Moses, chitchatting about the matatu ride, about nothing.

Over the previous six months, the board of directors for Blood:Water had led a thorough investigation to confirm the allegations against Moses. We immediately terminated the partnership with WWG, informed our donors of the misuse of funds, adjusted our reporting and accountability structures, and spent much time discussing ways to improve the due diligence and integrity of our work. In addition, the board unanimously recommended that Joel and I meet face-to-face with Moses to formally end the partnership. They wanted us to give him the dignity of closure, to offer him an opportunity to share his side of the story, and to show that relationships mattered to us—even relationships that hurt us.

Moses looked tired, defeated. He told me that his operation had shut down, that all foreign funding had been withheld. He rested his hand on his forehead and stared down at his desk.

I was still naive: I had expected an explanation of what happened and an apology from Moses. I received neither. He simply shared his frustration about the imposition that the investigations had been on his work. He was the one full of accusation.

Moses gave Elizabeth a nod as if it were her cue to speak. She told us that the women's groups had been asking about me and wishing that I would visit them so they could keep partnering with us. I knew these women. I loved them. I admired them and their accomplishments. I listened to what she was requesting, but I didn't know how to respond. I shifted in my seat, looking over to Joel for help.

"Moses," Joel said, "first and foremost, you are a brother to us. You have demonstrated some of the best community development we have ever seen. But WWG did not pass the audit, so we cannot fund you. You cannot keep two books or be dishonest about salaries."

Moses continued to look down at his desk. "WWG made mistakes," he answered quietly. "No, not WWG. Moses made mistakes."

I was relieved to hear him acknowledge his wrongs, even if he used the third person.

"Jena, we are thankful for the partnership," Moses continued. "Together, we have been able to do so many wonderful things for these communities. But the relationships are more important than the dollars."

I had trouble believing him since his motivation for dollars had clearly sabotaged our relationship.

He began to reminisce about the first time Joel and I met him at the Kisumu airport and he had walked right past me because he was looking for someone who looked like a director, not a twenty-two-year-old. He didn't want the relationship to end. He asked, "As you pass through to Lwala, could you please stay a night or stop by to say hello?" He said that I ought to meet his newest baby, whose name was Jena.

His invitation made me feel even more worn down. I wasn't angry at Moses—I was just horribly disappointed. His poor decisions meant that we wouldn't get to keep serving together in partnership, which was one of my greatest joys in the work of Blood:Water. To learn that he had named his daughter after me only made it hurt more. I would probably never meet her.

And then Moses closed the conversation. He wanted us to take a meal together and not speak about WWG anymore. He handed me a manila envelope and told me that it held the thoughts he couldn't say in person. I was eager to see if the letter was more satisfying than the conversation, but I tucked it away as Moses had asked.

We shared an awkward meal at "our" Chinese restaurant across the street where we had eaten together a dozen times before in more joyful circumstances. Then Joel and I said our goodbyes and boarded the bus to Nairobi.

After we found our seats, I pulled out the manila envelope to read Moses's explanation. The letter was written on WWG letterhead. Moses used formal language but gave no acknowledgment of wrongdoing or corruption on his part. No apology. No recognition of the friendship and partnership we had built over the last five years. Instead, it was a complaint that he had been wronged, followed by a demand for more money. I put my head in my hands and melted with defeat.

"I feel like several years ago, we went on a quest to kill a lion," Joel said to me after he read the letter. "And we have limped our way back to the road." I couldn't have agreed more.

Project: No. 488
Location: Nhongonhane, Mozambique
Partner: Lifewater International and Agua Para Todos
Drillers from Agua Para Todos (translated "Water for All") in Mozambique drilled a shallow well for a rural community outside the capital city of Maputo, where the only available water is from contaminated hand-dug wells. After this well was drilled, the community began planting gardens around it to grow crops during the dry season. *Photo Credit: Barak Bruerd, Blood:Water.*

23

Fool's Errand

As our work continued, I tried to find the enthusiasm for helping others that had once come so easily. But it felt tainted now, and the work of engaging American evangelicals began to wear on me in the midst of so many other challenges. I couldn't help but take their questions personally.

"I see here that your African partners are working intimately with the communities," a Christian family foundation representative said on the phone. "It says here that they are making home visits, providing clean water and health clinics, and sometimes even praying with them. But I still don't see where the gospel is being shared."

"What's the point in providing clean water for Africans," a woman asked me after a speaking engagement, "if they're just going to spend eternity in hell?"

"Before I make a donation," a potential donor told me on the phone, "I just want to make sure you're sharing the love of Jesus with these African communities."

We also faced the dilemma I'd first heard about on the tour bus with Jars of Clay: we were too corporate for Christians and too Christian for corporations.

"We need to understand your hiring policies and how you choose to serve beneficiaries to ensure that these funds will not be used for proselytizing," a representative of a major corporate brand would say.

That same day I might have the opposite conversation within the Christian community.

"You tell me you're a Christian organization," a pastor said. "But when I go to your website, I don't see the word 'salvation' anywhere on your front page." I explained that the band and I wanted to use language the whole world could understand, especially since words mean so many different things to different people. He responded with a question about whether or not I was ashamed of making a public stand as a Christian. I didn't feel equipped to share my whole faith journey while my integrity as an evangelical Christian was under investigation. What I really wanted to say was "People are dying while we discuss this."

Do we share Jesus in Africa? This is the most commonly asked question at Blood:Water. On the surface, the answer is obvious. Yes. We bring water to the thirsty and health care to the sick because of our love for Jesus. In that way, we are sharing the love of Jesus. The question, though, is loaded with spiritual innuendo. Are we evangelizing the Christian message to the people we worked with? As I'd discovered when Jars of Clay wrestled with similar queries about whether their music was "Christian," providing an answer to that question is complicated.

Many Christians have different definitions of evangelism, "sharing the love of Jesus," and what it means to be a Christian organization. The truth is that many of the people we serve in Africa already know Jesus and have dedicated their lives to the Christian story. What they have in abundance is faith. What they lack is stable work, clean water, and quality health care. As Joel wrote me once from Kenya, "Lwala needs a hospital, not faith. If anyone needs faith, it's me."

The love of Jesus is shared in Africa because my African friends share it with me every time we gather. We would be richly served here in North America by learning what our African brothers and sisters have to teach us about Christ. I often find that we are the lost ones.

But this answer was not satisfying to potential donors. I was meeting the Sleeping Giant Bono spoke about face-to-face. So, reluctantly, I spent nearly two years in meetings with board members, supporters, and African partners sorting, explaining, and debating Blood:Water's Christian identity. Out of those conversations came a statement of faith for our website to ease the concerns of our support base. We created the document and signed our names to it. Meanwhile, communities were thirsty for clean water.

The language we now used in conversation and in promotional materials reassured American Christians. But feeling as if Blood:Water was on trial had far-reaching effects on my own spiritual life. It made me insecure about the certainty of my beliefs and brought me into theological debates that I never intended to engage in. The church that had raised me, shaped me, and given me identity began to feel unfamiliar. The judgment behind the questions of who deserved help and what kind of help they should get made me worry that someday I wouldn't deserve it either. I was simmering with significant uncertainty about the goodness of God and the validity of hope, and I had nowhere to take them.

I didn't believe orthodoxy was a prerequisite to giving or receiving love. The greatest expression of my Christian faith was giving my whole self to ensuring that the least of these in Africa had a chance at life. If evangelical churches saw that as less important than telling people what they ought to believe, maybe I didn't belong in the evangelical church.

The thought terrified me.

. . .

James was in his final semester of graduate school at Vanderbilt and had just begun to receive job offers in the leadership field of international development. We were still unclear about which direction or job he ought to take, but we were looking at projects in Bangladesh and other parts of the world.

Maybe moving around the world and focusing on James's job will be my way out of Blood:Water, I thought.

One evening, James and I had dinner with Milton's younger brother, Fred, who was still in medical school at Vanderbilt, while Milton had moved to St. Louis for residency. After Blood:Water invested in the clinic's launch, Milton and Fred and a band of other community members officially formed the Lwala Community Alliance as the umbrella nonprofit to the clinic and community services. Joel was its first executive director and got the organization established, but now that Joel had officially turned in his resignation, Lwala's future was uncertain. The start-up clinic was performing basic services to the community, but its management and systems were underdeveloped and unsustainable.

"We still need someone who can facilitate the development of the clinic back home," Fred told us. "We need a new executive director."

I let Fred know that I would keep my eye out for any qualified candidates. *And good luck to him or her,* I thought.

"I actually know an ideal candidate," Fred replied carefully. I looked up from my plate with curiosity.

"You're married to him." He smiled.

I looked over at James to see his reaction. To my dismay, he'd perked up at Fred's words. He started to ask Fred about the details of the job. It would be a full-time paid position based in Nashville, with expectations to be in Kenya a third of the year.

"You're not seriously considering Lwala?" I asked James as we drove home from dinner.

"Of course I am," he answered, offended by my accusing tone. "It's an incredible opportunity and tied to a community we already know."

I stayed quiet, feeling my anger rise.

"I thought you, of all people, would be the most excited about this possibility," he continued. "We've been talking about how to have a common mission. You helped launch it, and I could be the one to take it to its next stage of growth. I'm excited about the challenge."

"It's a sinking ship, and you know it," I insisted. If Joel, filled with conviction and a radical commitment to serving among the poor, had called it quits, I knew James and I weren't equipped to take on such a task.

"It will break you," I warned James. But I was more afraid that it would break me.

James took the job, and in the season when I wanted to quit Africa the most, I instead became more connected to it. James had been to Lwala before with me, but he was about to dive further into the community than I ever had, spending about a hundred days a year in this small village with no paved roads, electricity, or running water. He was now leading one of the Africa-based organizations that Blood:Water supported. This meant we were both working in the same area, but we each had our own board, donors, and travel requirements specific to our respective organizations. We were in deep.

He first spent several weeks with Joel getting oriented to the small clinic staff, the local leadership committee, and the current operations of LCA. He met Caitlin, the American volunteer I'd met on my first visit to Lwala, who had since received her master's in public health and returned to Lwala to work alongside Joel. And he met another American volunteer, a medical student named Brooke. She had a degree in African studies and spoke fluent Swahili.

It was a challenging beginning for James as he quickly encountered one of the biggest issues that had discouraged Joel from moving forward: an underlying suspicion that there might be a Moses among the clinic staff. It didn't take long for James to realize that one of the founding village members of the clinic was pocketing a significant amount of money for his own gain. The project began to validate the fears and anxieties I had about sinking deeper into the mess of one community in Africa. After Moses's deceit, I didn't have the stomach to accept that corruption was happening in Lwala, too.

But James had an emotional stamina greater than Joel and me combined. He investigated the staff member in question, brought on a lawyer, and worked to untangle a complicated web of broken systems and untrusting relationships. He recruited Robert, a soft-spoken and humble Kenyan from a large missionary hospital, to provide the consistent leadership that this project lacked. He met regularly with the local village committee as they collaborated on the plans for the clinic. He held on to the ability to dream about what could be.

The committee spoke of a maternity ward to curb the high death rate of mothers and babies during delivery. James knew it would take a while to rally the funds necessary for such a facility, but in the meantime, he commissioned Brooke to begin teaching the village's traditional birth attendants key safety interventions for mothers and babies during delivery. Since Brooke taught classes in Swahili, she instantly became a beloved teacher among the village women. Her commitment for the people of Lwala was infectious to all. Brooke loved Africa. When her time at Lwala finished at summer's end, she took off to visit her dear friend in Tanzania. She planned to join Lwala again on her next break from school. The whole community turned out to say goodbye.

James and Robert continued to work on gaining access to HIV medications. The Kenyan government had them, but there were many hoops to jump through to get Lwala on the list. They had small victories along the way. Even Leah's story had been turning in slow but remarkable ways. The new clinic hosted an HIV support group, and Leah was one of its first members. She hadn't realized how many other neighbors were HIV positive, and she felt far less alone. She was taking her medications as prescribed, receiving nutritional support, and getting stronger. This was a story that the Lwala community had dreamed to write.

Meanwhile, James and Robert continued to uncover inefficiencies, corrupt local politics, and insurmountable complexities. I was furiously trying to raise more money through Blood:Water to continue what we began in Lwala, but I also had a nagging sense that it wouldn't make any difference.

One afternoon while I was on the road fundraising with the band, I received a call from James in Lwala. It was about Leah. She had been battling tuberculosis, and one of her lungs had just collapsed. It was the middle of the night in Kenya, and James was keeping vigil by Leah's bedside at the hospital. It did not look as though she was going to make it through the night. TB is an all-too-common communicable disease in the developing world, and it is nearly impossible for someone with HIV to overcome without treatment. I cried in defeat and begged God to save her.

James kept me updated every hour. We waited. Leah survived the night. We felt a sensation that might have been hope.

When the world plays by rules that are neither logical nor compassionate, you need to look for miracles instead of happy accidents. Sometimes recognizing small triumphs is the only thing that keeps hope alive.

．　．　．

It was the end of James's first summer in Lwala when a bus traveling from Kenya to Tanzania crashed and killed more than twenty passengers. Brooke was one of them.

James and I were hardly able to believe that Brooke was gone.

"I was just with her," James kept saying. "We just had the ceremony for her community of graduates. I was just with her."

James had to communicate with her family back home and work with the Kenyan authorities to identify the unidentifiable body. It was the worst of responsibilities.

We flew home from Kenya and arrived an hour late to the funeral in Philadelphia after torrential floods made roads impassable. We awkwardly walked into the small room where Brooke's family and friends were seated facing one another in a circle to honor the Quaker tradition of her faith, tearfully sharing memories of their daughter, sister, and friend. No one knew who we were, and due to our late entrance, we had to publicly introduce ourselves. We were the strangers who represented the place that had taken Brooke's life. It was horrible.

But it was not grief that I felt most intensely. It was anger. It was an inner rage that a woman with such great love was given only death. It was a pointed fury at a culture that allowed buses to be dangerously top-heavy from cramming in more people and luggage than they could hold. It was a disgust for every senseless death I had witnessed in the past five years. If I let myself think too much about it, I was angry at the entire continent of Africa.

As I witnessed the grief of Brooke's parents, I couldn't help but imagine the devastation that my death could bring to my own parents—my loving and protective mom and dad who pray me through every plane flight and celebrate each time I call to tell them I've landed. Looking around the room at Brooke's loved ones, I understood in a new way that when you choose a calling, you don't do so in isolation. The people you love are a part of your choice, too. They are the ones who rejoice the most with you when life goes well, and they are the ones who will bear the heaviest burdens should the world's brokenness overtake you.

I used to believe that justice was worth fighting for, no matter what. Then I sat in a room with a devastated family, a family who would not have been grieving if only one young woman had not committed to serve a small group of village women across the ocean. If only she had not dreamed, too.

"What do you care about?" Steve Garber had asked me when I first met him. "What do you *truly* care about?"

My answer at the time dripped with idealism.

"We have entered the Culture of Whatever," he had said. "Ironically, the more we know, the less we care . . . The greatest challenge is to attach yourself to the cares of the world and still keep going. To know the world and love it still."

In the rubble of my heart, I mulled over Steve's question: Once I come to know the world in all its doubt and darkness, can I love it still?

I thought of the communities in Marsabit that worked tirelessly to construct the rain tanks only to face a year of drought. I thought about my dear friend Lillian who compassionately cared for village communities only to have her life taken in an instant of reckless driving. I thought about Moses's shameless ability to deceive a trusting young woman from America while using donations to fund porcelain toilets in his home. I thought about the women's groups who would no longer progress in their water projects because of Moses's greed, and the employment struggles that John Gideon and Elizabeth were facing because of his bad decisions. I thought of the girls in Lwala who were being raped by their schoolteachers, the babies who died in their first moments, the women who had so little power in life that they could not protect themselves from a deadly disease. I thought about Leah and how many times she had cheated death, knowing that there would be a night when she does not win. I thought about the American church holding their wallets tight, stuck in the weeds of wrong questions. I thought of the convictions that crumbled from Joel's heart to the muck of the Lwala dirt. And the life that was lost in Brooke.

Cynicism won me over. I really was the girl Most Likely to Devote Her Life to a Lost Cause. But it was no longer a compliment. Africa was a fool's errand, and I was the fool who thought that my childish compassion on a San Francisco street corner could fix a continental crisis. Love the world in all its doubt and darkness? As I limped my way home, my answer was an easy no.

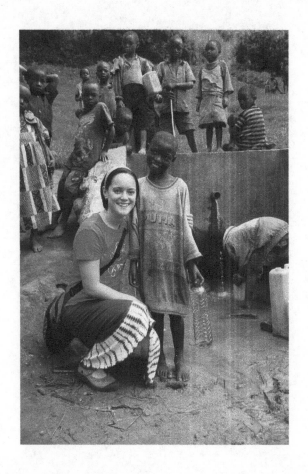

Project: No. 569

Location: Gicumbi District, Rwanda

Partner: African Evangelistic Enterprise

The volcanic mountains of northern Rwanda have an abundance of artesian springs. When carefully protected and managed like this one, these springs can provide sustainable safe water with very little maintenance cost. *Photo Credit: Barak Bruerd, Blood:Water.*

24

The Third Way

"I'm not sure I believe in as much as I used to," I told Steve Garber as we walked around the Tidal Basin in West Potomac Park in D.C. It was April and canopies of blossoming Yoshino cherry trees were overhead. Crowds of tourists surrounded us. I confessed to Steve a fountain of doubts. Disappointment and disillusionment. I admitted my desire to quit—not just Blood:Water, but perhaps the evangelical church, too. Just as he has since the first time I introduced myself to him years ago, Steve listened, pondered my questions, and offered abounding wisdom.

"The world is a tough place to live, Jena," he said as he squeezed his arm around my shoulder. "But there is nowhere else to live."

It was as straightforward an answer as anyone had given me. I remembered the evening James and I sat around a living room with a dozen or so friends from church soon after Brooke's funeral. The small group leader was facilitating a discussion around a Bible passage, and we were expected to chime in with answers. A lot of smart people in the room had Bible verses and theological substance to back their insights. The problem for me was that I didn't trust answers anymore, not after I couldn't trust my own intuitions about Moses, not after seeing someone as good and true as Brooke die young. I said as much, maybe too much, and the room went quiet.

They decided to pray for me, which was a compassionate thing to do. But they offered prayers about seeking truth and finding my way when I really needed someone to say, with no intention to correct or fix or save: "I sometimes feel that way, too." Or, "Those uncertainties are legitimate." Pat answers and prayers only confirmed my suspicion that doubt and discouragement were not welcome evangelical Christianity.

It was satisfying to hear Steve admit such an unromantic truth.

Steve pointed toward the water, the paths around it lined with cherry blossoms as if pink snow had descended.

"Just look at this for a moment," he said quietly. The view was glorious indeed. "You know as well as I do that underneath this beauty is the stench of a sausage-making factory." Steve was referring to his favorite quote about politics, attributed to Otto von Bismarck: "Laws are like sausages. It is better not to see them being made." Steve had lived in Washington, D.C., for twenty years and knew well the underbelly of our nation's dealings.

"But since the world *is* a tough place to live," he continued, "we have to live with what is proximate."

I asked him what he meant by that.

"People have wanted to make the world a better place for thousands of years. It often seems like the world wins. That makes it hard to keep going."

I did feel as though I was losing to someone or something.

"You know too much now," Steve went on. "You know that Africa, like Washington, is more complex and more disappointing than you had hoped it to be. Like a lot of people, you want to throw your hands in the air and give up so you can protect your heart from further wounds."

That's exactly what I want to do, I thought.

But Steve continued. "The other option would be to choose to enter the world still, knowing what you know. That means believing that it is better to do something than to do nothing. That justice somewhere is better than justice nowhere. You can choose proximate mercy for a certain group of people, even though you know that as hard as you try, you will not be able to achieve all you set out to achieve in the world."[9]

Was this a defeatist's manifesto, a compromise on the greater ideals? I couldn't be sure then, and I continue to wrestle with this today. Steve was the first one, though, to offer me a way to approach the world that was more realistic, more sustainable, and more responsible than the options I thought I had left. It was neither idealism nor cynicism. It was a third way.

"Choosing to live proximately does not mean you've lowered your standards," Steve concluded. "It means you've decided to be honest about the world. And still live by hope."

I had once thought hope was easy—belief in the good came easily to me. Now I realize it was passion that came easily. When I was a young adult, my passions were a gift. They propelled me forward. But at some point, the wind disappears, and hope must take over while you wait, expectantly, in still waters.

True hope is always hard. It is not a passive wishing. It is an active exercise, a choice, an intention. Hope means giving up apathy and despair and instead embracing the uncertainty that terrifies you. It is the sacrifice of keeping your heart soft.

Why would you build a rain tank when you have lived for a year under cloudless skies? Why would you teach your neighbors how to care for water when there is no water to care for? Why risk playing the fool by believing in a good God when the earth continues to stand dry and children die watching for rain? When I look at the deserts of Africa, sometimes I wonder if the tears of the grieving are the only drops of water that come. I pray, but with disbelief.

As I grappled with how to view this reality, I thought about Paul Farmer, the American doctor dedicated to providing health care to the poor in Haiti and other places around the world. Dr. Farmer is known in Haiti for walking mountains beyond mountains, door-to-door, hour-by-hour, to visit and ensure that his patients are taking their tuberculosis medications.

One of the greatest risks for those with TB is not taking pills at the right time, so adherence to the medication is crucial. It is the same with HIV therapies. If your doctor comes to your door, there's a much greater chance that you'll remember or agree to take the pills.

Farmer has been unconventional not only in the practice of seeing his patients in their homes but also for trying to work toward radical transformation in the lives of the poor. Many people believe it is inefficient for the most qualified medical provider in an area to spend his time with just a few patients, especially patients whose survival is questionable.

In response to such criticism, Farmer said, "I have fought the long defeat and brought other people on to fight the long defeat, and I'm not going to stop because we keep losing."[10]

In the wake of Moses's betrayal, our struggles in Lwala, and Brooke's death, I came to understand better what Dr. Farmer meant. To pour resources into small African organizations instead of large established international agencies is to dwell in the valleys with people at work rather than enjoy the mountaintops of big promises and fat checks. To fight for clean water and HIV/AIDS support in some of the most difficult places in the world is a long, slow sail.

A vision for change is thrilling when you stand behind a soup kitchen counter or in a classroom buzzing with ideas or in the back room of a tour bus that overflows with dollar bills. But when you're face-to-face with human depravity—sometimes others' and oftentimes your own—it is extremely difficult to keep pressing forward with any conviction that it is worth it.

I couldn't decide if fighting the long defeat was a devastating way to look at vocation, or if it was simply the more honest and, therefore, more sustainable way.

In a world where the winners are the ones with the money and the power and the privileges, then the losers are the materially poor, the oppressed, the forgotten, the meek, and the marginalized. To wear the jersey for the under-dog is to watch others point their fingers and say: *Surely, you will not win.* And if those are the rules of the game, if losing is guaranteed, do I want to be on the side of the losers and wage the long defeat? If the losers include Leah in Lwala and Pamela the widow in Kano Plains and HIV-positive Bill from Spokane and Mark in a Colorado shelter and one homeless man on the streets of San Francisco, then yes, I want to be on the losing team.

We don't seek to love so we can win. We seek to love for love itself. That truth above all freed me to keep my commitments to Blood:Water, to my faith, and to Africa.

·   ·   ·

As I considered Steve Garber's invitation to live proximately, my approach to the world and my work in it shifted. I understood the value of focusing on smaller places and particular changes. I wanted to live with the hard truth about human limitations while still believing that all our work—even if we lose, even if it is merely proximate—is worth fighting for.

This way of looking at the world means admitting that at some point along our vocational journey, we will not feel the rush of serving as we did once, but we will stay with it anyway. It means admitting that the world is indeed a hard place to live, and it will likely break our heart if we keep engaging with it, but we will choose to hope anyway. It means admitting over and over, sometimes every day, *Yes, the pain of this journey is real. Let's keep climbing anyway.* And, for me, it means accepting that even the place that raised me, the church, would cause pain, but I would love it anyway.

When you choose to keep walking in a proximate direction, you define success differently than before. And that means there's more to celebrate. I have learned that truer triumph comes from the small than from the grandiose. I have seen as much empowerment happen in the grassroots organizing of a village water committee as from the expert interventions of outsiders. I have witnessed the lasting change that happens when comprehensive quality health care is provided for a handful of HIV-positive clients compared to the haphazard fixes that are scattered to thousands of people.

Even as a young girl in the privacy of my bedroom, I had a hunch that the God of the Universe cared about the small things as much as the big ones. I saw that small things mattered to Jesus: a mustard seed, a few loaves of bread, twelve friends. He was drawn not to the powerful or successful, but to the meek, the humble, the oppressed. That's where abundance flowed.

The faithful actions of loving one person at a time, working for justice one place at a time, providing water one village at a time—that is how we love the whole world. That is the third way.

．．．

Flying back to Marsabit two years after the drought, I saw a different land. Day in and day out, the people of Marsabit had continued with utter resilience to survive. They faithfully built the rain tanks and repaired the dams as dust devils swept across their land. They developed health and hygiene clubs, dug pit latrines, and carried on with a commitment to improve their lives regardless of the circumstances that they could not control. Many people in the United States, myself included, would consider an empty rain tank a failure, but with dignity, responsibility, and hope, those communities had pressed on.

The rains had finally come one October. The skies filled the tanks and the dams with water as if it were manna from heaven. Because the people of Marsabit had worked throughout the drought to construct the catchment systems, they were able to collect every drop.

Marsabit and its people reflected an earth where all things can be made new. As I celebrated with the community—that one small place—I prayed for new life to keep growing in me as well.

．．．．．

James and I stopped to visit Elizabeth in Kisumu on our way to Lwala. After WWG shut down, she had found a part-time job as an x-ray assistant, working in a multistory building in Kisumu's small downtown. A simple desk and a large x-ray machine wrapped in a plastic cover took up most of the room. The yellow ceiling light made the space feel stale and lifeless. Elizabeth's spirit seemed that way, too. It hurt to see one of Kenya's most talented community teachers cooped up alone in a room with a machine instead of with people; it was a betrayal of Elizabeth's gifting.

"I want to recruit her," James said as we traveled on to Lwala. Together, Blood:Water and the Lwala Community Alliance were working on plans to construct rain tanks for thirteen area schools, but we needed someone who could organize the students, teachers, and parents and teach the village about water, sanitation, and hygiene. I loved the idea.

In a matter of weeks, Elizabeth came down to visit Lwala and the rest of the small community health team. She interviewed with Robert and negotiated a way to spend the weekdays in Lwala and be home in Kisumu with her son on the weekends.

Just as she had done with the communities across the Kano Plains, Elizabeth gathered village men and women in a small church with wobbly benches. Using masking tape name tags, butcher block paper, and group rules, the community began to learn things that would save their lives and those of their families.

Soon Elizabeth met Leah and was struck by her joy and her unwavering drive to become a leader in the community. The HIV medication, matched with clean water, nutrition, and the social encouragement of an HIV support group had created a Lazarus effect in Leah's body and spirit. She was thriving.

In time, Elizabeth recruited Leah to assist in the WASH trainings. To my great delight, a new movement of redeeming change had begun in Lwala, led by two women graced with second chances. It felt like proximate healing. It felt like something worth fighting for.

Project: No. 765
Location: Twapia, Zambia
Partner: Seeds of Hope International Partnerships [SOHIP]

When surface water is abundant but contaminated, filtration technologies like these biosand filters are a cost-effective way to provide safe water. Because of the health improvements they experience from filtering their water and incorporating hygiene behaviors like hand-washing, many community members in Twapia, Zambia, have joined SOHIP's program to become certified community health promoters in order to better advocate and support change in their community.

Photo Credit: Barak Bruerd, Blood:Water.

25

All the Good That You Will Do

"Do not depend on the hope of results," wrote the monk Thomas Merton to a young activist, but instead, "struggle less and less for an idea, and more and more for specific people."

Merton's advice reminds me of the I-Thou and I-It relationship that Jewish philosopher Martin Buber wrote about. The I-Thou relationship occurs when two people see each other simply as people created by God in his image. There is no qualification of "poor" or "rich" or "us" or "them." I-Thou sees the humanity and the divinity within each person. Conversely, I-It exists when a person sees the other as an object to be used to serve his or her interest. It gives a person permission to define, label, and objectify the other person. To romanticize Africa is to make an "it" of the place and the people. To be human with one another is to dare to take seriously the I-Thou relationship.

Even before I could articulate it, I have longed to live out the I-Thou relationship in my thoughts and interactions. Yet idealism stood in the way. My romanticism for the virtues of justice, health care, and preferential option for the poor had to be shattered in order for me to understand what I-Thou truly meant. As a college student, it was easy for me to see someone as a brother or sister in the loving, general sense of the word. But the true test of I-Thou came when Moses betrayed, when the church caused pain, when those I trusted left. It came when I realized that the same brokenness of the world was in the *I* who wanted to serve. My vision of grandiosity fell apart, and I knew the grief of letting go of the idea of saving the world.

I am still picking up some of the pieces of my idealism and reworking them. But James and I continue to commit our lives to social justice around the globe, and we invite many others to join in the journey even as we are still learning. We do believe that the world changes when we give love lavishly. We hold fast to the hope that someday all things will be renewed.

I often think about what my life would have looked like had I missed that San Francisco homeless man's humanity. Or had I turned around on that Colorado mountain. Or had I realized how hard a vision can be to see through.

As a twenty-one-year-old, I cofounded Blood:Water with the belief that we could eradicate HIV/AIDS and provide safe water for all. If we could rally enough people to care, surely there would be resources in the world to make these things happen. Like other Americans, I imagined Africa as it appeared in travel magazines, in the headlines of newspapers, and in the argument of why children should finish their dinners. We tend to sentimentalize places and people who are different from us until we truly know them. But communities in Africa don't want our pity. They don't want our charity. Like all of us, they want to be known.

The Old Testament prophet Isaiah gives us a way to move beyond pity and into action:

> Is not this the kind of fasting I have chosen:
> to loose the chains of injustice
> and untie the cords of the yoke,
> to set the oppressed free

and break every yoke?
Is it not to share your food with the hungry
and to provide the poor wanderer with shelter—
when you see the naked, to clothe them,
and not to turn away from your own flesh and blood?
Then your light will break forth like the dawn,
and your healing will quickly appear;
then your righteousness will go before you,
and the glory of the Lord will be your rear guard.
Then you will call, and the Lord will answer;
you will cry for help, and he will say: Here am I.[11]

The call is to *loose* the bonds of injustice, *undo* the thongs of the yoke, *let* the oppressed go free, *share* your bread with the hungry, *bring* the homeless poor into your house, *clothe* the naked. But let me be a witness that these things do not happen all at once. The challenge is to wake up each day and live out your vocation in the same way true change happens in Africa: slowly by slowly, brick by brick. Faithfully entering the world does not require an advanced degree, a fancy job title, or endless resources. Vocation is a calling, an action, to be expressed wherever your feet are today.

According to my childhood history, my feet were supposed to stay close to home. I welcomed this plan. Until in an unexpected moment of forgetfulness, I broke my own rules.

One might imagine that I've changed, that along with my vision for one thousand African wells came a new courage, an undiscovered gutsiness, a joy in taking risks. The truth is, I've never felt equipped to do anything extraordinary in my life. I battle fear every time I get on a plane. I experience so much failure and self-doubt that I have come to expect it. But the path to providing water for a thousand African communities taught me that it's less about having it all together and more about the unwavering commitment to keep walking.

As Merton goes on to write, "All the good that you will do will come, not from you but from the fact that you have allowed yourself, in the obedience of faith, to be used by God's love."[12]

Loose, undo, share, bring, clothe. As these actions flow within and beyond one another, our lives will tell a marvelous story.

Project: No. 932

Location: Mapalo, Zambia

Partner: Seeds of Hope International Partnerships [SOHIP]

Community members work with SOHIP to install a hand-pump in their community. The dramatic changes that water, sanitation, and hygiene brought to this slum community of 65,000 people included the first year in living memory with zero recorded cases of cholera. As a result, the community decided to change their name from *Chapulukusu*, or "Cursed," to *Mapalo*, meaning "Blessed." *Photo Credit: Seeds of Hope International Partnerships.*

26

One Thousand Wells

On May 10, 2011, the pews of Nashville's historic Ryman Auditorium were filled with more than a thousand people eager to celebrate the completion of a dream. Seven years after Dan's phone call pulled me out of my college classroom and into the charge of bringing clean water to one thousand African communities, we had done it. In fact, we had exceeded it.

The dream for the 1000 Wells Project began with one dollar. Others caught the vision and set up bake sales, bike rides, and benefit concerts. Over the years, that one dollar became twenty dollars and one hundred dollars, and today, more than 25 million dollars. Those dollars were invested into twenty organizations across Africa to drill 207 new wells, repair 449 broken wells, construct 181 rain catchment tanks, protect 114 springs, and serve 87 communities with biosand filters. They paid for tools like drill rigs, trucks, motorcycles, and computers for partner organizations to reach their communities. They paid for trainers like Elizabeth to offer villagers across eleven countries lifesaving knowledge about water, sanitation, and hygiene. Thousands of children like Joseph began to attend school and report the disappearance of stomachaches. HIV-positive women like Leah were given a second chance at life because their living conditions improved and medical care was available.

Every person in the auditorium that night was critical to the success of the 1000 Wells Project, and ultimately, the launch of Blood:Water. Jars of Clay shared the stage with other Nashville artist friends and with Kenya's beloved musician Eric Wainaina. Michel, whose Rwandan organization MOUCE-CORE built nearly a hundred rainwater catchment tanks, sat next to Lulu, a young girl from California who raised money through lemonade stands. Deleo, whose well-drilling organization provided 86 new and repaired wells across the war-torn region of northern Uganda, sat next to Ken, the filmmaker who took a risk on us before we had any means to tell our story. A host of other representatives from our partners in Kenya, Uganda, Rwanda, Zambia, and Central African Republic cheered with us along with Steve Garber; Bobby the road manager; Joel; Blood:Water board members and staff; the group of cyclists who rode their bikes across America for us; the family foundation from Kansas City; Fred from Lwala, whose father's dying wish gave us all life; my loving parents; and James, my partner in mission. The collection of stories within the room was one of the most beautiful pictures of community I have ever seen.[13]

If you want Africa to be a lost cause, keep judging success by rain or drought. Judge it by what is left to do. Partnering directly with local people who are capable, compassionate, and hardworking and applying the values of dignity, relationship, and excellence—now that's where you'll see true success.

One thousand wells didn't come the way we had imagined, but setting sail doesn't always mean you'll get where you thought you were going. Together, we had learned hard lessons about partnering with grassroots organizations in Africa. We had become more convinced than ever that real change happens with Africans leading the way. We had discovered hidden heroes and equipped them with the skills and resources necessary for them to be agents of change in their communities. Blood:Water's projects across Africa had brought clean water to more than 632,000 men, women, and children. Their lives had changed for the better, and in the process, so had mine.

When I had asked Dan if we could begin with the 10 Wells Project instead of the 1000 Wells Project, he insisted that we should choose a number we didn't feel comfortable with. As I stood onstage looking at the faces in the pews, I was thankful for his insistence on discomfort.

Reaching one thousand was not the end of the water crisis in Africa. It was not the end, but just the beginning, of the work of Blood:Water. By that point, in 2011, we had built a team at Blood:Water. I was learning a new joy in seeing others take the lead in fulfilling our mission.

Our celebration was a time to pause in the midst of the mission and recognize publicly that God was at work. Because one thousand communities were finding their way to self-confidence and achievement. Tens of thousands of Americans were learning that their lives were implicated in the injustices of the water and HIV/AIDS crises in Africa. And the dancing women across Africa had shown us that love is always worth celebrating.

So we danced that night as if dancing around the first well we built. We sang an anthem to community, a Jars of Clay song borne out of the same artist's heart who understood who his neighbor was:

> *We must all believe*
> *Our lives are not our own . . .*
> *God has given us each other*
> *And we will never walk alone*
> *In the shelter of each other*
> *We will live*

In the beginning days of Blood:Water, I thought the vision was mine to accomplish. The truth is, it never was mine. The work of healing and redeeming a broken world belongs to God. I have a small part to play and I am responsible for that part, but in the end, it's not on my shoulders. In all my years at Blood:Water, I have never drilled a well. I didn't need to.

My calling is to do the one more thing in front of me. And then the next. If I can step into that, I want to be there. If stepping into this calling means stepping into hard times, I still want to be there.

I had taken on a mountain as daunting as the first one I faced as a teenager in the Rocky Mountains. I lost a lot of myself as I climbed: the unshakable faith of my youth, the belief in the right intentions of others, the simple assumptions of how to do good in the world. Even now, I carry a quiet grief over the loss of the idealism I held as a young adult. It was what fueled me to keep going, and I miss that straightforward resolve.

But in its place is the beautiful realization that I do not need to climb any mountain alone. On my winding journey, God was there—in the form of friends who came alongside to share the load, through a set of values that served as a compass for all of us, and in the grace of clean water flowing through our hands.

My faith is messier now than it once was. My questions are bigger. Some of my convictions have eased into mystery, even as my understanding of God has grown. I've found a home in the liturgical calendar, the open doors of the Episcopal church, the common prayer, and tried and true sacraments of Christianity. Some days, I am living out the actions of a faith I don't feel, trusting the movements and practices to carry me through. I take in the words of theologians I trust—like Frederick Buechner, Wendell Berry, Barbara Brown Taylor, and Becca Stevens—with the hope that their creeds will somehow, over time, become my own. I know now that courage is less about driving through war zones in northern Uganda and more about choosing to believe in a good God in the midst of a nearly blinding brokenness.

So slowly by slowly, we build hospital wings, though HIV and cholera still persist. Brick by brick, we bring ten thousand liters of water, even though one hundred thousand are needed. Each day, we wage the long defeat.

The good news is that when we care for our proximal part in the world, the God of heaven knits these small pieces together into something beautiful. But we are not called to change the world. We are called to love the world. And to love the world, we are the ones who must change.[14]

Epilogue

James and I hop on a motorbike to visit the homesteads around Lwala. A local nurse and community health worker are on another motorbike ahead of us. As we ride along the uneven and muddy road, we slow to greet familiar faces. We stop at a circle of homes to sit with new moms and hold babies whose lives would have been in danger without the medical interventions and safe delivery techniques in the new maternity ward. They hug me and call me NyaLwala, daughter of Lwala.

The rain comes and we take cover in a school. We watch the downpour fill the rain catchment tanks. The students laugh at our surprise visit and entertain us with stories about the health clubs at their schools. We wave to neighbors walking by, familiar faces like Leah, who make this place a home to us.

As the rain lets up, we go on to visit a group of young people wearing neon green shirts, a sign they have completed WASH training and made commitments to change. They invite us to visit their homes and tour their hand-dug latrines and nearby hand-washing stations. We play with their healthy children and celebrate the community's vision for wholeness of life.

In the beginning years at Blood:Water, we took a risk to fund the opening of the Lwala clinic and drill its first borehole. It was a bare-bones start, but the Lwala community pressed forward toward a vision of redeeming and restoring.

Eight years after our initial investment in Lwala, nearly two hundred Kenyans work together daily to break down the barriers of extreme poverty and HIV/AIDS in this rural place. What was once an empty lot of ambitious dreams became a project reaching twenty thousand people. Lwala continues to hold grief, the unbearable stories that accompany our choice to wage the long defeat. But side by side we hear whispers of encouragement. We see glimpses of redemption. We each find a reason to continue.

Acknowledgments

My deepest gratitude is for my husband, James, my partner in life and mission. Thank you for encouraging me to push beyond my comfort zone, but always with the assurance of your hand in mine. For living with me through the angst of writing, for teaching me about the value of an outline, and for coauthoring so much of this story. (And for sweet Jude, who in so many ways, is our greatest adventure.)

My parents, Gus Lee and Diane Elliott-Lee, built a love and a family that made space for a young girl's dream to flourish. You have been ever selfless and supportive, and I am so grateful.

Thank you to Jars of Clay for believing in a college girl with a "25-page manifesto." Your families became family for me when I needed it most. Dan and Katie Haseltine, Charlie and Sonja Lowell, Stephen and Jude Mason, Matt and Kristen Odmark—thank you for embracing me into your world. And to Aaron and Cari Sands for being the glue that kept it all together!

Special thanks to Steve Garber for caring about the long narrative of my life. To Gary Haugen for teaching me about leadership, vision, and joy in service. (Thanks to Ruthie McGinn, too. You're a star). And to Reverend Becca Stevens, for showing me how to love the whole world, one person at a time.

Eight summers in the Rocky Mountains with Cheley Colorado Camps served as the greatest playground of my youth. To my Cheley sisters and

257

brothers whose memories are scattered across a thousand miles of Colorado trails—you dear friends, lift me up where earth and heaven meet.

To each of the million plus individuals in Africa who has taken part in the Blood:Water narrative, this story is yours. A very special thanks to our early partners: Lifewater International, Seeds of Hope International Partnerships, Lwala Community Alliance, MOUCECORE, Divine Waters Uganda, and Water for Good. Thank you to Leah Oyugis, Elizabeth Akinyi, Milton Ochieng', Fred Ochieng', and the Baxter family for letting me tell your stories.

To every individual who took a risk on the Blood:Water vision, this story is yours, too. Your contributions, mentorship, and advocacy over the last decade have filled our cup to overflowing. (The pages that follow are simply some of the many names who have made this work possible.)

Blood:Water is only as effective as its people—and my, do we have incredible people! For the 25+ staff who have given your days and years to building Blood:Water over the last decade, I can't thank you enough. A very special thank-you to Aaron Sands, Barak Bruerd, Amy Adams Hann, Matt Ward, Kellie Lutito, Victor Huckabee, Lauren Hitch, and Pamela Crane-Hoover for being the core team to launching the 1000 Wells Project into a reality. And, to our founding board members: Collin Brown, Lon Cherry, Rob Curwen, Reagan Demas, Steve Garber, Brad Gibson, Rich Hoops, Dr. Clydette Powell, and Joel Vikre. I am grateful for those who are leading the way today, especially Jake Smith, Katherine Hofstetter, and Courtney Baker. Special thanks to Mike Hamilton, Chris Bolton, Stuart McWhorter, and Carrie Horton for providing encouragement and backend support along the way.

Thank you to Dan Raines and Kathryn Helmers at Creative Trust, and to Donald Miller for insisting that Kathy and I meet. I am in such good hands! Elisa Stanford was the best editing partner through the writing process, helping me find my voice in the piles of words, and working with me and James through multiple drafts over late nights and early mornings. And thanks to Amy Tan for offering her generous support.

Acknowledgments

I am grateful to the team at Howard Books and Simon & Schuster, especially Jonathan Merkh, Jennifer Smith, Bonnie MacIsaac, and my wonderful editor, Beth Adams. And thanks also to Jessica Wong for her early enthusiasm—our time was too short!

The wonderful readers of my early manuscript provided me invaluable feedback: Courtney Baker, Mary Anna Brown, Katherine Falk, Katie Harris, Cooper Kandler, and Jessica Pearson. Asante sana to Fred Ochieng', Damianus Japolo Nyakinye, and Elizabeth Akinyi for being my Kenyan readers with important edits. Thanks to Barak Bruerd for compiling the photos and stories of the water projects. And to Ken Byers for his creative marketing support.

I am thankful for the loving congregations of St. Augustine's Chapel and City Church of East Nashville, the staff and faculty of Whitworth University, and the community of Nashville.

For my lifelong friends: Amy Aaron, Rachel Schlabs, Alyssa Dillard, Sarah Sandifer, Holly Wielkoszewski, Kara Hanger, Katy Byers, Autumn Petersen, Erin Gallion, Elizabeth Paul, Anna Engeln, Katie Harris, and Jessica Pearson. And for my family: Eric and Becky Lee, Jim and Allie Nardella, and RJ and Jalene Salus. And always, for Elan Vie Salus.

S.D.G.

I wish I could name all the people who made the early days at Blood:Water possible. Thousands of people allowed their stories to become part of ours. To honor the thousands, here are a few:

A.G. Silver	Aaron Sawyer	Adam Goodman
Aaron Phaneuf	Aaron Smith	Adam Taylor
Aaron Sands	Abigayle Craigg	Adrian Hitt

Acknowledgments

Adrienne Moscheo

African Leadership

Africare

Aida Samir Kouko

Aimee Abizera

Al Andrews

Alex Beh

Alex Schmitt

Alice Demas

Alison Krauss

Allen Kuo

Allie Mikels

Alyssa Aviles

Alyssa Dillard

Alyssa Womack

Amanda Fisher

Amber Morey

Amie Hadaway

Amy Aaron

Amy Casey

Amy Gibson

Amy Grant

Amy Huckabee

Amy Kiehl

Amy Marie Hann

Andi Ashworth

Andrew Osenga

Andy Lowell

Angela Skahen

Anna Hatch

Anne Cregger

Anne Jackson

Anne Lee

Anne Marie Miller

Anne Pageau

Anthony Catalano

Antoine Rutayisire

Apple Computer

ARAMET

ARASI

Arden Bailey

Ashleigh Harb Roberts

Ashley Buffey

Ashley Cleveland

Ashley Lee

Athanase Ndayisaba

Audrey Milicevic

Austin Manuel

Avril Thomas

Baker Books

Barak Bruerd

Barbara Latimer

Barrett Ward

Barry Simmons

Beliefnet

Benjamin Kola Oyoo

Beth Hamilton

Bethany Hertrick

Bethany Pickard

Bethany Stallings

Betsy DeLaney

Betty Gatere

Betty Mirembe

Bill Bassett

Bill Evans

Bill Robinson

Bill Young

Blake Stockard

Bo Bartholomew

Bob Briner

Bobby Simmons

Bono

Brad Phillips

Bradley Gibson

Brandon Bargo

Brandon Brown

Brandon Heath

Brenda Koinis

Brian Elliott

Brian Mulder

Brian Pageau

Brian Williams

Brianna Benson

Brianna Rieck

Brianne Olson

Brittany Pulei

Brody Bond

Caedmon's Call

Caitlin Glover

Caitlyn Pugliese

Calvin College

Cameron Strang

Cara Baker

Cari Sands

Carlee Nestelberger

Carol Nowlin

Caroline Smith

Carrie Horton

Carsten Bradley

Cassie Elmer

Catherine Winter
Cocke

Cathy Cherry

Charles Peters

Charlie Lowell

Charlie Peacock
(Ashworth)

Chase Baker

Chase Livingston

Chelsey Dailey
Goodan

Chris Bolton

Chris Clements

Chris Metzger

Chris Pereira

Chris Pochiba

Chris Pritchett

Chris Rice

Chris York

Christianity Today

Christine Burger

Christopher Jackson

Christopher Lanning

Christopher Williams

Chuck Pryor

Clair Brothers
Production

Claudette Uwimana

Cliff Young

Clydette Powell

Cody Henderson

Coldplay

Collin Brown

Cosma Gatere

Courtney Baker

Courtney Lancaster

Craig Brown

Craig Burger

Craig Goldman

Craig Parker

Craig Smith

Criselda Sweet

Criselda Vasquez

Crystal Downing

Curtis Wickre

Dan Haseltine

Dan Raines

Dan Russell

Dan Stevens

Dana Chavey

Danica Mercer

Daniel Finney

Danielle Young

Darren Wendell

Dave Dillard

Dave Kiersznowski

David Braud

David Downing

David Hofstetter

David Maina

David McCollum

David Pierce

David Sparvero

David Van Buskirk

David Wilcox

Deb Go

Debbie Barnett

Debbie Robinson

Dedra Herod

Dee Lafferty

Deleo Ocen

Dennis Haack

Derek Webb

Diana Barth

Diana Garcia

Diane Lee

DJ Smith

Don Donahue

Don Miller

Don Pape

Donald Miller

Drew Holcomb

Drew Nelson

Duane Hatch

Dustin Burkhart

Dustin Conway

Dwight Gibson

Ebralie Mwizerwa

Edana Hough (Nelson)

Edward Haseltine

Edward Kiwanuka

Elizabeth Beinhocker Overstreet

Elizabeth McCormick

Elizabeth Rogers

Elizabeth Sherwood

Ellen Smith

Emily Boyd

Emily Gray

Emily Korst

Emily Theis

Endel Liias

Eric Ness

Eric Wainaina

Erik Pelttari

Erika Ottenbreit

Erin Gallion

Erin McDermott Perkins

Erin Morris

Erin Perkins

Erin Roberts

Erin Todd

Erin White

Essential Records

Eva Kemp

Evans Chiyenge

Evelyn Raines

Fawn Brown

Flavia Feruka

Francis Feruka

Frank Ramirez

Fred Smith

Gabe Roberts

Gabe Ruschival

Garrett Buell

Gary Grubbs

Gary Haugen

George Burkhardt

George Patterson

Gina Francisco Rayburn

Ginger Gibson

Greenville College

Greg Bargo

Greg Rittler

Gregg Mwendwa

Gus Lee

Hank Habicht

Hannah Holland

Hanson

Haylee Hartman

Heather Snodgrass

Heather Warfield

Henry Pritchett

Ian Pietz

ICDI

Isaiah Fish

Jackie Marushka

Jacob Childerson

Jacqueline March

Jacquelyn Maruschka

Jake Goss

Jake Smith

James and Sheena Grosshans

James Nardella

Jamey Escamilla

Jamie Bruce

Jamie Schwartzendruber

Jared Angaza

Jason Bennett

Jason Dominy

Jason Hecht

Jay Johnson

Jay Parks

Jay Schwartzendruber

Jay Williams (deceased)

Jay Wright

JD Atkinson

Acknowledgments

Jeanne Goskie
Jen Tyler
Jennifer Robins
Jennifer Vasquez
Jenny Dyer
Jeremy Cowart
Jeremy Davis
Jeremy Lutitio
Jerry Jenkins
Jerry McNeish
Jesse Olson
Jesse Pickott
Jessica Abt
Jessica Bargo
Jessica Dowden
Jessica Mahoney
Jessica Miller
Jessica Shearer
Jessie Miller
Jessie Tyree
Jim Blankemeyer
Jim Chaffee
Jim Hitch
Jim Hocking
Jim Latimer
Jim Odmark
Jimmy Abegg
Jimmy Wheeler
JJ Heller
Joann Cadicamo

Joe Ed Conn
Joel Griffith
Joel Schoon-Tanis
Joel Vikre
John Blanton
John Davis
John Fischer
John Foreman
John Huie
John Karenzi
John McBride
John Thomas
Jon Reno
Jonathan May
Josh Shicker
Joshua McNeilly
Josias Hansen
Jude Mason
Judy Lanning
Julia Nusbaum
Julia Pruveadenti
Julia Stronks
Julie Lewis
Justin Enerson
Justin Hastings
Justin McRoberts
Justin York
Kaiti Jones
Karen Pritchett
Karen Ramirez

Karl Feller
Kate Etue
Kate Pilman
Katherine Falk
Katherine Hofstetter
Kathy Schoon-Tanis
Katie Ellwood
Katie Haseltine
Katy Lee
Kay Shorten
Keith Wright
Kellie Lutito
Ken Carpenter
Ken Germer
Ken Heffner
Kevin Twit
Kiely Concannon
Kimberley Frey
Kirk Schauer
Kristen Odmark
Kristin Flow
Kyle Chowning
Kyle Reiter
Kylie Coyne Foshee
Lance Robinson
Larry Warren
Laura Blucker
Laura Page
Lauren Hitch
Lauren McBride

Laurie Odmark
Lavonne Stevens
Leeland
Leigh Ann McWhorter
Levi Humble
Lewis Lavine
Libby Perry
Lindalyn Hutter
Lindsay Nobles
Linkin Park
Lisa Bond
Lisa Nelson
Lisa Phaneuf
Lisa Ralph
Lisa Williams
Little Big Town
LMichael Green
Lon Cherry
Lori Morris
Louie Giglio
Lucas Hendrickson
Luka Milicevic
Lulu Cerone
Lynn Hickernell
M. Aaron Hines
Macy Rentschler
Madeleine Hemphill
Mandy Quiram
Marc Wheat
Marcus Womack

Margie Gordner
Mark & Diane Button
Mark Bortz
Mark Brinkmoeller
Mark Hann
Mark Joseph
Mark Rodgers
Mark Schilcher
Marti Bolton
Mary Brinkman
Matt Clark
Matt Lynch
Matt Morginsky
Matt Odmark
Matt Provo
Matt Ruff
Matt Turner
Matt Ward
Matt Wertz
Matthew Kaemingk
Matthew Perryman
  Jones
Matthew Sterling
Maya Bakke
Meg Beasley
Meg Garber
Megan Kolacinski
Megan Russom
Melanie Hager
Melinda Gunter

Melissa Barber
Melissa Eisenbrandt
Melissa Foss
Mendy Myers
Michael Corcoran
Michael Dean
Michael W. Smith
Michel Kayitaba
Michelle Conn
Mike Barrow
Mike Donehey
Mike Hamilton
Mike Lenda
Mike Mutungi
Missi Martin
Mitch Goskie
Mitch Lee
Monica Grubbs
Morgan Bortz
Moses Pulei
MOUCECORE
Nadia Kist
Nancy Holland
Nancy McNeish
Nancy Powell
Nancy Wickre
Naomi Lowe
Natalie Grant
Nate Larkin
Nettwerk Management

Nicole Boymook

Nicole Provo

Nina Williams

Nita Andrews

Os Guinness

Pamela Crane-Hoover

Paper Route

Pat Klever

Patricia Grimm

Paul Coleman

Paul Marshall

Penny Hunter

Peter Greer

Peter York

Phil Keaggy

Porter DeLaney

Rachel Clark

Rachel Lenda

Rachel Stockard

Randy Brothers

Randy Dowell

Raymond Harris

Reagan Demas

Rebekah Deal

Redlight Management

Relevant Media Group

Rich Hoops

Rich Klopp

Richard Swoboda

Rick Warren

Rob Curwen

Robbie Maris

Robbie Pinter

Robby Schwindt

Robert Beeson

Robert Holland

Robert Thompson

Roberta Parks

Roger Parrott

Ruthie Dean

Ruthie McGinn

Ryan Bennett

Ryan Skoog

Ryane Williamson

Sally Hall

Sam Moore

Sam Newcomer

Samantha Smith

Sandra McCracken

Sandra Obrey

Sara Groves

Sarah Bartholomew

Sarah Miller

Sarah Raines

Sarah Roper

Sarah Shryer

Scott Calgaro

Scott Morris

Scott Mottice

Seabird

Seth Willard

Shannon Briano

Shannon Cowart

Shelby Steelhammer

Shep Owen

Simone Grauer

Sonja Lowell

Stephanie Gay

Stephen Gause

Stephen Leiweke

Steve Beck

Steve Carlson

Steve Garber

Steve Haas

Steve Koinis

Steve Mason

Steven Trusty

Stuart McWhorter

Summer Curwen

Susan Swoboda

Suzanne Williams

Switchfoot

Tara Bruerd

Taylor Bruce

Taylor Mobley

Ted Haddock

Tenth Avenue North

Terry Hemmings

Terry McBride

Theresa Johnson

Acknowledgments

Thomas Nelson

Thrice

Thuy-An Julien

Tiffany Arbuckle

Tiffany Broaddus

Tim Noll

Toby Mac

Todd Bragg

Todd Wahrenberger

Tom Grimm

Tracey Collins

Traci Hoops

Trevina Tadros

Troy Groves

Tyler Edmondson

Tyler Sevlie

Tyrus Ridgway

Victor Huckabee

Vince Gill

Vincent Okeng

Warren Pettit

Water for Good

WaterAid

Wayne Haughey

Wendell Berry

Wendy Habicht

Whitney Kuhn

William Mwizerwa

Yes

Yvonne Carter

Zachary Hazlett

Zachary Kaymenyi

Zondervan

Notes

1 Matthew 25:31-40. New International Version.

2 Frederick Buechner, *Wishful Thinking: A Seeker's ABC* (New York: Harper-Collins, 1993).

3 "Not Much to Celebrate in New Barna AIDS Survey," press release, World Vision, November 25, 2002, http://www.worldvision.org/worldvision/pr.nsf/stable/new_barna.

4 Allan H. Smith, Elena O. Lingas, and Mahfuzar Rahman, "Contamination of Drinking Water by Arsenic in Bangladesh: A Public Health Emergency," *Bulletin of the World Health Organization* 78, no. 9 (September 2000): 1093–1103.

5 Jamie Skinner, "Where Every Drop Counts: Tackling Rural Africa's Water Crisis," *International Institute for Environment and Development Briefing*, March 2009, http://pubs.iied.org/pdfs/17055IIED.pdf.

6 For more on Roger's model of sailboat leadership, see Roger Parrott, PhD *The Longview: Lasting Strategies for Rising Leaders* (Colorado Springs: David C. Cook, 2009).

7 Dan Mitchell (March 30, 2002). *NPR Weekend Edition Saturday* interview, npr.org.

8 We later learned that Steve was quoting an article by Stanley Hauerwas and Allen Verhey. Steve also quotes it in his own book, *Visions of Vocation:*

Common Grace for the Common Good (Downers Grove: InterVarsity Press, 2014).

9   For more on Steve's philosophy of vocation, see Steve Garber, *The Fabric of Faithfulness: Weaving Together Belief and Behavior* (Downers Grove: InterVarsity Press, 2007) and *Visions of Vocation: Common Grace for the Common Good* (Downers Grove: InterVarsity Press, 2014). These books have been highly influential in my own life.

10 Tracy Kidder, *Mountains Beyond Mountains: The Quest of Dr. Paul Farmer, A Man Who Would Cure the World* (New York: Random House, 2003), 288. Kidder's book on Dr. Farmer received the Pulitzer Prize.

11 Isaiah 58:6-9. New International Version.

12 Thomas Merton, *The Hidden Ground of Love: The Letters on Religious Experience and Social Concerns*, selected and edited by William H. Shannon (New York: Farrar, Straus, Giroux, 1985). You can also read the young activist's response to Merton's letter at http://jimandnancyforest.com/2014/10/mertons-letter-to-a-young-activist.

13 For a video clip from that incredible night, see http://vimeo.com/m/49932125.

14 I am grateful for my priest, Reverend Becca Stevens, who shared this with me and speaks prolifically around this subject. She has also written about it in her books. See Becca Stevens, *The Way of Tea and Justice: Rescuing the World's Favorite Beverage from Its Violent History* (Nashville: Jericho Books, 2014).

DEAR FRIEND,
AT BLOOD: WATER, WE OFTEN TALK ABOUT
BEING IMPLICATED IN THE LIVES OF OTHERS.
PERHAPS AFTER READING ABOUT MY JOURNEY
AND OUR FRIENDS IN AFRICA, YOU FEEL
IMPLICATED, TOO. I WOULD LIKE TO PERSONALLY
INVITE YOU TO STEP INTO THE BLOOD: WATER
STORY AND HELP US WRITE THE NEXT
BEAUTIFUL CHAPTER TOGETHER!

BLOODWATER.ORG

P.O. BOX 60381 NASHVILLE, TN 37206, 615.550.4296.

About the Author

Jena Lee Nardella is the cofounder of Blood:Water, which she started in 2004 at the age of twenty-two with band Jars of Clay. Following her vision and leadership, the organization has brought clean water to more than a million people in Africa and provided health care for more than 62,000 people in HIV-affected areas. Jena has been honored as one of *Chronicle of Philanthropy*'s "40 Under 40," *GOOD Magazine*'s "GOOD 100," and *Christianity Today*'s "33 Under 33" Christian leaders shaping the next generation of faith. In addition to speaking and writing as an advocate for social justice issues around the globe, Jena currently serves on the core team for Praxis, a New York–based venture group helping entrepreneurs build high-impact organizations. She and her husband James, and son, Jude, live in the San Francisco Bay Area.